# Norton
## FROM 1946

# Road Tests and Features from
# The Motor Cycle & Motor Cycling

Compiled and introduced by Cyril Ayton

BAY
VIEW
BOOKS

Published 1988 by
Bay View Books Ltd
13a Bridgeland Street
Bideford, Devon  EX39 2QE

Reprinted 1991

ISBN  1  870979  00  1



Printed in Hong Kong

# Contents

# Introduction

*In 1967 complaints about the roughness of the long-stroke Norton twin were answered by the 750 Commando, premiered at the Earls court show in November. A design/development team of Bernard Hooper and Bob Trigg headed by Norton Villiers' new director of engineering, Dr Stefan Bauer, made no changes to the 20-year-old engine; instead they installed it in a brand-new frame which satisfactorily disposed of the vibes problem. The engine and gearbox, plus rear fork and pivot, were mounted in a sub-structure depending from three large rubber bushes. These absorbed the shocks and trembles of the engine most effectively (though convulsive movements at under 2,000rpm could be alarming) throughout the 10-year lifespan of the Commando, during which swept volume reached 829cc and peak power climbed to 65bhp at 6,5000rpm.*

During the Second World War, Norton, like all the other motorcycle manufacturers, issued regular pronouncements through the weekly press about the models that were to surprise and delight the post-war rider. It was indicated that the new bikes would be little short of breathtaking. There was talk of the stringent demands of war throwing up new manufacturing techniques and materials that would be harnessed to the post-war effort.

After the war, Norton, like so many (though not all) of the other makers, came out with a range of motorcycles that might have been in store since 1939, so largely unchanged were they in comparison with their pre-war forebears. Nobody seemed to mind. It was enough that a few – a very few – new motorcycles were available to be bought.

In fact Norton was not the worst offender. BSA, for instance, managed to imply in wartime advertising that the clutches on its M20 side-valves had been honed to a condition of near-indestructibility during the course of the North Africa campaign and would, therefore, be something of a revelation to owners post-war. But at least BSA managed to fit telescopic forks to its first post-war bikes, and gave them a new paint job and general smartening-up – all clearly distinguishing the new breed from the old. At Norton the first bikes to appear out of khaki (the models 16H side-valve and 18 overhead-valve), in August 1945, seemed almost regressive when compared with what had been revealed to "insiders" in 1939 of the factory's plans for the following year. In 1945, however, there were few insiders – and they kept quiet – among the thousands who read of Norton's range for the first full year of peace. Much was made of the (1939-style) cradle frames – of the advantages of common enclosure for previously separate components of the 10-year-old gearbox. There was no sign of telescopic forks, despite an announcement in January 1944 about a new design incorporating provision for "hydraulic means of damping the return movement of the fork." At Bracebridge Street there had obviously been some over-production of wartime girder forks and other impedimenta which the directors thriftily decided should be absorbed during manufacture of the early post-war models.

At *Motor Cycling* they received – or claimed they received – letters from Continental agents for British motorcycles pleading for production of all those really *new* models that had been discussed, albeit in rather vague terms, in recent months and promised for delivery early in the days of peace. The Continentals, it seemed, wanted to see plenty of chromium, and spring frames. "The present types of machines will not continue to please," they declared, in quoted and convincingly laboured English. Graham

*Charles Markham, Motor Cycling's chief roadtester, on the 1947 Model 30 International. According to the Green 'Un, top speed of the handsome sportster, with long-stroke ohc motor of early 1930s design, was 97mph. The Motor Cycle docked 11mph off that figure in its test report.*

Walker, the Green 'Un's editor, and respected confidante of the manufacturers, clearly was unused to this sort of complaint from his home-based readers, who in the main appeared happy to carry on with the convivial wartime practice of queuing to buy food and clothes and petrol – and, now, motorbikes. "It is very obvious," wrote Mr Walker sternly "that Continental motorcyclists fail to appreciate how wholehearted has been the devotion of our manufacturers to the war effort . . ." Quite right: so why shouldn't Nortons flog off those old forks and other bits and pieces?

*Arthur (always listed as A.J.) Humphries and brother Harry (who like most sidecar passengers of the time was seldom mentioned at all) were among the top trials sidecar teams of the 1950s, with a factory-supported 490cc alloy-engine single and Canterbury 'chair'. This 1955 shot shows Arthur but not Harry, who had been sidelined by a leg injury. His replacement performed well enough for the couple to take the premier sidecar award in a severe Victory Trial, held as usual during February in the Long Mynd area of Shropshire. Note the headgear favoured in a pre-helmet decade. The Humphries brothers went on to win the British Experts Trial of 1955.*

*Nineteen-year-old John Surtees was one of the stars of the fourth post-war Bemsee/Motor Cycling "Silverstone Saturday" meeting, held at the Northants circuit in April 1953. Riding Manx singles, he outrode a host of top factory riders and was only beaten, by a matter of yards, by John Storr, another Norton rider, in the major solo races of the day. He is pictured on his 350 model.*

Not that any hint of such hard-headed business practice filtered through announcements in the "books". There the tone was one of scarcely contained excitement in purveying news that, in the case of Nortons, centred on use of the cradle frame for the two bikes on offer and reversion, for the side-valve model, to an arrangement of full enclosure for the valve gear that had been originally introduced in 1938 and then abandoned for the duration of the war. However teles were there in 1947, and the pre-war spring heel, made a little neater, was to be seen on the new ES2, a machine tested – and heartily approved of – by Torrens of *The Motor Cycle* towards the end of 1946.

Norton's major post-war programme change occurred with the introduction of the 500 twin in 1948, subsequent to the arrival at Bracebridge Street of Herbert Hopwood as chief designer. Norton was not alone in turning to the ohv parallel twin at this time in an attempt to cream off some of the spectacular sales at home and abroad being notched up by the Triumph concern. Their version – the complete motorcycle – was probably the closest rival of all to the Meriden models in unity of style and practicality. So good was the Dominator design that it endured, with periodic enlargement and improvement, into the 1970s as the power unit for the last of the Commandos.

No other significant design was to come, if one excludes the 250cc Jubilee twin of 1958 from that description. This, too, was mainly Bert Hopwood's work, with help from Doug Hele and Bill Petcher, but the machine was, according to him, flawed by management insistence on its being decked out with items taken from the two-strokes produced in the AMC factories. In time the Jubilee grew into the 350 Navigator that became, in 1964, the 400cc electric-start Electra.

The articles in this book are, like those in the companion book on Vincent-HRDs, taken from *Motor Cycling* and *The Motor Cycle*, the latter in the 1960s dropping *The* from its title (which was restyled typographically to a more striking outline) in an attempt at greater impact on a dwindling readership. This change never seemed an entirely happy one. In the same way, the titling for *Motor* and *Autocar*, magazines which lost the definite article in similar circumstances, remains as hybrid transatlantic, reminding one of Americans who talk about Albert Hall, never the Albert Hall.

The writing and presentation of the articles represent the differing approach of the two magazines. *The Motor Cycle,* always the market leader, and conscious of its seniority, played down personality, agonized after accuracy, and probably was less fun to work for, and to read.

Torrens' article on the 1947 model ES2 was a rare instance of a signed piece about a single model. Perhaps the privilege (self-conferred, for he was the editor) went to his head for there was much about "Willing William", a 1925 16H, and "Rhoda", the first of the TT-winning ohc Nortons, and even some pertinent information concerning his inside leg measurement, before he got down to the serious business of reviewing the ES2. In later years anonymity ruled in published writings about Nortons (and other makes). Even the photographs chosen to accompany road-test write-ups were mainly close-ups – very rarely on-the-road shots giving a glimpse of the tester at work. Not so, however, at *Motor Cycling* where, although the test reports were unsigned, one or more revealing photographs would indicate, to the regular reader, the identity of the tester/writer.

There were other quirks to distinguish between the weeklies. *Motor Cycling* in the early post-war years was not averse to borrowing a slightly "breathed on" model – the extra breath perhaps amounting to no more than an unbaffled silencer – and publishing a "flash" reading of top speed achieved during the best of several runs. This sort of thing was disapproved of at *The Motor Cycle*, in whose hands a near-identical model might emerge as several mph slower. A case in point concerns the 1947-48 plunger-frame Model 30 ohc International tested by *Motor Cycling*. The report was decorated with rousing pictures of hatless testers, chin an inch or two above the tank. Top speed, they found, was 97mph. At the Blue 'Un the Inter received standard two-page treatment, with decorous "static" photographs, and was credited with 86mph.

There was talk of oil leakage from cam box and lower bevel box – "elimination would have been appreciated" – that impresses in its steely restraint. (I understand this sort of treatment for it accorded with both magazines' policy of "See no evil . . ." but the insistence on the excellence of the 7in-diameter front brake fitted to those early post-war Nortons, with supporting figures on stopping distances recorded that put them in the Vincent-HRD class, baffles me.)

In the Featherbed era that began in the 1950s Vic Willoughby arrived at *The Motor Cycle* and took over much of the road-testing together with an export-type Featherbed Dominator 500 lately the occasional personal transport of editorial director Arthur Bourne. At *Motor Cycling*, at about the same time, sports editor Cyril Quantrill published a happy-go-lucky yarn about his four years of Continental jaunts with a very special 596cc ohc Norton sidecar outfit under the title "Is there a better 'bigger banger'?" It was not a heading that would have found much favour with *The Motor Cycle*'s sub-editor – and had it, unthinkably, been used there would have been a great weeding-out of quotation marks – but the story was a very entertaining one that, in sharp contrast with Blue 'Un practice, named names in the Norton hierachy, described with relish well-lubricated meals in three-star hotels, and implied pretty clearly that working on a motorcycling paper – *this* motorcycling paper, at least– meant that you could count on more than a few perks.

Other entries in this book deal with the Manx racers and the servicing of various roadsters. There is nothing about the last – should it be called the current? – two-wheeler bearing the Norton name, the rotary-engine Interpol, for the adequate reason that by the time this interesting machine had arrived on the scene, the two magazines had departed

*Two weeks after completing an engineering apprenticeship 21-year-old Phil Read won the 1960 Senior Manx Grand Prix at a record-breaking 95.38mph on a Norton prepared by Bill Lacey. Engaging Lacey, already renowned for wonders performed with Mike Hailwood's bikes, had been a shrewd move on Read's part: the Manx win was the culmination of a successful season on outstandingly fast and reliable machines. At the end of the year he threw up a secure job to become a professional racer.*

*A 1959 model 350 Manx featuring newly designed vertical drive shaft incorporating needle races for top and bottom bevels (and dispensing with the Oldham couplings familiar on all Carroll-designed ohc units since 1930).*

The Motor Cycle's Vic Willoughby on a 1962 650SS. Developed from the previous year's US-market Manxman, the 650SS had a 68 x 89mm engine running on an 8.3:1 compression ratio and was equipped with two downdraught carburettors. A curious belt and braces arrangement was the retention of the magneto, in addition to the new alternator (the latter being sole equipment on standard 650s). Top speed was 110-plus at over 6,000rpm. Finish was in "traditional" Norton style, with silver tank and black and chrome elsewhere, in contrast to a plethora of colours on other Nortons.

# Full Range

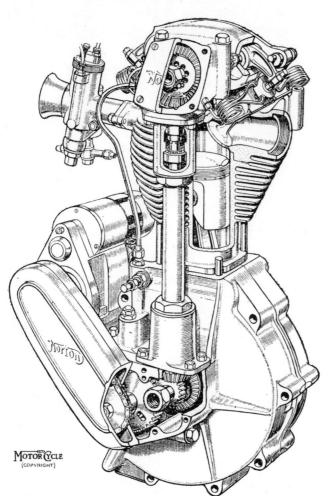

The famous overhead-camshaft Norton engine, power unit of Model 30 and Model 40

## Side=valve, Overhead=valve and Overhead=camshaft Machines: New "Roadholder" Forks Standard Throughout : Spring Frames on Five Models

ing feature is the little panel for the speedometer head that is mounted across the top of the telescopic front forks. The speedometer head is thus set forward of the steering head in the best possible position for ease of reading. The various control cables pass through rubber-bushed holes in the panel, a particularly neat arrangement. Another interesting little detail is that the steering dampers are spring loaded so that there is no rattle when "off."

The 82×120mm, 633 c.c. Big Four is provided with sidecar gear ratios, which

Hairpin valve springs are fitted to the standard overhead-camshaft models, which are available in 490 c.c. and 348 c.c.

NO fewer than 10 models are included in the Norton range for 1947. There are two side-valve mounts and four overhead-camshaft machines. The capacities are 348, 490, 499 and 633 c.c. There are machines for tourist, sportsman, racing man and, a little later in this case, those who compete in trials. They range from the famous 16H side-valve, which has won many an old-time speed event and helped to win the war, to the square-headed 348 c.c. and 499 c.c. Manx models, victors in races almost without number.

All models are fitted with the cradle frame which has given the Norton such a reputation for steering and road-holding, and all have new hydraulically controlled telescopic front forks. Also, throughout the range there is now a prop-stand, which can best be described as a specially low-lift central stand. What will please many is the standardization of spring frames on the 490 c.c. overhead-valve E.S.2 and on each of the four overhead-camshaft models.

The 16H, which blossomed forth with the famous cradle frame for this year, becomes doubly attractive with the new "Roadholder" front forks. It remains its simple, straightforward self—a machine of staunch reliability and easy maintenance. Like the 633 c.c. side-

valve, the Big Four, and the two overhead-valve models, the 490 c.c. Model 18 and the E.S.2, it has 3.25×19 Dunlop Universal tyres, a 2¾-gallon fuel tank and a ½-gallon oil tank. Gear ratios on the 16H are 4.9, 5.92, 8.65 and 14.5 to 1 solo; and sidecar, 5.45, 6.6, 9.65 and 16.2 to 1. The compression ratio is quoted as 4.8 to 1.

All except the Manx models, which have remote-needle racing Amal carburettors, have lever-type throttle stops so that for starting from cold there is no setting of the twist-grip to get the easiest possible start; it is merely a matter of leaving the twist-grip "shut" and moving round the little throttle-stop lever. All these machines have, of course, that simple and ingenious Norton oil-bath primary chain case, which comprises two neat steel pressings held together by a single hexagon and rendered oil-tight by a synthetic rubber washer. Other points of note are the detachable rear portion of the back mudguard, the twin petrol taps which render it unnecessary to drain the tank previous to removal, the wing-nut-type filler caps and the way the rear chainguards are carried well down to ensure greater protection of the chain.

Lucas Magdynos and rubber-mounted batteries are standard other than on the racing and trials machines. An interest-

are 5.45, 6.6, 9.65 and 16.2 to 1. It has a 4.5 to 1 compression ratio. In view of the machine being produced specially with sidecar work in mind there are swept-back, touring-type handlebars.

Both the 490 c.c. overhead-valve Model 18 and E.S.2 machines have a 6.45 to 1 compression ratio and are available with sidecar or solo gears, namely, 4.64, 5.61, 8.2 and 13.8 to 1; and 5.15, 6.24, 9.12 and 15.3 to 1. The E.S.2 has the simple, effective Norton plunger-type rear springing.

Next comes the overhead-camshaft 490 c.c. Model 30. This has the same sets of gear ratios as the 490 c.c. overhead-valve models, but, in common with the Model 40, the 348 c.c. overhead-camshaft, has the long, deep tank of thrilling ap-

# of Nortons for 1947

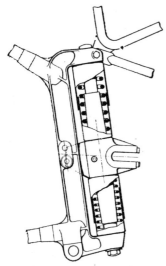

**Norton plunger-type rear springing is standard on the 490 c.c. overhead-valve E.S.2 and on the overhead-camshaft models**

pearance—a 3¾-gallon tank—a 3.00×21 Dunlop ribbed front tyre and a 3.25×20 Dunlop Universal rear tyre. Compression ratios are 7.23 to 1 and 7.33 to 1, and in each case there is a 1mm compression plate so that the owner can raise the ratio to approximately 7.6 to 1 on the 490 c.c. model, or 7.8 to 1 in the case of the three-fifty. With the latter machine the gear ratios are 5.15, 5.66, 6.85 and 12 to 1.

Like the E.S.2 and the Manx models, these machines have rear-wheel springing as standard. A detail point is that the primary chain cases on these o.h.c. models are finished in black and chromium.

The racing models, the Manx machines, are equipped all ready for the fray, even to the provision of racing number plates with built-in fixings. There are two, the 79.62×100 mm. (499 c.c.) and the 71×

88 mm. (348 c.c.), both at the same price. Magnesium light-alloy crankcases and aluminium-alloy cylinders and cylinder heads are standardized. These last are the famous "square heads," which in plan view measure approximately 10in × 9½in overall. The engines are built and tuned in the experimental department. The 499 c.c. has a compression ratio of 7.23 to 1 and is provided with three compression plates, two of them 1½ mm. thick and the third ½ mm. Thus a ratio up to approximately 9 to 1 is possible. Plates of the same thickness are provided in the case of the 348 c.c. machine; this has a ratio of 7.33 to 1, which can be raised to approximately 9.5 to 1.

### The New Front Forks

Among the features of these machines are a 4½-gallon fuel tank floating in rubber—the bolts run right through the tank with rubber mountings top and bottom—cone-type front brake with aluminium alloy brake plate, long pressed clutch and front brake levers (the latter is 7⅜in from fulcrum to end), Dunlop racing tyres, light racing three-plate clutch with Ferodo bonded-asbestos linings, special racing four-speed gear box without kick-starter and Smith's rev counter mounted on the front forks. Tyres are 3.00×21 ribbed front and 3.50×20 and 3.25×20 studded rear on the 499 c.c. and 348 c.c. models respectively. Dunlop mudguard pads—"seats" is more apt in view of the size—are standard, so are sponge-rubber pads for the tank top. Quick-lift, large-diameter filler caps are fitted to both the fuel and oil tanks. The brakes are 8in diameter and have 1½in wide linings; the standard models have 7in diameter, 1¼in wide brakes. All the overhead-camshaft models have hairpin valve springs.

The gear ratios standardized for the 499 and 348 c.c. Manx models are respectively 4.42, 5.36, 5.86 and 7.82 to 1, and 5.16, 5.67, 6.85 and 9.14 to 1.

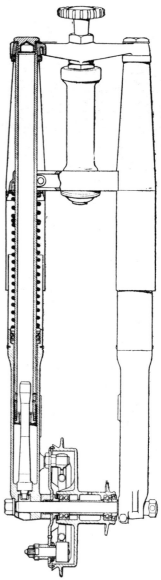

**A part-sectional view of the new hydraulically controlled "Roadholder" front forks such as were used in the Manx Grand Prix and which are now standard on all models. An interesting feature is the employment of two springs, of different rates, in each leg**

Lastly, and most important, there are the new front forks. How efficient the Norton telescopic front forks—the "Roadholder" forks—are was demonstrated in remarkable fashion in the Manx Grand Prix. On all sides there were approving comments on the way the many new "Manx" Nortons which competed were holding the road and steering to the proverbial hair.

Unlike the pre-war racing Norton telescopic forks, the "Roadholder" incorporates hydraulic damping. The construction is one of most praiseworthy sim-

**Ready for the fray! The "Manx" Nortons, specially built and specially tuned, are available to all. They are of 499 and 348 c.c., and have magnesium crankcases, light-alloy cylinders and cylinder heads and megaphone exhaust systems**

Plunger-type rear springing, "Roadholder" front forks—the latest E.S.2 Norton. A specially low-lift central stand is fitted as a prop-stand

plicity. There are the usual main fork tubes. These are of $1\frac{11}{32}$in outside diameter and 7 gauge; in the case of the racing, the "Manx," models, they are of chrome-molybdenum, and on the other machines, Reynold's A quality. The slides which carry the wheel spindle are of light alloy, which on the racing models is polished. At the lower end of each fork tube, operating on the aluminium, is a steel bush 1in long and $1\frac{13}{32}$in in diameter. This bush is held in place by the restrictor plug which is screwed into the end of the fork tube and is arranged so that it is free to rotate.

The upper bush, which operates on the steel fork tube, is of phosphor-bronze and has a length of $1\frac{1}{2}$in. Immediately above is a Super Oil Seals oil seal. There are two main springs. The long one is of 40 to 45lb per in deflection, and the short one, the buffer spring at the top, of 200lb per in.

Hydraulic damping is effected with delightful simplicity. Extending up from the base of each slider is a double-acting restriction plunger. This, it will be noted from the drawing, has a parallel portion which occupies the restrictor plug when the forks are in their normal, static-load position. It is parallel over a distance of 2in. Hence over the initial travel of the forks there is substantially free movement so far as the hydraulic side is concerned—merely the action of the fork springs. A greater deflection and, on upward travel, the long gentle tapered portion of the plunger enters the restrictor plug and provides a gradually increasing damping effect. At extreme deflection, owing to say, an unusually severe road shock, a parallel portion enters the restrictor plug and there is complete cut-off,

with oil trapped to form a buffer.

On downward movement of the sliders—that is, on rebound—a short, steep taper comes into operation, followed by, in extreme cases, a parallel portion. Again there is a hydraulic buffer, but in this instance it is provided in the annulus between the main tube and the slider. As the phosphor-bronze and steel bearings approach each other, the upper, the phosphor-bronze bearing, covers ports in the main tube. At a distance of $1\frac{5}{8}$in from the bottom of the fork tube there are $\frac{3}{16}$in holes and at $1\frac{3}{16}$, $\frac{1}{8}$in holes. Thus there is progressive cut-off of the oil in the annulus and, finally, complete cut-off, the $\frac{1}{8}$in holes being covered by the bush and oil trapped in the annulus to form a cushion.

"Castrolite," half a pint per leg, forms the hydraulic and, automatically, the lubrication medium. Steering-head adjustment is carried out by slackening the top hexagon on the steering stem and the pinch bolts which fix the main tubes to the lower cross-member and screwing down the adjuster nut. An interesting point is that with the new Roadholder forks there is a saving of no less than 14lb in unsprung weight as compared with the old girder-fork arrangement. The total travel of the forks is $5\frac{3}{8}$in, of which approximately $3\frac{3}{4}$in is the maximum upward travel from normal load position. These are "theoretical" measurements, the hydraulic buffers preventing metal-to-metal contact.

## PRICES

| Model | List Price £ s | | Purchase Tax £ s d | | |
|---|---|---|---|---|---|
| 16H, 490 c.c. side-valve .... | 125 | 0 | 33 | 15 | 0 |
| No. 1 (Big Four) 633 c.c. s.v. | 128 | 5 | 34 | 12 | 6 |
| 18, 490 c.c. o.h.v. ........ | 130 | 0 | 35 | 2 | 0 |
| E.S.2, 490 c.c. o.h.v. ..... | 142 | 0 | 38 | 6 | 9 |
| 30, 490 c.c. o.h.c. ......... | 181 | 0 | 48 | 17 | 5 |
| 40, 348 c.c. o.h.c. ......... | 174 | 0 | 46 | 19 | 7 |
| 30 Manx, 499 c.c. o.h.c. .... | 235 | 0 | 63 | 9 | 0 |
| 40 Manx, 348 c.c. o.h.c. .... | 235 | 0 | 63 | 9 | 0 |
| 500 Trials, 490 c.c. o.h.v. .. | 135 | 0 | 36 | 9 | 0 |
| 350 Trials, 348 c.c. o.h.v. .. | 135 | 0 | 36 | 9 | 0 |
| Speedometer ............... | 4 | 0 | 1 | 1 | 7 |

Makers: Norton Motors, Ltd., Aston, Birmingham, 6, England.

# Road Impressions of New Models

# 490cc Spring-Frame ES2 Norton

A Fast, Lively Sports Mount, Fitted with the New. Norton "Road= holder" Front Forks : Speed with Safety : Easy Starting and Excellent Slogging Powers

By "TORRENS"

Telescopic front forks, rear springing—the new spring-frame 490 c.c. E.S.2 Norton

OVER many years has the Norton held an important place in my affections. First, I only knew the make by repute and as a result of watching machines win hill-climbs and speed trials. Then I owned "Willing William," a 1925 16H Norton, which was used for almost everything from "covering" a London-Edinburgh trial to tackling "impossible" hills on Exmoor. Never did that 70 m.p.h. side-valve let me down. Also, there was "Rhoda," the first of the T.T.-winning overhead-camshaft Nortons, which I took just as she was, except for a special-ratio gear box, and used for a holiday hill-hunting on Exmoor. An overhead-camshaft Norton, too, was my choice when I carried out a lengthy series of tests of tyres of differing section—a cradle-frame camshaft Norton, because that was the machine which was outstanding in both steering and road-holding and which alone, in my experience, would enable me to detect precisely what difference tyres could make to a motor cycle.

### Easy Starting

What of the new E.S.2 Norton, with its telescopic front forks and plunger-type rear springing? This machine has the Norton cradle frame which has been eulogized ever since it was introduced. Like its forebears, the E.S.2 is a lusty performer. Wisely, the makers of the Norton have never gone in for mere discs of flywheels. They have made machines with plenty of flywheel, its accompaniment—flexibility—and high performance. Among other things those flywheels spell an engine which can be spun by means of the kick-starter and, therefore, can be counted upon to start really easily. The machine tested was started second kick from cold by—if she will excuse the description—a slip of a girl. Were all machines of the type one-half as easy to start there would be little criticism of the single cylinder engine as regards starting.

The only point which anyone could raise is that the engine can kick back heartily if there is too large a throttle opening; with a large throttle opening, as is to be expected, the ignition needs retarding.

Where the Norton scores is that it combines both liveliness with slogging power. There is nothing mettlesome about it, yet it can hold its own, if desired, with almost anything on the road. It is a machine of the 80 m.p.h. class. At the other end of the scale, however, it will amble along at some 15 or 16 m.p.h. in top gear, which is 4.64 to 1. There is some transmission flutter as one opens up, but no harsh snatching.

For a fast sports mount the riding position is "touring." The footrests in their lowest position (10¼in from feet to ground) are but a bare 20½in below the level of the peak of the saddle, which is not adjustable. The handlebars are adjustable for angle and, within the range of the 1½in-centre clips, for height. With my 5ft 10½in and some 31in from foot to crutch it was not possible to obtain a riding position that gave me full comfort and at-one-ness with the machine.

The motor cycle, with its road-holding and its excellence of steering, does not call for any holding. The way it swirls round bends is delightful, and the same

This view shows the new Norton "Roadholder" front forks and the front portion of the famous cradle frame. The lamp brackets are of built-in type

**The engine remained pleasantly free from oil leakage during the 550-mile test**

applies to straight-ahead speed work; it is a cradle-frame Norton. Not once, but several times I found that the machine had tucked some 50 miles into 60 minutes —had done so without the rider seeking specially high averages. And it is a safe motor cycle in another aspect; the brakes are some of the best I have used. They are extremely light in operation, but relentless in action. There is no roughness, but retardation that is foreign to all but outstandingly well-braked spring-frame machines. When the brakes are applied there is no rear-wheel bounce. The wheel remains on the road to provide one with stopping power.

### Speed with Safety

Both the front and rear suspension are comparatively stiff and show their full value when the machine is driven hard. The rear springing is of plunger type. How much it adds to the machine is demonstrated by the speed with safety of the motor cycle and by that smooth, effortless braking.

Already the steering on corners and at high speeds has been remarked upon; at the walking speeds which are so often a feature of town work the steering is particularly good. The rider can trickle along feet-up at speeds which the speedometer will not register and, starting off from rest, he will have his feet on the footrests immediately the clutch begins to bite.

At the intermediate speeds I was not so impressed by the steering. I found, as was confirmed by riding hands-off, that the machine tended to wander a little, which is something that experience in other directions suggests would probably be overcome by the use of lighter front fork springs. [The Works state that rather lighter springs have been standardized.—Ed.] With the machine tested the forks did not respond appreciably to minor road irregularities.

Ever since I have known Nortons, the make has been famed for its ease of gear-changing. Unless the foot gear change has been used as a hack-change, the gears, up and down, engage without a sound and without the slightest degree of skill being demanded. With the machine under review the gears were silent in operation— it was impossible from the gear box angle to tell which ratio was in use—and the gear change was good. The latter missed perfection, however, owing to slight clutch drag. Examination suggested that the clutch lever fitted had insufficient movement to ensure that if the clutch freed completely there was still the necessary backlash in the control cable. The gear ratios, which are 4.64, 5.61, 8.2 and

13.8 to 1, are very well chosen indeed.

With a five-hundred sports mount a matter that looms large in the eyes of so many is the ease or otherwise with which the machine can be put on the stand. In the case of the Norton there is a low-lift central stand so designed that it is properly accessible to the foot. To put the machine on the stand, all that is necessary is to place the right thigh against the cheek of the saddle and give a quite-gentle push backwards. The weight of the machine with a "full" oil tank and the fuel tank rather more than two-thirds full came out at 399lb. Twin fuel taps are fitted to the tank, so there is no need to drain the tank should it be desired to remove it

This last is one of the many little refinements found on the machine. For instance, the rear-brake pedal is adjustable for angle by means of a stop; there is a very neat speedometer panel mounted at the top of the telescopic front forks, with the speedometer dial in just about the ideal position; the control cables run through rubber-bushed holes in the panel; a rubber-mounted type of Lucas battery is fitted, which means that the cells are readily accessible for topping-up; there are excellent "tommy-bar" filler caps; and hand adjusters of effective type for brakes and clutch; an unusually comprehensive tool-kit is provided; the rear-chain adjusters are really accessible, and the back portion of the rear mudguard is quickly detachable.

The exhaust is well toned down and the note pleasant. There is a certain, but not annoying, amount of "clack" from the engine. How pleasantly free from oil leaks the latter remained will be seen

**A close-up of the plunger-type rear suspension. Note how the rear chain guard is carried downwards, the breather for the rear chain, the adjustable stop for the brake pedal, and the mudguard, which is detachable just below the lifting handle. Since the test was carried out, the makers have standardized a spring-up rear stand and the central stand, of low lift, becomes a prop-stand**

## Road Impressions
### of New Models—

from the photographs, which were taken at the end of some 450 miles.

While the present—or recent—pool petrol has probably been the worst to date as regards the tendency for engines to knock on it, the Norton, in spite of its high efficiency, did not pink readily, and there was still that Norton cart-horse-like pulling on hills. The engine will also rev. and many a time the machine was taken well into the "sixties" in third before top was snicked in. At first I felt that the balance was not up to the standards achieved with sundry single-cylinder engines of to-day. At 60 m.p.h. there appeared to be a fair amount of vibration, which tailed off at higher speeds. Transferring the hands to near the middle of the handlebars, however, suggested that the vibration was more apparent than real —by this I mean that the particular bars, which are bent into the form of a squat M, were doing most of the vibrating and that the engine itself is quite well balanced.

Driving light with the well-tucked-in 7in

Neat speedometer panel at the top of the telescopic front forks. It is doubtful whether the speedometer dial could be in a better position from the rider's point of view

head lamp proved to be very good indeed. There was useful width to the beam, plus sufficient light forward for fast riding. As with other machines I have tested post-war, the pilot bulb in the head lamp could not be relied upon. The bulb was slack in its holder and while turning the bulb through 180 degrees effected a cure, this was only temporary.

Fuel consumption at a maintained 30 m.p.h. over the undulating roads I use as my standard test worked out at 80 m.p.g At a maintained 40 m.p.h. it was 73 m.p.g.

On one journey the engine started cutting out at medium and long throttle openings. Since there had been a considerable amount of hard driving, a stop was made to examine the sparking plug.

There were no signs of excessive heat, but another plug was fitted, just in case. The cutting out continued. It was cured, without a further stop, by the simple expedient of placing a gloved hand over the bell-mouthed air intake of the carburettor —doing so with the throttle well open— that old but useful tip for clearing an obstructed jet

The machine is an excellent example of a fast overhead-valve single, one which can be counted upon to give lasting service. It is lively, superbly braked and endowed with bend-swinging which is enthralling.

Makers: Norton Motors, Ltd., Bracebridge Street, Birmingham, 6 Price, with speedometer, £146. Purchase tax (in Great Britain) £38 6s 9d on machine and £1 1s 7d on speedometer.

## Road Tests of New Models

# 490 c.c. Mode

### A High-performance Race-bred Mac

FEW engines have so enviable a reputation (and are sought after so much) as the overhead-camshaft Norton. The power unit fitted to the Model 30 "International" is the basis of the famous "Manx" model which gives such a good account of itself in road races all over the world. Perhaps the most notable characteristic of the "Manx" engine is its capacity for sustained high speeds under racing conditions without being

**Every inch a race-bred roadster, the Norton is the nearest approach possible to a racing machine in road trim**

over-stressed and with a measure of reliability that is extraordinary.

This feature is apparent with the Model 30. No matter how hard the machine is ridden the engine feels always to be working well within its limits and to be capable of going on and on relentlessly eating up the miles. Even when deliberately over-revved in the lower gear ratios the engine retains its "solid" feeling; indeed, some difficulty was experienced in deciding the maximum speed in bottom gear—the speed given in the performance data is the figure considered to be usable with no chance of harmful effects, but, if it were desired, over 50 m.p.h. could be reached without audible protest from the engine.

In the higher gears the Norton is correspondingly rapid, although it would obviously have a higher maximum speed in third and top ratios if the exhaust were unsilenced. In addition, acceleration could be improved upon were a higher octane fuel available.

Starting was easy at all engine temperatures providing certain points were borne in mind. When cold, the T.T.-type carburettor required to be copiously flooded, the air lever to be closed, the throttle fractionally open and the ignition half retarded; then with the easily-operated exhaust-valve lifter in use a first-kick start was assured. Similar tactics were used for a warm engine except that it was unnecessary to flood the carburettor. The engine was rather susceptible to both air and ignition controls.

On first acquaintance it might be considered that the Norton was inclined to be intractable and harsh under low-speed traffic conditions. Actually this was not so if the ignition control was used intelligently. In fact, properly driven, the Model 30 proves as suitable for town work as any average single-cylinder.

A trace of clutch drag made low speed gear changing slightly heavy, and it was not usual to obtain an absolutely clean change from bottom to second gears. However, changing from second to third and third to top and vice versa was as effortless as it should be bearing in mind the closeness of the ratios. The gear-change pedal is nicely positioned and the positive-stop mechanism has a pleasing, "taut" movement.

The riding position is a happy compromise between the average racing and touring layouts. The saddle is high—32in from the ground with the machine unladen—and the handlebars, measuring 29in from tip to tip, are wider than average. The footrests are far enough below the saddle to give a comfortable leg position, yet there is no chance of their grounding when the machine is heeled well over.

The result is that the rider sits over the machine and feels master of his destiny at all speeds and under all road conditions.

For high-speed road work few riders would ask for more than this machine offers. It will cruise effortlessly and indefinitely in the seventies and do so with a degree of riding comfort that has to be experienced to be appreciated. The well-known cradle frame now fitted with the proved plunger-type rear springing and the post-war Roadholder front fork gives hairline steering, first-class road-holding and excellent stability.

A particularly good point is that these qualities are apparent throughout the speed range—from walking pace to maximum. Though the rear springing is relatively "hard," it makes all the difference to comfort over such "hazards" as cobbles and tramway inspection covers at town-traffic speeds. Similarly, although the Norton has the feel of a big machine it can be manœuvred and weaved in traffic at a walking pace as readily

**The overhead-camshaft "International" engine has hairpin valve springs and a T.T.-type carburettor**

# 30 NORTON

## h Spring-frame and Telescopic Forks

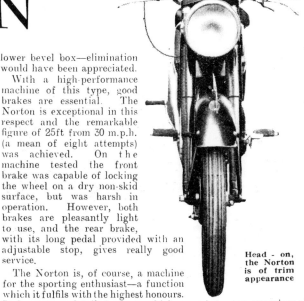

**Head - on, the Norton is of trim appearance**

as many machines of half its size. At the other end of the performance range, front and rear suspensions work so well and the steering is so good that it is well to keep an eye on the speedometer. Incidentally, the speedometer is mounted in an instrument panel bridging the fork legs and can be read with a minimum of distraction.

Fast cornering with the machine well heeled over could be indulged in with complete confidence and there was not the slightest "chopping-out" or wavering on bumpy surfaces.

Top gear—4.64 to 1—is on the high side for a five-hundred, and coupled with the surging, effortless power of the o.h.c. engine endows the Model 30 with its easy seventy-mile-an-hour gait so much appreciated on long-distance journeys. The third ratio—5.62 to 1—is very well chosen for a machine of this type and is the gear to use on gentle up-grades, against head winds, and when the mood is such that the ultimate in acceleration is required at speeds in excess of a mile a minute. The intermediate ratios are smooth and noiseless, and no greater compliment can be paid to the excellent third gear than to say that it can easily be mistaken for top.

The "solid" feeling of the Norton is coupled with a sensation that the engine is "remote," for although the valve gear is audible it passes unnoticed and there is no vibration until about 65 m.p.h. in top gear is reached. At this speed and above there is a slight tremor at the handlegar grips.

A vegetable-base oil is used in the dry-sump lubrication system of the Model 30. Oil leakage occurred from cam box and lower bevel box—elimination would have been appreciated.

With a high-performance machine of this type, good brakes are essential. The Norton is exceptional in this respect and the remarkable figure of 25ft from 30 m.p.h. (a mean of eight attempts) was achieved. On the machine tested the front brake was capable of locking the wheel on a dry non-skid surface, but was harsh in operation. However, both brakes are pleasantly light to use, and the rear brake, with its long pedal provided with an adjustable stop, gives really good service.

The Norton is, of course, a machine for the sporting enthusiast—a function which it fulfils with the highest honours. It has many detail features which appeal to any experienced rider and make so much difference to pride of ownership. This 1947 edition of a famous breed is in keeping with the tradition of its illustrious predecessors. As a high-speed road machine it embodies every feature desired by the enthusiast plus the suitability for racing, if required, in, say, the Clubman's T.T.

# Information Panel

## 490 c.c. Model 30 Norton

### SPECIFICATION

**TYPE :** Norton, Model 30.

**ENGINE :** 490 c.c. (79 x 100 mm.) single-cylinder, overhead-camshaft. Dry-sump lubrication.

**CARBURETTOR :** Amal T10 T.T. type ; twist-grip throttle control ; handlebar air-lever.

**GEAR BOX :** Norton, with positive-stop foot control. Bottom, 10.8 to 1. Second, 6.1 to 1. Third, 5.1 to 1. Top, 4.64 to 1.

**CLUTCH :** Norton multi-plate with vane-type shock absorber.

**TRANSMISSION :** Chain. Primary $\frac{1}{2}$ x .305in. Secondary $\frac{5}{8}$ x $\frac{1}{4}$in.

**IGNITION :** Lucas magneto with manual control.

**LIGHTING :** Lucas Magdyno ; 8in headlamp.

**FUEL CAPACITY :** $3\frac{3}{4}$ gallons. Oil Capacity : 6 pints.

**TYRE SIZES :** Front, 3.00 x 21in Dunlop ribbed. Rear, 3.25 x 20in Dunlop Universal.

**BRAKES :** Both 7in diameter by $1\frac{1}{4}$in wide ; hand adjusters.

**SUSPENSION :** "Roadholder" telescopic fork with hydraulic damping ; plunger-type rear springing.

**WHEELBASE :** $54\frac{3}{4}$in. Ground Clearance : $4\frac{1}{2}$in unladen.

**SADDLE :** Terry.

**WEIGHT :** 421lb, with 2 gallons of fuel and fully equipped.

**PRICE :** £194 10s., plus Purchase Tax (in Britain)—£247 0s.4d. Speedometer extra £4 plus £1 1s. 8d. Purchase Tax.

**MAKERS :** Norton Motors, Ltd., Bracebridge Street, Birmingham, 6.

### PERFORMANCE DATA

**MAXIMUM SPEED :**

| | |
|---|---|
| First : | 47 m.p.h. |
| Second : | 69 m.p.h. |
| Third : | 80 m.p.h. |
| Top : | 86 m.p.h. |

**ACCELERATION :**

| | 10-30 m.p.h. | 20-40 m.p.h. | 30-50 m.p.h. |
|---|---|---|---|
| Bottom | 3 secs. | $3\frac{1}{2}$ secs. | — |
| Second | — | 5 secs. | $4\frac{4}{5}$ secs. |
| Third | — | — | $6\frac{4}{5}$ secs. |

Speed at end of quarter-mile from rest : 72 m.p.h.
Time to cover standing quarter mile : $16\frac{3}{5}$ secs.

**PETROL CONSUMPTION :** At 30 m.p.h., 96 m.p.g. At 40 m.p.h., 88 m.p.g. At 50 m.p.h., 68 m.p.g. At 60 m.p.h., 51 m.p.g.

**BRAKING :** From 30 m.p.h. to rest, 25ft. (surface : dry tar macadam).

**TURNING CIRCLE :** $17\frac{1}{2}$ft diameter.

**MINIMUM NON-SNATCH SPEED :** 16 m.p.h. in top gear.

**WEIGHT PER C.C. :** 0.86lb.

**R.P.M. IN TOP GEAR** at 30 m.p.h. : 1,706.

# TWO NEW NORTON

A machine with a world-wide reputation—the handsome 490 c.c. overhead camshaft "International" model

## The Side-valve and Overhead-valve Units Redesigned for 1948

WHEREVER motor cycles are discussed, the name Norton is almost sure to be voiced. But when Nortons announce, as it were in one breath, the birth of two new engines, then indeed must the tongues of motor cyclists work loose; for the occasion is an important one.

Greater mechanical quietness, increased power and the prevention of "whip" are the main objects behind the creation of the new engines now being fitted to overhead-valve models 18 and ES2, and to side-valve model 16H. The other side-valve machine, the "Big 4," will have a unit built on the same lines as that for the 16H.

### New Timing Gear

Both new engines—one an overhead-valve and the other a side-valve—retain a bore and stroke of 79 × 100mm, giving a capacity of 490 c.c. But an entirely new timing gear has been evolved and is used for both power units. A mainshaft pinion drives two cam pinions which, of course, revolve at ½-engine speed. Cam followers have been dispensed with and, instead, the cams operate directly on flat-based tappets, which in turn operate pushrods or side-valves, depending on which engine one has in mind. The inner faces of the cam wheels are indented, or "dished," thus making room for the reciprocating movement of the tappet bases. This arrangement ensures a very neat timing chest, and avoids waste space that might cause resonance. Moreover, simplification of the timing gear, together with its rigidity and generous size, should make for mechanical quietness.

Further width is saved by the mainshaft pinion's being retained by a nut actually carrying the worm gear that drives the oil pump. This nut contains three holes into which a special tool may be inserted as a "spanner." The nut has a left-hand thread which ensures that inertia forces keep it tight.

The flywheels on both models are of smaller diameter than before, but are of greater width. Thus the same kinetic energy is retained; but the new flywheels allow a redesigned, longer-skirt piston to be used, with consequent reduction in piston slap and in wear of the cylinder bore.

To increase rigidity, the tubular pushrods for the overhead-valve engine are shorter and of larger overall diameter. The cross-section thickness of the pushrods is such that they are now lighter as well. They are also more widely placed, and their covers are positively sealed by means of heat-resisting washers at the top and synthetic rubber washers at the bottom.

Apart from having an inspection cover, which, when removed, allows valve clearances to be adjusted, the rocker box on the overhead-valve engine is now cast in one piece. Rockers have been stiffened, lightened and made smaller, and now operate on fixed shafts. Oil is pressure-fed to the rocker box from a synthetic rubber T-piece inserted in the return pipe beneath the oil tank. From the T-piece a pipe carries the oil up and under the petrol tank to a banjo union on the near-side of the rocker box. Then, through drillings in the box, the oil passes to the rockers.

A description of the cycle as it affects each rocker is as follows: From the drilling fed by the banjo union, the oil passes into a drilling along the stationary rocker shafts. Each rocker, being mounted on a plain bearing at its ends, leaves a small annular ring of space round the middle of the shaft. Into this annular space, from within the shaft and through a further drilling, the oil passes, thus lubricating the plain bearings.

Another oil-way passes from the inside of the shaft to its outside (here indented with a tiny annular ring) and feeds lubri-

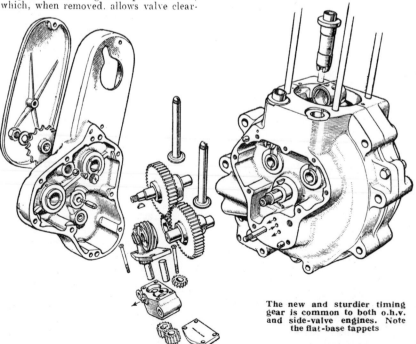

The new and sturdier timing gear is common to both o.h.v. and side-valve engines. Note the flat-base tappets

# ENGINES

A very famous side-valve, the 16H, is now further improved

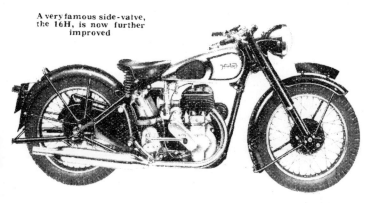

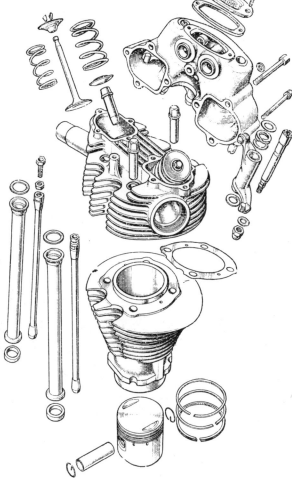

cant through the off-side plain bearing. along a drilling in the rocker arm, through the ball-end and into the push rod cup itself.

Surplus oil collecting on the timing side of the rocker box passes down inside the push-rod covers and into the timing case. Oil collecting in the valve spring wells passes through internal drillings in the head and barrel, and returns to the crank case.

### Side-valve Cylinder Head

Valve springs and stems on the side-valve model are now contained in a new, die-cast, aluminium-alloy compartment or chest—shaped rather like a pair of inverted trouser legs. The openings at the top of this valve chest are large enough to allow the withdrawal of valves and springs in situ when the barrel is removed. Synthetic rubber washers seal the bottom of the chest, and metal-bonded asbestos washers seal the top. There is a space between the chest and the cylinder barrel for a free flow of air. An inspection cover is incorporated.

A new cylinder barrel is used on the side-valve unit and a small part of the valve-seating area is machined out in order to suit the geometry of the valves, which are now inclined towards each other slightly at their heads

The side-valve cylinder head is of heat-treated aluminium alloy, generously finned, the continuity of fins being maintained wherever possible. A 14mm sparking plug with a long reach ensures not only that there is little break-up in combustion chamber space but also that sufficient bulk of metal is retained for dissipation of heat.

Solid, soft aluminium cylinder-head gaskets are used for both engines.

All models are now fitted with an 8in, domed head-lamp glass. This provides a better beam of light and improves appearance. Solid type clutch and front brake levers are standard.

The famous overhead-camshaft models continue unaltered for 1948. These comprise Models 30 and 40 "International," and 30 and 40 "Manx." Of 499 c.c. and 348 c.c., the "Manx" models are specially built to racing specification, with aluminium-alloy heads and barrels, and are specially tuned. Their slightly gentler brothers, the "Internationals," have engines of 490 and 348 c.c., and are,

The redesigned rocker mechanism. Rockers have been stiffened and lightened and now work on fixed spindles

of course, fully equipped road machines.

All models continue to have the well-tried Norton cradle frame, and Norton "Roadholder" front forks are fitted throughout. A spring-frame is standard on the ES2 and overhead-camshaft models

### Sports-touring Sidecar

Included in the 1948 range is the Model G sports-touring sidecar. Later on, redesigned trials machines will be announced. It will be seen that, with their new programme, Nortons continue to cater for many types of rider—from the out-and-out racing man to the family sidecarrist. Makers are Norton Motors, Ltd., Bracebridge Street, Birmingham, 6. Prices are as follows:—

| Model | Basic Price | | | Total Price | | |
|---|---|---|---|---|---|---|
| | £ | s | d | £ | s | d |
| 16H, 490 c.c. s.v. | 134 | 10 | 0 | 170 | 16 | 4 |
| No. 1, "Big 4" s.v. | 138 | 0 | 0 | 175 | 5 | 2 |
| 18 490 c.c. o.h.v. | 139 | 10 | 0 | 177 | 3 | 4 |
| ES2, 490 c.c. o.h.v. | 152 | 10 | 0 | 193 | 13 | 6 |
| 30, 490 c.c. o.h.c. | 194 | 10 | 0 | 247 | 0 | 4 |
| 40, 348 c.c. o.h.c. | 187 | 10 | 0 | 238 | 2 | 6 |
| 30 M, 499 c.c. o.h.c. | 248 | 0 | 0 | 314 | 19 | 2 |
| 40 M, 348 c.c. o.h.c. | 248 | 0 | 0 | 314 | 19 | 2 |
| Model "G" sidecar | 46 | 0 | 0 | 58 | 5 | 4 |
| Speedometer extra | 4 | 0 | 0 | 5 | 1 | 8 |

For long one of the most popular models in the range—the push-rod Model 18

## ROAD TESTS OF NEW MODELS

# 490 c.c. Overhead-valve

### A Machine Capable of Effort

FOR many years the overhead-valve Nortons have maintained a reputation in touring spheres of staunch reliability, of being capable of high average speeds, and of having handling qualities and brakes well above the average. The 1949 490 c.c. ES2 adds another attribute to the list—mechanical quietness.

The valve-operating mechanism was redesigned in 1947. In its new form, with flat-base tappets bearing directly on the cams, it is now commendably quiet : so much so that when the engine is ticking over or running light, the predominant sounds, apart from the exhaust, emanate from the primary chain and the piston.

One of the ES2's most appealing characteristics is its capacity for maintaining high average speeds for long periods without the engine giving any indication that it is being overstressed. Mile after mile can be covered with the speedometer needle on the 70 mark, yet the engine feels always to be working effortlessly

brake, clutch and ignition controls are well placed and require no great hand-reach for their operation.

It might be imagined that with the machine's high-speed cruising propensities and high gearing the ES2 would be intractable in traffic. Provided reasonable use is made of the ignition control, the engine is extremely flexible and docile. It was unusually responsive to the ignition lever and pleasantly free from pinking. The engine was smooth except for a bad vibration period between 60 and 70 m.p.h. in top gear. Acceleration under normal conditions was decidedly brisk. With the rider really trying, as, for example, when the acceleration figures were taken, the performance was most exhilarating ; some idea of the power available in bottom gear (13.84 to 1) can be judged by the fact that the urge caused the tail end of the machine to snake even on a surface of coarse-chipped macadam. When snap gear changes were made, the front fork legs were made to extend to their fullest extent.

*Left : Saddle height on the ES2 is 31in. The riding position affords excellent control at all speeds*

*Below : The renowned "Roadholder" fork gives exceptionally positive steering. Note the 8in head lamp with domed glass*

and well within its limits. During the 600-mile test, 50 m.p.h. averages were commonplace, and the reliability throughout 100 per cent ; the tools were required only to set the controls to suit the rider at the beginning of the test and to readjust the horn, which developed a flat note. The brakes, which have finger-type adjusters, were reset twice.

Starting at all engine temperatures was certain at the first or second kick, and the control setting simple. With the engine cold, the carburettor required to be only lightly flooded ; the air lever was then closed and the throttle fractionally opened by turning the lever-operated throttle stop on the side of the mixing chamber. After use of the exhaust-valve lifter to ease the piston over the top of the compression stroke, a long swinging kick assured a positive start. In cold weather, kick-starting required some physical effort. When the engine was hot, it was necessary to retard the ignition about one-third and, provided that the throttle was barely open, first- or second-kick starting was again certain.

The saddle height, 31in, is greater than average. The riding position, in point of fact, can almost be described as a compromise between racing and touring. Of the rather wide (29in from tip to tip) variety, the handlebars are carried in split clamps on the top fork bridge. The position of the grips provides a comfortable wrist angle. In the horizontal-rear setting, the footrests were excellently positioned for a shorter-than-average stature rider and at such a height from the road that there was no danger of their grounding when the machine was heeled well over on fast corners and bends. Tests with tall riders revealed that they, too, had an excellent riding position.

Few machines provide greater comfort at sustained high speeds than does the ES2. The relative positions of handlebars, saddle and footrests cause the rider to sit "over" the machine in such a way that he is in full command at all speeds. The

# ES2 NORTON

## High-speed Cruising

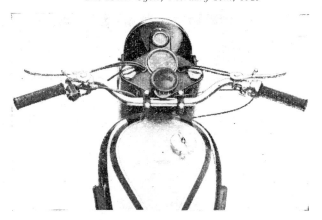

A lusty engine in itself is not sufficient to encourage high average speeds. First-class steering and road-holding and excellent brakes are also necessary. In these respects the Norton earns full marks. The combination of the well-known Norton cradle frame, the Norton plunger-type rear-springing, and Roadholder front fork, provides steering and road-holding that are altogether exceptional. The characteristics of the fore-and-aft suspension are rather hard, and over cobbles and pot-holes taken at traffic speeds only a slight measure of comfort is afforded. At the other end of the scale, the suspension comes into its own. Steering is positively hair-line on corners and bends, irrespective of whether the surface is smooth or bumpy. There was no "chopping" or "snaking," and fast, zestful cornering could be indulged in with the greatest confidence. The Norton also handled easily at a walking pace or even more slowly, and could be manœuvred easily in traffic.

The brakes were almost up to racing standards. Braking from high speeds could be accomplished smoothly and quickly. There was no harshness and no "fading." The solid-type front brake lever gave a delightfully positive feel. It was a little heavy in operation. The braking figure of 27ft 6in is the mean figure, achieved as a result of six tests, on a road surface of dry, coarse-chipped tarmac.

An especially noteworthy feature of the Norton was the excellence of the gear change. There was just the merest suggestion of clutch drag—which was so slight, however, that neutral could always be selected easily or bottom gear engaged quietly when the machine was stationary with the engine idling. At low engine revs (as, for example, in traffic), top gear generally had to be "fed" in by maintaining a light pressure on the gear control until the clutch was fully engaged. At high speeds the change was light and instantaneous, and slick gear changes could be made just as rapidly as the controls could be operated. In fact, so easy was the change that clean, sweet changes could be made whether the clutch was disengaged or not.

The clutch was smooth and sweet in taking up the drive, but driving comfort would have been enhanced had it been a little lighter in operation.

As has been remarked, the machine was ridden at higher-than-average cruising speeds during the test. Apart from a trace of

*Neat speedometer mounting on the Norton. The handlebars are of the wide, flat variety, measuring 29 in from tip to tip. Solid-type front brake and clutch levers are fitted*

oil flung from the rear chain on to the rear tyre and rim, and a slight drip of oil from the primary chain case, the machine remained remarkably clean. The engine and gear box proved completely oil-tight, and both filler caps were liquid-tight.

Fitted under the gear box is a sturdy spring-up centre stand. When the camber is such that the machine can be leaned in towards the rider, or the road is flat, it can be operated without undue physical effort; otherwise the effort required can be considerable.

The speedometer is mounted in a panel bridging the fork legs. In this position it is easily read. The instrument was accurate at 30 m.p.h. and approximately 2½ m.p.h. fast at 50 m.p.h. At all speeds the needle remained rock steady.

With its domed glass, the 8in head lamp gives a long wide beam, and it was possible to maintain daylight average speeds after dusk. The ammeter registered a slight charge when all lights were on at 32 m.p.h. in top and showed that the discharge was balanced at 30 m.p.h. A T-type battery is fitted. Topping-up is especially simple, since the lid can be raised by moving only two spring clips.

To sum up, it can be said of the ES2 that it is a machine which is capable of unusually high average speeds. It has an engine that is lively and powerful and the machine's handling and braking qualities are almost good enough to provide the criteria by which, in general, these features might be judged.

---

# Information Panel

### SPECIFICATION

**ENGINE** : 490 c.c. (79 x 100 mm) single-cylinder o.h.v. Fully-enclosed valve gear. Ball and roller bearings supporting mainshafts. Compression ratio, 6.6 to 1. Dry-sump lubrication ; oil capacity, 4 pints.

**CARBURETTOR** : Amal, with lever-operated throttle-stop for easy starting. Twistgrip throttle control. Gauze air-filter in air intake.

**IGNITION AND LIGHTING** : Lucas Magdyno, with manual ignition advance and retard control. 8in diameter head lamp with domed glass.

**TRANSMISSION** : Norton four-speed gear box with positive foot control. Top gear 4.66 to 1. Third, 5.64 to 1. Second, 8.24 to 1. Bottom, 13.84 to 1. Multi-plate clutch with Ferodo inserts. Primary chain, ⅜in x 0.305in in pressed-steel oil-bath case. Secondary chain, ⅝ x ¼in. R.p.m. at 30 m.p.h. in top gear, 1,810.

**FUEL CAPACITY** : 2¾ gallons.

**TYRES** : 19 x 3.25in Dunlop front and rear.

**BRAKES** : Both 7in diameter by 1⅛in wide ; hand adjusters.

**SUSPENSION** : Norton "Roadholder" telescopic front fork with hydraulic damping. Plunger-type rear-springing.

**WHEELBASE** : 56½in. Ground clearance, 5in unladen.

**SADDLE** : Lycett. Unladen height, 3 1in.

**WEIGHT** : 371lb, with approximately ½-gallon of fuel and fully equipped.

**PRICE** : £152 10s., plus Purchase Tax (in Britain)—£193 13s. 6d. Speedometer extra £4, plus £1 1s. 8d. Purchase Tax.

**ROAD TAX** : £3 15s. a year ; £1 0s. 8d. a quarter. Half duty if only standard ration is used.

**MAKERS** : Norton Motors Ltd., Bracebridge Street, Birmingham, 6.

**DESCRIPTION** : *The Motor Cycle*, October 30th, 1947.

### PERFORMANCE DATA

**MEAN MAXIMUM SPEED** : Bottom : 32 m.p.h.
Second : 53 m.p.h.
Third : 74 m.p.h.
Top : 78 m.p.h.

| ACCELERATION : | | | | | 10-30 m.p.h. | 20-40 m.p.h. | 30-50 m.p.h. |
|---|---|---|---|---|---|---|---|
| Bottom | ... | ... | ... | ... | 2.6 secs | | |
| Second | ... | ... | ... | ... | 4.4 secs | 4 secs | 4.4 secs |
| Third | ... | ... | ... | ... | — | 6.8 secs | 6.2 secs |
| Top | ... | ... | ... | ... | — | 7.6 secs | 7.4 secs |

Speed at end of quarter mile from rest 69 m.p.h.
Time to cover standing quarter-mile, 18.6 secs.

**PETROL CONSUMPTION** : At 30 m.p.h., 97.6 m.p.g. At 40 m.p.h., 81.6 m.p.g. At 50 m.p.h., 66.4 m.p.g. At 60 m.p.h., 54.4 m.p.g.

**BRAKING** : From 30 m.p.h. to rest : 27ft 6in (surface, dry tar macadam).

**TURNING CIRCLE** : 15 feet.

**MINIMUM NON-SNATCH SPEED** : 19 m.p.h. in top gear, with ignition fully retarded.

**WEIGHT PER C.C.** : 0.74 lb.

### Road Tests of Current Models

# THE 497 c.c. VERTICAL TWIN MODEL 7 "DOMINATOR"
# NORTON

ONE of the major attractions at the Earls Court Show last November was the new Model 7 "Dominator" Norton. For several years it had been common knowledge that the famous Bracebridge Street, Birmingham, factory was developing a 500 c.c. o.h.v. vertical twin-cylinder design, but here it was at last, no longer on the secret list and included in the 1949 range. And somehow the name chosen for it seemed particularly apt, for it was a machine of masterful appearance.

Naturally enough, the first question everyone asked was, "What will she do?" That was a subject for specula-

### A Machine With an Imposing Appearance and an Impressive Performance

The off-side of the "works" showing the transverse vertical cylinder - head finning below the rocker box, directing air on to the plugs, the new induction manifold and the compact gearbox.

tion, but with a reputation second to none for single-cylinder machines of superlative performance it could safely be assumed that Norton Motors, Ltd., had taken no chances when re-entering the multi-cylinder field after more than 40 years. Now "Motor Cycling" supplies the answer to that query in what is probably one of the most eagerly awaited test reports ever to be published.

On the "Dominator" displayed at the Show the carburetter was bolted direct to the cast-iron cylinder head, feeding a common induction tract. An important modification since made on

(Left) Dennis Hardwicke discovers the "Dominator's" ability to stand up to mile after mile of wide-open throttle work. (Below) With its bold, sweeping rear mudguard, and deep section fuel tank, the Model 7 presents a well-balanced appearance.

the production machines now going through the works is to be seen in the bifurcated light-alloy induction manifold giving separate feeds to each cylinder. The machine offered to us for test, equipped with this new carburation system, was the pilot production model, and one which had covered many thousands of miles on the road, whilst the power unit had put in many additional hours on the dynamometer. The results recorded below are, therefore, the more remarkable because they represent figures recorded and impressions gained after the equivalent of approximately two

The Editor makes a note of mental impressions gained following a fast 125-mile non-stop run on the Norton Model 7.

This forward view of the engine shows the cast-in inclined push-rod tunnels and the widely spaced exhaust ports.

seasons' hard usage by a private owner.

Prior to our test, valve clearances were measured to check that they were at the correct .002 in. inlet and .008 in. exhaust, tyre pressures were set at the recommended 21 lb. per sq. in. front, and 23 lb. per sq. in. back, footrests lowered (the three "Motor Cycling" testers involved are all long-legged) and brake and gear-change pedals adjusted to suit.

The first portion of the test consisted of a 125-mile run over a circuit which includes L o n d o n traffic, narrow straggling country villages, twisting secondary roads and many miles of a trunk highway on which wide throttle openings can be used for long periods. It is a circuit warranted to reveal any shortcomings in navigation or comfort, and one which is exceptionally hard on power units. Thanks to a combination of good road-holding, high maximum speed and really remarkable acceleration the "Dominator" covered the course in a time which certainly surprised the very experienced tester aboard.

With relatively high saddle and footrests, the riding position is almost identical with that of the Norton "International" model and is one which gives complete confidence in

high-speed cornering, an impression assisted by the specially shaped 3¾-gallon fuel tank, which provides a natural grip for knees and thighs. The characteristics of the Norton plunger rear-suspension system and "Road-Holder" telescopic front forks are sufficiently well known to make detailed description superfluous.

## Starting

The power unit proved to be an easy starter on its 6.7-to-1 compression ratio. From stone cold, a touch on the carburetter tickler and two "prods" on the kick-starter, with the air lever closed, produced an even tick-over. At all other times one kick, without flooding and with air wide open, was all that was needed. When cold, the tank-mounted oil-pressure gauge registered 80 lb. per sq. in. at 30 m.p.h. in top gear, but when the lubricant reached working temperatures the gauge remained steady at 70 lb. per sq. in. for all normal running, dropping to 40 lb. per sq. in. at tick-over speed. The engine was flexible, being quite happy at 20 m.p.h. in its 5-to-1 top gear and pulling away without pinking when the throttle was opened. The non-snatch limit in third gear (6.05) was 12 m.p.h., whilst in second gear (8.85) it was below walking speed.

Carburation was clean throughout the range; indeed, the most outstanding impression gained by each of the testers was the smooth rapidity with which the machine would accelerate from 30 to 85 m.p.h. or more with the rider normally seated and wearing full kit. The only detectable vibration throughout the range was a very faint tremor felt through the knee-grips, but not through the footrests, at approximately 75 m.p.h. in top.

The maximum speeds recorded on the accompanying testers' report sheet and

taken by stop-watches were, of course, obtained "lying down to it," so far as was possible with the standard footrests. The pillion seat and rests shown in the photographs are "extras"; an attempt was made to use these to get flatter, but it was found that the wide saddle then fouled the knees, so the normal position was maintained throughout the timed tests. Whilst in its element at high speeds, the "Dominator" nevertheless proved to be an equally pleasant machine in congested areas, slow-speed steering being very good indeed and the power unit unflurried in top gear when observing 30 m.p.h. limits.

Considering the large mileage already covered when our test was undertaken, the unit was reasonably quiet mechanically and the exhaust note, whilst not particularly subdued, was mellow and deep-toned. The unusual timing gear, with its separate, short chain drives to the automatic advance magneto and single camshaft, runs very quietly. Slight piston tap and valve-clearance click were noticeable when cold, but were not detectable on the road. The valve clearances, incidentally, remained unaltered after nearly 500 miles of brutal misuse, the machine being deliberately driven hard on the assumption that any o.h.v. Norton is likely to be so treated by a private owner!

The gearbox, like the engine, is of completely new design, and full marks must be awarded to the excellent short-travel change mechanism with its absence of lost motion. Gears could be engaged with absolute certainty and ease, even when pursuing racing tactics. Another very useful feature was the ability to find "neutral" by just tapping the change lever. The clutch, with its in-built shock absorber, also deserves high praise for, throughout the long series of acceleration tests—made the

### BRIEF SPECIFICATION OF THE "DOMINATOR" MODEL 7, 497 c.c. O.H.V. TWIN NORTON

**Engine:** Vertical twin, o.h.v., single chain-driven camshaft, 66 mm. bore by 72.6 mm. stroke = 497 c.c.; compression ratio, 6.7 to 1; dry sump lubrication by gear-pump; totally enclosed and positively lubricated valves and rockers; forged high tensile steel cranks with cast iron central flywheel; ball bearings on timing side, roller on drive side; H section R.R.56 Hiduminium light-alloy connecting rods; phosphor bronze small-end bushes; split big-ends with steel-backed micro-babbitt bearings; flat top light-alloy pistons each with one scraper and two compression rings; fully floating gudgeon pins; iron monobloc cylinder and iron head; Lucas magneto driven by separate chain; automatic advance; Amal carburetter.

**Transmission:** Separate Norton four-speed gearbox with built-in positive-stop foot-operation; ratios, 5.0, 6.05, 8.85 and 14.88 to 1; primary chain, ½ in. by .305 in., rear ⅝ in. by ¼ in.; oilbath primary chain-case.

**Frame:** Cradle-type; plunger-pattern rear springing; Norton "Road-Holder" hydraulically controlled, telescopic front forks; steering damper; spring-up central stand; bolt-up front stand; Lycett saddle; fully adjustable handlebars; side lifting handles.

**Wheels:** WM2/21 front rim, WM2/19 rear; Dunlop tyres, front 27-in. by 3-in.; rear 26-in. by 3.50-in. triple-studded; brakes, 7 ins. by 1¼ ins. front and rear; finger adjustment.

**Tanks:** Petrol 3¾ gals., oil 7 pints; both with quick opening, hinged filler caps; reserve fuel tap; petrol tank chromium plated with matt silver top and nose panels; recessed rubber knee grips; oil-pressure gauge in fuel tank top.

**Equipment:** 6v. Lucas separate gear-driven 45w. dynamo lighting with c.v.c.; electric h.t. horn; 8-in. headlamp with bulbous glass and dipping filament.

**Dimensions:** Saddle height, 30 ins.; wheelbase, 55 ins.; overall length, 86½ ins.; width, 27 ins.; ground clearance, 6½ ins.

**Weight:** 438 lb.

**Price:** £170 plus £45 18s. purchase tax. (Total price, £215 18s.)

**Extras:** Smiths 120 m.p.h. speedometer, £4 plus £1 1s. 8d. purchase tax. (Total, £5 1s. 8d.)

**Annual Tax:** £3 15s. (£1 0s. 8d. per quarter).

**Makers:** Norton Motors, Ltd., Bracebridge Street, Birmingham, 6.

---

more numerous because of the multiplicity of testers—it showed an ability to withstand abuse with no sign of "fade" and without need for adjustment.

The testers were frankly puzzled by the braking figures recorded from 30 m.p.h. in top gear—a standard feature in "Motor Cycling" tests. These returns showed what might be termed a "good average," yet each rider was under the impression before measurements were taken that the brakes came in the "very highly commended" class. Certain it is that they provided extremely rapid and safe retardation from high speeds, with that race-bred feel which inspires confidence. The matter remains a mystery, although the trio were of the united opinion that the front brake did not compare favourably with the rear stopper, and that it would be interesting to try the same machine with a "Manx" front anchor.

The "Dominator" is not light at 438 lb., but the weight is very well distributed, the steering being effortless at, or even below, walking speed; indeed, one of the testers managed that trick so beloved by cyclists when he balanced

feet on rests at a traffic light stop and managed to move off again without footing! The only time the weight was noticeable was when manhandling the machine in the garage, or when putting it on its central stand. The latter fitment is easy to "find" with the toe of one's shoe, but the existing lifting stay would be more conveniently placed were it nearer the saddle. As it is, however, if the steering damper is nipped up to prevent the forks swinging round, it is an easy lift from the near, rear side.

Whilst the "Dominator" never needed the steering damper on the road the testers were of the opinion that the front wheel on all "90-m.p.h.-or-over" machines (or, for that matter, of all motorcycles with any pretensions of going places quickly) should be balanced. Whilst it in no way affected the steering, the front wheel of the "Model 7" could be "felt" at high speeds, but we deliberately refrained whenever possible from making any alterations to the machine "as received," other than those relating to riding position. Actually, the only change made was that of plugs when, after a particularly gruelling set of acceleration tests, the engine refused to stop on the cut-out button. The plugs showed signs of whiskering, but

new ones of the same type subsequently gave no trouble. The only other "casualties" at the end of a very tough test consisted of a broken filament in the rear lamp, and a cracked toolbox mounting clip.

At the completion of the test a routine check was made on accessibility. The rubber-mounted tank is designed for quick detachability, and it was found that it could be removed in under three minutes and replaced equally quickly—it is simply a matter of one spanner, two petrol pipe unions, two horizontal bolts and then one can adjust valve clearances in comfort. Carburetter main jet, slides and throttle needle, front chain tensioner and clutch adjustment are all easily get-at-able; indeed, the only inaccessible fitting is the contact breaker, which is partially masked by the primary chain case; the points, however, can be checked for gap without difficulty. The rear wheel is made accessible by removal of a section of the rear guard, it only being necessary to slacken two pins and remove two nuts when the blade lifts away. The standard tool kit, carried in a very roomy metal case, is of good quality and comprehensive.

To sum up, the "Dominator" embodies all the speed qualities of the Norton race-bred tradition, and its smooth flexibility also makes it a delightful machine for town travel or lazing through the lanes.

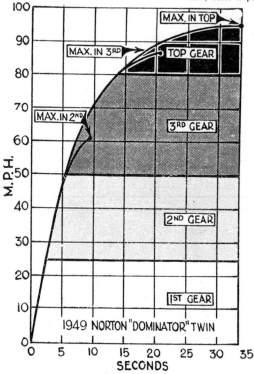

1949 NORTON "DOMINATOR" TWIN

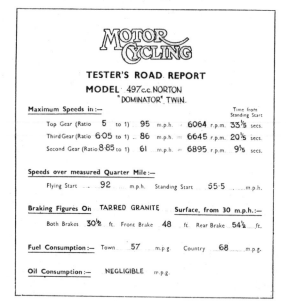

## TESTER'S ROAD REPORT
### MODEL 497 c.c. NORTON "DOMINATOR" TWIN.

**Maximum Speeds in:—**

|  |  |  |  | Time from Standing Start |
|---|---|---|---|---|
| Top Gear (Ratio 5 to 1) | 95 m.p.h. | = 6064 r.p.m. | 33⅕ secs. |
| Third Gear (Ratio 6·05 to 1) | 86 m.p.h. | = 6645 r.p.m. | 20⅕ secs. |
| Second Gear (Ratio 8·85 to 1) | 61 m.p.h. | = 6895 r.p.m. | 9⅕ secs. |

**Speeds over measured Quarter Mile:—**

Flying Start 92 m.p.h. Standing Start 55·5 m.p.h.

**Braking Figures On** TARRED GRANITE **Surface, from 30 m.p.h.:—**

Both Brakes 30½ ft. Front Brake 48 ft. Rear Brake 54½ ft.

**Fuel Consumption:—** Town 57 m.p.g. Country 68 m.p.g.

**Oil Consumption:—** NEGLIGIBLE m.p.g.

# Norton Vertical-twin

## E. A. Sitwell Questions Mr J. E. Moore, AMI.Mech.E, About the Engine Design of the "Dominator".

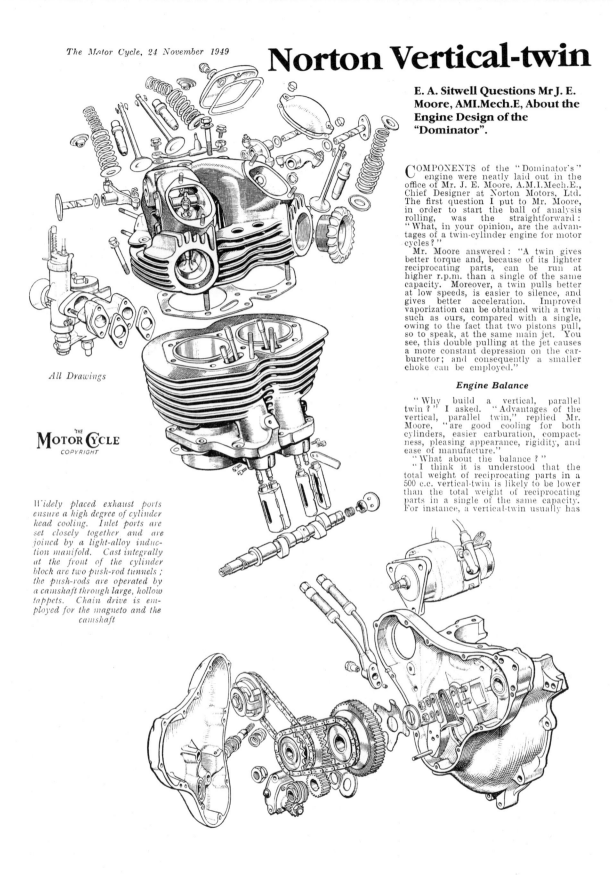

*All Drawings*

**MOTOR CYCLE**
THE
COPYRIGHT

*Widely placed exhaust ports ensure a high degree of cylinder head cooling. Inlet ports are set closely together and are joined by a light-alloy induction manifold. Cast integrally at the front of the cylinder block are two push-rod tunnels; the push-rods are operated by a camshaft through large, hollow tappets. Chain drive is employed for the magneto and the camshaft*

COMPONENTS of the "Dominator's" engine were neatly laid out in the office of Mr. J. E. Moore. A.M.I.Mech.E., Chief Designer at Norton Motors, Ltd. The first question I put to Mr. Moore, in order to start the ball of analysis rolling, was the straightforward: "What, in your opinion, are the advantages of a twin-cylinder engine for motor cycles?"

Mr. Moore answered: "A twin gives better torque and, because of its lighter reciprocating parts, can be run at higher r.p.m. than a single of the same capacity. Moreover, a twin pulls better at low speeds, is easier to silence, and gives better acceleration. Improved vaporization can be obtained with a twin such as ours, compared with a single, owing to the fact that two pistons pull, so to speak, at the same main jet. You see, this double pulling at the jet causes a more constant depression on the carburettor; and consequently a smaller choke can be employed."

### Engine Balance

"Why build a vertical, parallel twin?" I asked. "Advantages of the vertical, parallel twin," replied Mr. Moore, "are good cooling for both cylinders, easier carburation, compactness, pleasing appearance, rigidity, and ease of manufacture."

"What about the balance?"

"I think it is understood that the total weight of reciprocating parts in a 500 c.c. vertical-twin is likely to be lower than the total weight of reciprocating parts in a single of the same capacity. For instance, a vertical-twin usually has light-alloy con-rods; and a shorter stroke is, of course, employed than in a single. Therefore, although the theoretical balance is identical in practice there are lower inertia forces in the twin for a given r.p.m., with consequent smoother running. In balancing an engine, the aim should be to make the reciprocating and rotating parts as light as possible relative to the flywheel mass, in order to achieve smoothness at high r.p.m. This has been our aim with the Norton twin."

"I see you use a built-up crankshaft and flywheel assembly," I said. Mr. Moore replied: "We favour the bolted-up arrangement on the score of simplicity of manufacture. That statement, however, needs further explanation: we think that, with a really high-efficiency engine, forged crank cheeks are desirable and this dictates the building-up, since it would be impracticable to use a forged one-piece crankshaft and flywheel assembly because of the excessive machining that would be required after forging."

"What material is used for the shaft?"

"The shaft is made of manganese-molybdenum and has toughened journals. We use this material because of its high tensile strength, which is about 65 tons per square inch."

"And the flywheel—what is that made of?"

"Cast-iron — an entirely suitable material, and more than strong enough for the job, especially since a flywheel is intrinsically strong in section."

"What are the dimensions of the wheel?"

"They are 7in × 1½in."

"Will you please explain the construction of the crankshaft and flywheel assembly?"

"Certainly. As you see, the wheel is sandwiched between the bobweighted crank cheeks, each of which has a flange for fixing purposes. These flanges are specially large in diameter in order to promote rigidity in the whole assembly. Four bolts and two studs pass through the flanges and the flywheel, holding all three together. To ensure accurate alignment, there is a large-diameter central dowel."

"How are the nuts on the studs and bolts locked?"

"The end of each bolt is centre punched over its nut; also, the two locking plates that you can see, one on each side of the flywheel, are turned up against the stud nuts. These plates, incidentally, secure the dowel endwise."

### Two Main Bearings

"Have you the dimensions of the crank journals?"

"Yes; 1½in dia. × 1in long."

"Concerning the main bearings, why did you go in for two and not three? In other words, why not a central bearing as well as one at each end of the crankshaft?". Mr. Moore answered, "Our tests have proved that entirely satisfactory results are obtained with two main bearings and a centrally disposed flywheel. With this arrangement there is greater simplicity of construction. Moreover, a central bearing would increase the over-all width of the engine."

"What can you tell me about the bearings you employ?"

"For ease of manufacture of both crankcase and mainshaft, the bearings are both the same diameter. Dimensions are 72mm × 30mm × 19mm, which, you will agree, make the bearings particularly robust. On the driving-side we have a roller journal, and on the timing-side there is a ball journal. We prefer to use a roller journal on the driving-side, as it is the higher loaded of the two bearings and has to look after the driving torque."

"I suppose there is an oil seal for the driving-side main bearing?"

### Light-alloy Con-rods

"Yes; a synthetic rubber, spring loaded oil seal."

"What allowance is made for differential expansion between the mainshaft and the crankcase owing to temperature changes?"

"There is end play on the driving-side of the crankshaft of between 5 and 10 thou when cold."

"As you have already suggested, the con-rods are made of light-alloy . . ."

"Yes; each con-rod and end cap is a forging of R.R.56, a material chosen for its lightness and high tensile strength."

"What can you tell me about con-rod length and piston speed?"

"As you know, bore and stroke of the

F. W. BEAK

*Pistons are made of Lo-Ex aluminium alloy and give a compression ratio of 6.7 to 1. The hollow, fully floating gudgeon pins are located by circlips in the orthodox manner. Connecting rods are forgings in R.R.56 light-alloy and there are steel-back shell bearings at the big-ends. The cast-iron flywheel is bolted between the bobweighted crank cheeks, which are forgings. Large main bearings, roller on the drive-side and ball on the timing-side, carry the crankshaft assembly*

*Norton 500 c.c. vertical-twin*

# MODERN ENGINES

## The Norton Vertical-twin
### continued

engine are 66mm and 72.6mm respectively, giving a total capacity of 497 c.c. Each con-rod is 6in long, and the ratio of con-rod length to crankshaft throw (i.e., to half the stroke) is 4.19. This we have found through development is the best compromise for keeping the piston speed down (consequently reducing wear), and at the same time keeping con-rod angulation to a minimum."

"Why do you use loose shells for the plain big-end bearings?" "For ease of replacement and servicing."

### Flat-top Pistons

"What are the shells made of?" "They are steel backed, Micro-Babbitt shells. The steel gives us rigidity and the Babbitt part a good bearing surface."

"How are the shells located?" "By the little nicks or grooves in the con-rod. Each groove holds a small offset abutment of the shell, of which complete location is thus ensured."

"Anything special about the small ends?" "No; they each have an orthodox, pressed-in, phosphor-bronze bush. Fully-floating gudgeon pins are used, located by circlips."

"I see you employ a pair of flat-top pistons. Will you please give me further information about them?"

"Each piston has a full skirt, is form-turned oval, and is made of Lo-Ex aluminium-alloy, which has an expansion coefficient of 0.0000105 per deg. Centigrade. Clearances when cold are 6 thou at the top of the skirt and 4 thou at the bottom. Compression ratio is 6.7 to 1, which we think is as high as we can go on pool petrol. Both pistons are flat-topped in order to conform with combustion chamber characteristics. Each has one $\frac{5}{32}$in slotted scraper ring and two $\frac{1}{16}$in compression rings.

Here Mr. Moore paused to take a breath, and I continued for him: "But there is a right- and a left-hand piston. I always remember that one!"

"Correct," Mr. Moore said. "You see, because of the V-section formation of the cylinder-head, the valve clearance pockets in the top of each piston are not at right angles to the gudgeon pin; therefore, as you say, there is a right- and a left-hand piston."

### Maximum Cooling

"Now we come to the barrel block," I said, "which, as one can see, incorporates push-rod tunnels in front and has air spaces not only between each cylinder barrel itself, but also transversely between the bores and the push-rod tunnels." Mr. Moore said: "Yes, the aim, of course, has been to provide maximum cooling. The block is a one-piece casting of close-grained cast-iron. It is spigoted into the aluminium-alloy crankcase."

"To what depth?" "One inch."

"How is the block held down?" "By

seven $\frac{3}{8}$in diameter and two $\frac{5}{16}$in diameter studs. Incidentally, the joint of the crankcase is slightly offset from the centre line in order to accommodate a central holding-down stud."

"I see the barrel block is very slightly spigoted into the cylinder head. I presume this is for added rigidity?" "Yes; and, of course, for gas-tightness." Mr. Moore went on: "The cylinder head is of patented formation designed for maximum cooling, and it is held to the barrel by seven bolts and three head studs. It is made of cast-iron and has an integral rocker box. We use a copper-asbestos gasket between the head and the barrel. To allow a full flow of air at the front of the head, the exhaust valves are widely disposed. I liked your original description in *The Motor Cycle* last November, when you wrote: '. . . the cylinder head as it were opens its arms wide to the incoming flow of air.' As you know, there is a flow of air between the combustion chambers and also transversely between the exhaust and inlet valves. In plan, the port axes converge towards the rear, making a total angle of 50deg. The valves make a total angle with each other of 58deg, which means that they are fairly upright; and it follows that we can use shallow combustion chambers."

"Why is it good to have shallow combustion chambers?" I asked. "Because," Mr. Moore replied, "the surface of the chambers is reduced, and thus they keep cooler and give better combustion."

### Hollow Rockers

"What can you tell me about the rockers and their shafts?" I asked. Mr. Moore picked up a flanged rocker shaft and said: "Each shaft is pushed in, and its flange is pulled up to the flat face by two $\frac{1}{4}$in pins. The rockers themselves are hollow and oscillate round the stationary shafts."

"What are the rockers made of?"

"Three per cent nickel steel, case-hardened in the bore. At the valve end of each rocker is a hardened steel adjuster with a lock-nut. At the other end is a fixed, hardened steel ball which seats in the push-rod cup."

"Anything special about the valve springs?" "No; there is, of course, an inner and an outer coil spring—wound in opposite directions to prevent trapping."

"Can you give me a load figure for the springs?" "Yes; the initial seat load exerted by a pair of springs is 88 lb."

"I see that each of the two rocker-box covers on the exhaust side is held down by two $\frac{5}{16}$in studs, and that the single inlet-side rocker box cover is secured by a stud protruding from the inlet cavity. That seems to complete the information about the rocker box. Now the valves—what are they made of and why?"

"The valves are made of Silchrome, a

material chosen because it withstands heat extremely well."

"What are the valve dimensions?" "Port diameters are $1\frac{1}{32}$in, and stem diameters are $\frac{5}{16}$in. Incidentally, each top spring-cup is taper-cotter retained, and the bottom spring-cup is an inverted cup located by the head of the valve-guide."

"What is the valve-guide material?" "Chilled cast-iron, which provides a good bearing surface. The guides are pressed in."

"Obviously," I said, "there is no need for valve-seat inserts, since the head is made of cast-iron." Mr. Moore answered, "That is correct."

### Two Induction Ports

"Why," I asked, "do you now employ two induction ports? I remember there was only one in the original design." Mr. Moore replied: "As you remark, the cylinder head now has two induction ports—one per valve—and there is a short aluminium induction manifold connecting with a single, flange-fitting Amal carburettor of 1in bore. The two induction ports give a higher volumetric efficiency —better cylinder filling—than one, and therefore the general performance of the engine is higher. Obviously, with the present arrangement, the gases have a longer *straight* port in which to gather speed before reaching the valve. The two Tufnol distance pieces between the manifold and the head are put there, of course, for purposes of heat insulation."

I picked up a push-rod. "You tell me," I said, "that the push-rods are made of $\frac{5}{16}$in light-gauge high-tensile steel tubing. In order to save reciprocating weight, why not use light-alloy rods?"

"Because it is doubtful," Mr. Moore answered, "if there would be any saving in weight by the time we had increased the section (in the alloy) for strength." He continued "Each rod has a hardened steel cup at the top to hold oil and to take the ball on the rocker end. There is a hardened steel ball at each lower end. You will notice, of course, that the two pairs of rods are of different lengths."

### Massive Tappets

"What are the main points about these massive, car-type tappets?" "We use this patented type of tappet because it has a large bearing surface with consequent reduced wear. Also, we can do without tappet guides. The tappets are hollow and made of cast-iron. They have chilled rubbing surfaces. Each pair forms a complete circle, of which each half forms a complete tappet and moves independently. Bolted to an extension of each cylinder spigot is a retaining plate sandwiched between the lower ends of each tappet in order to prevent rotation. Incidentally, these plates effectively prevent the tappets from falling out when the cylinder block is lifted. In the top of each tappet there is a small cup which takes the ball end of the push-rod and holds oil. The tappets are particularly robust, but they are also light: you will see that windows are cast in the sides to reduce weight."

"Yes," I said; "and I also notice that the tappets are slightly chamfered fore-and-aft at their lower ends. Is this also to save weight ?"

"Yes."

"Another question: the tappet housings are hollow milled at each lower end, obviously in order to provide sufficient clearance for the rotating cams. Why are the housings not machined straight across ? Clearance could surely still be achieved ?"

"Because we wanted to provide plenty of fore-and-aft support for each tappet on its initial thrust by the cam."

Discussion reached the camshaft. Mr. Moore said: "The camshaft is carried on two widely spaced, plain, phosphor-bronze bearings. It is made of forged, case-hardened Ubas steel, and, in order to reduce weight, it is machined hollow. Designed for efficiency and quietness, the cams have quietening curves. Neutral diameter of each cam is 1 9/16 in. Each cam is individually tested for hardness."

I looked at the timing gear, and Mr. Moore went over the main points. He explained: "This pinion on the end of the mainshaft drives an intermediate gear on a fixed shaft at half engine-speed. Integral with this intermediate gear are two chain sprockets, of which one drives the automatic advance-and-retard magneto at the rear, and the other the camshaft in front. Both chains have straight-sided links. The camshaft chain has a slipper-type tensioner, for which the straight-sided links are particularly suitable. Dimensions of the magneto chain are 3/8 in pitch × 0.155in width, and of the camshaft chain, 3/8 in pitch × 0.225in width."

"Why use chains and not gears ?" I asked. "For quietness in operation," Mr. Moore replied. He went on: "A slight adjustment of the magneto chain can be made by moving the instrument. The dynamo, which is in front of the engine, is driven by a spring-loaded fibre wheel which is carried on the cam-shaft and forms a slipping clutch drive. Slip occurs only on inertia overloads."

### Lubrication System

"Now I think we should come to the lubrication. Would you please enumerate its general characteristics ?"

"Certainly. The system is actuated by a double-action gear pump; and pressure that is built up at the big-ends is controlled by a pressure release valve. Oil pressure is linked up with adequate oil volume. A by-pass from the return pipe lifts oil to the rocker box. Prevention of cylinder lubrication bias has been one of the chief aims in the design of the system; and this aim, as you will see in a minute, has been successfully achieved. Total quantity of oil in circulation is 5 pints."

"Thank you. Now let us follow the oil in detail through the system."

"Right. First the oil falls by gravity from the tank to the gear pump, which is driven by a worm off the mainshaft. This pump then forces the oil through a nipple, which is sealed by a taper synthetic rubber washer, into a horizontal drilling in the timing cover. From here the oil passes to a small chamber in the timing cover; and this chamber is fitted with a spring-loaded synthetic rubber oil seal. When the timing cover is in place,

the end of the mainshaft fits snugly into this very oil seal."

At this point I interrupted and said: "Won't the synthetic rubber oil seal wear, with the revolutions of the main-shaft ?" Mr. Moore answered: "This is an excellent application for a spring-loaded oil seal of this type, (a) because the seal is lubricated, and so there will be very little wear; (b) because pressure created within the chamber assists in closing the seal down to the shaft; and (c) because, if there is any wear in the rubber, the spring will take it up."

Having dealt with that point, Mr. Moore continued: "The oil has reached the chamber I have already described. Now it passes into the hollow crank-shaft, and through drillings in the crank members, to the big-ends, which it lubricates under pressure. Oil released from the big-ends is thrown centrifug-ally to lubricate the cylinder walls, and the surplus drains into the sump at the rear of the crankcase, whence it is picked up by the scavenge pump and returned to the tank."

"What is the pressure at the big-ends, and how is it maintained ?"

"The pressure is about 80lb per. sq. in when cold, and it is maintained by a large, spring-loaded, piston-type pressure release valve connected with the horizontal drilling in the timing cover already described. To prevent foreign matter from getting in the valve, there is a gauze filter on its input side. At the pressure mentioned, oil exhausts into the timing chest and lubricates the timing gear. Thence the oil passes through suitable drillways to the *middle* of the engine at the rear. Thus there is no cylinder lubrication bias, as the oil goes straight down to the sump *without* running excessively down the timing side crankcase wall, whence it would in-evitably be flung up by the crankshaft cheek."

### Oil Lifted to Rockers

"A by-pass on the return pipe next to the oil-tank lifts oil up to a T-piece which distributes the lubricant to two banjo unions, one on each side of the rocker box at the top. Oil is led through drillings directly to each hollow rocker shaft, from which it emerges at an annular ring in the middle and feeds the shaft via a scroll. The oil then drains from the lowest points of the rocker box to the crankcase, via the push-rod tunnels on the exhaust side (lubricating the tappets, etc.), and down a drilling in the head and barrel on the inlet side."

"How do you control the amount of oil in the rocker box, to prevent too

much oil from getting into the valve guides ?"

"It must be remembered that the oil in the rocker box is not there under pressure. It is only *lifted* there from the return side of the system; and it is present in the rocker box in a quantity sufficient only for lubricating the rockers. The valve-guides are lubricated by oil mist only, and no level of oil is built up in the rocker box."

"Where is the oil filter ?"

"In the oil-tank. It is a wire gauze, removable type of filter."

"How do you prevent oil from drain-ing into the crankcase when the machine is not being used ?"

"We do not find it necessary to employ a ball-valve. Oil just does not leak past the gears in the Norton pump."

"Good," I said. "That seems to deal with the lubrication system. Now would you please describe how the crankcase breathes ?"

### Power Output

Mr. Moore said: "The engine breather is incorporated in the camshaft. Centre of the camshaft, as you see, is increased in diameter, so that heavy particles of oil will be flung off, and the air immediately surrounding this centre portion will be as free as possible from oil. The raised portion is drilled radially with four holes, which are the pick-up points, so to speak, for the air to be breathed, and lead to the main drilling in the camshaft. Keyed to the end of the camshaft nearer to the driving side of the engine is a spring loaded valve containing small ports which, as the camshaft revolves, coin cide with a stationary ported plate in the crankcase. The stationary ports are connected by a drilling in the rear of the crankcase, and by a pipe, to the open air. With its mechanical arrange ment, the breather exhausts at all en gine speeds on the down-stroke of the pistons, and the ports are closed on the up-stroke. Air, some oil mist, and probably a little moisture are breathed out by the engine. We do not, incident ally, utilize the breathings to lubricate the rear chain, and the exit pipe points merely to the ground."

"That seems to have cleared up most things," I said. "Now, what is the power output of the engine ?"

"The output is 29 b.h.p. at 6,000 r.p.m."

"And a pretty good figure," I said. "Another question that occurs to me is to ask why there is no engine-shaft shock-absorber." "Because," Mr. Moore answered, "we have in the clutch a rubber vane type of shock-absorber which has been a feature of Nortons for many years."

### Instruction Book Data

"Fine. I think those are all the questions I have to ask, except for a few on such instruction book details as mag-neto and valve timing, etc."

I took down the following information, dictated by Mr. Moore :—

*Magneto timing:* Set, in the fully ad-vanced position, at 31 deg before t.d.c.

*Valve timing:* Exhaust opens 57.5 deg before b.d.c. and closes 22 deg after t.d.c. Inlet opens 22 deg before t.d.c. and closes 57.5 deg after b.d.c.

It is necessary for the valves to be timed with the tappet clearance set at 10 thou (*not* the working clearance) when cold, because of the quietening curve ramps on the cams. Final work-ing tappet clearances when cold are 3 thou for the inlet and 5 thou for the exhaust.

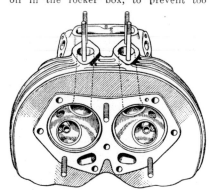

*New cylinder head with separate in-duction ports. Combustion chambers are unusually shallow.*

*Graham Walker entering Windy Corner when testing the Junior Race winner.*

# SO LONG, SYNOVITIS!

Testing the T.T. Winners Cures a Bad Attack of Editor's Elbow

WHEN the "New Look" Norton made its first appearance at Blandford on April 29, it created a sensation. But that was a mild affair compared with the sensation created two weeks ago by the overwhelming Norton victories in the Junior and Senior T.T. Races. Even when full allowance is made for the superb artistry of Bell, Duke, Lockett and Daniell it is obvious the latest Bracebridge Street models have "got something"—and all over the world there are enthusiasts who want to know what that "something" is.

Well, I will do my poor best to describe it, because once again I was one of those fortunate few given the opportunity to test the winning mounts immediately after the Races. In previous years, through sheer enthusiasm, I'm afraid I have tended rather selfishly to devote a lot of space to what I was able to do on the models rather than to how the models did their stuff, and why. I don't intend to do that on this occasion for two reasons; first, space is short, due to printing difficulties; secondly, the Norton team and "Professor" Joe Craig have evolved a gear change-to-revolution rate technique which, in my experience, is unique, and it would be unfair to publish the details. Suffice to say I have tried out the formula and it undoubtedly had an important effect upon the lap times put up by the Norton team.

### The Mystery

But that formula, of course, is not the answer to the question, "What is this mysterious 'something' which makes the new Norton such a potent device?" To answer that question fully would demand several pages—which I haven't got—plus a great deal of data, which I am not at all likely to get! I have, however, a simple explanation which can be given in a sentence: A new frame which enables all the power to be used all of the time allied with more power than ever before—power which is produced over a wider revolution range than hitherto. In other words the power curve is less like Vesuvius and more like Table Mountain, and the frame appears to run on rails rather than on a rippling road.

The "old" Norton was good enough to win the 1938 and 1947-8-9 Senior T.T. Races. When describing test runs on the machines which won these events, in all sincerity I used up most of the complimentary adjectives in the English language. What words, then, can I now

## By *GRAHAM WALKER*

use in attempting to analyse the qualities of the latest models? Frankly I don't know, because the new design sets a new standard in road holding, braking and overall engine performance so far as my experience runs.

When I set out on Artie Bell's "Junior" winner the morning after the race I followed the usual routine—from Windy Corner down the reverse way of the course to Waterworks Corner, back again to Hillberry and "in reverse" again to my starting point. My first impression was one of extreme comfort—an ideal position and almost featherlight brake, clutch and carburetter controls. My next was one of amazement at the complete absence of bumps in the road—and I was deliberately looking for them. Moreover, so far as the power unit was concerned it might not have been there for all the vibration I could feel.

### 112 m.p.h.—

But that it was very *much* there was quickly proved by revs which represented 112 m.p.h. at the bottom of the Mountain Mile—and those revs were a long way below those recorded by Bell on other parts of the course during his record-breaking ride. Indeed, I have heard rumours that at the bottom of Bray Hill his speed was higher than that associated with more than one potential 500 c.c. Race-winner in other post-war years. But it was coming *up* the Mountain Mile that I got my most vivid impression of power, for I was moving at 100 m.p.h. in third, and actually got into top before I eased up for the bend after the Mountain Box—and that, with my weight and frontal area, was phenomenal.

I had another lasting impression—the speed with which around 110 m.p.h. could be reached in top gear at two spots where on earlier Junior winners I had never bettered 104. The rapidity with which the rev counter needle mounted after a momentary flick back when changing up was clear indication of the "flat" power curve giving the remarkable acceleration.

As for the steering, "pluperfect" is an overworked adjective, but unless I resort

to Americanese and write "perfect plus" I am going to be stumped for a description. It is, *in excelsis*, of the type which enables the jockey to alter direction by thought transference rather than by conscious muscular movement—and all racing men will know what I mean by that. In this connection, I speak highly of the modern seating arrangement with its back-stop which prevents all strain on the fingers when accelerating. Daniell's Prize Presentation crack about "going to sleep on the model" cannot be improved upon as an apt description of its comfort.

And what of Geoff Duke's "Senior" job? Again, experienced racing men will know what I mean when I say there is often a world of difference between Junior and Senior mounts identical in all but engine capacity. I have known 350 c.c. machines which were docile easily-handled devices, but which with an extra 150 c.c. between the engine plates became unmanageable brutes on full throttle. "Something to do with engine torque" the technicians will tell you, but in my ignorance I have always had the suspicion that it was due to frame warp under transmission tug, or to steering angles which were safe up to a certain optimum speed but geometrically went for a Burton at higher-velocities.

### —and then 118 !

That point has certainly not been reached with the new Senior Norton which, rumour again has it, was touching nearer 130 than 120 m.p.h. at the bottom of Bray Hill during the race. I have never before ridden a big 'un which, from the handling viewpoint, gave me the impression I was aboard a supersafe lightweight. It was, in fact, an uncanny experience, because although circumstances dictated I should have only a short run from the Mountain Box down to Waterworks and back, that was far enough to enable me to touch 118 m.p.h. on the downward journey and, coming back, to take the righthand sweep before the Cutting miles an hour faster than I have ever done before, and for the first time in my life to exceed 110 m.p.h. up **the Mountain Mile. Oh, brother, what a bicycle !**

# 596 c.c. Norton Big

### ROAD TESTS OF NEW MODELS

A Lusty Side-valve Providing Excel

FOR day-in, day-out reliability, without the need for constant maintenance, a large section of the sidecar public contends that the side-valve engine provides the perfect answer. Certainly, experience with the 596 c.c. side-valve No. 1 Norton, the famous Big Four, goes a long way towards bearing this out.

The maximum cruising speed of the outfit under test was 50-53 m.p.h. with a 10½-stone passenger in the Swallow, all-metal sidecar. Average speeds under fair give-and-take conditions generally worked out at approximately 40 m.p.h. The machine would maintain its 50-53 m.p.h. all day long, apparently

*The Big Four Norton was found to be almost as lively with a full sidecar load as it was with the sidecar empty*

without effort. It gobbled up the miles in an easy, effortless fashion, the low-revving characteristics of the engine giving an impression of lusty power.

Acceleration was brisk rather than "sparkling" in the modern sense. But the machine accelerated in a way which again gave that feeling of limitless power. The Norton was almost as lively with a full sidecar load as it was with the sidecar empty. Another feature was that acceleration uphill was not much below that attainable on the level. There was at all

*The engine was quiet mechanically, and remained oil-tight. Tappets and piston were barely audible when the engine was idling*

times a sturdy "force" on tap irrespective of the conditions, and irrespective of the number of miles already covered that day. The maximum speed and acceleration figures were taken on a gusty day with a heavily garbed rider and a 10½-stone passenger.

True, as a result of much full-throttle driving, the exhaust pipe discoloured badly below the port and the silencer also discoloured. Nevertheless, signs of overheating were never evident on the road and the engine would idle as reliably at the end of a brutal ride as it would at the beginning. The engine in the test machine was smooth right through the throttle range, though vibration was, of course, apparent when the engine was revved to the point of valve-float.

Low-speed torque developed by the engine was altogether exceptional. The engine would pull slowly and evenly down to speeds of round 15 m.p.h. in top gear, and the outfit would trickle along quietly and effortlessly at 12 m.p.h. in third. On hills, third gear was rarely required. Such was the torque that the outfit would chuff its way up steep gradients in a fussless manner at a steady 30 m.p.h., or accelerate, quite happily, up the speed scale.

### Starting from Cold

The engine was extremely sensitive to the ignition advance-and-retard control. With the lever in the full-advance position (forward and with the tension off the cable—a good point), there was a tendency to pinking if the throttle was snapped open or handled hamfistedly on up gradients. With the ignition lever and throttle used in unison, however, pinking could easily be avoided.

Engine starting from cold was easy provided that the air lever was closed and the ignition lever left in the full-advance position. It was unnecessary, and, indeed, undesirable (as with most side-valve engines these days) to flood the carburettor since this could result in wetting the plug. On the side of the carburettor mixing chamber is a tommy-bar type throttle stop which, when turned to the right, gave the correct throttle opening for making a cold start. An exhaust valve-lifter lever is fitted on the left handlebar. It was easy to use and, when the valve was raised, the engine could be spun without undue muscular effort or knack. The engine usually fired at the second or third kick when cold and was a certain first-kick starter when warm.

After the engine had been running for a minute or so following a cold start, the air lever could be fully opened and the throttle stop turned to its normal position. With the ignition set at about three-quarters retard, the engine would idle in the best "gas engine" fashion. On full advance the tickover was equally smooth and reliable, though slightly faster, of course.

In delivery tune, the engine was commendably quiet mechanically. When idling, the tappets and piston were barely audible. Later in the test—which embraced over 800 hard miles—the tappets became slightly noisier, but mechanical noise, generally speaking, had not increased. The exhaust noise prohibited the use of maximum acceleration in built-up areas.

The clutch freed perfectly under all conditions and was smooth in its take-up of the drive. Bottom gear could be effortlessly and silently engaged from

# Four and Sidecar

## ngine Characteristics for Sidecar Work

neutral when the machine was stationary and the engine idling; and neutral was equally easily found from either bottom or second gear. Quiet in operation, the new gear box provided an excellent gear change. Snap changes, if desired, could be noiselessly effected between any pair of gears both upward and downward. Pedal movement was light and short. The pedal could be moved by the rider merely pivoting his right foot easily on the footrest.

A first-class riding position was provided by the relationship between the saddle, handlebars and footrests. All the controls, and especially that for the front brake, were well placed for easy operation. They were light to use, with the exceptions of those for the clutch and front brake, which were rather heavy.

### Standard of Comfort

Under dry-weather conditions, the brakes when employed in unison were up to required standard. They were smooth in operation, with just the right degree of "sponginess." When the machine was ridden in the rain, or on roads that were awash, the efficiency of the front brake became seriously impaired.

Steering and road-holding of the test outfit were good, though slightly more sidecar toe-in would have been appreciated. Corners and bends could be swung effortlessly at speed. The standard of comfort provided, too, was high.

Greater than average protection from road water was provided by the deep-section front and rear mudguards. The engine remained oil-tight. Illumination provided by the Lucas headlamp was very good; the dynamo balanced the full lamp load when the machine was being driven at 30 m.p.h. in top gear.

*Finish of the Swallow all-metal sidecar was in red and black. The sidecar was roomy and comfortable for a passenger of average build*

The pilot-bulb filament fractured when the speed figures were being taken. The tool-kit provided is better than average and the tool-box dimensions are really sensible, allowing a repair outfit and other spares to be easily carried.

The sidecar was roomy and comfortable for a passenger of average build. Locker dimensions were adequate for one weekend size suitcase and a travelling valise. It was felt that the entry to the locker could have been wider with advantage. Moderate protection was provided by the celluloid screen. There was considerable draught inside when the hood was raised. The bolts holding the body to the chassis came loose on one occasion. It was not always possible to lock the lid of the locker without a great deal of fumbling because of the tongue of the lock not mating perfectly with its socket. Finish of the sidecar was red and black.

## Information Panel

### SPECIFICATION

**ENGINE :** 596 c.c. (82 mm x 113 mm) single-cylinder side-valve. Fully enclosed valve-gear. Detachable aluminium-alloy cylinder head. Dry-sump lubrication. Oil capacity, 4 pints.

**CARBURETTOR :** Amal, with tommy-bar type throttle stop for easy starting. Twistgrip throttle control. Gauze-type flame-trap fitted to air intake.

**IGNITION AND LIGHTING :** Lucas Magdyno, with manual ignition advance-retard control. 7in diameter Lucas head lamp with pre-focus light unit and domed glass.

**TRANSMISSION** Norton four-speed gear box with positive foot control. Top gear, 5.47 to 1. Third, 6.61 to 1. Second, 9.67 to 1. Bottom, 16.25 to 1. Multi-plate clutch with Ferodo inserts. Primary chain, ½in x 0.305in. in pressed-steel oil-bath. Secondary chain, ⅝in × ¼in; guard over top run. R.p.m. at 30 m.p.h. in top gear, 2,120.

**FUEL CAPACITY :** 2¾ gallons.

**TYRES :** 19 x 3.25in Dunlop front and rear.

**BRAKES :** Both 7in diameter by 1¼in wide ; hand adjusters.

**SUSPENSION :** Norton "Roadholder" telescopic fork with hydraulic damping.

**WHEELBASE :** 54½in. Ground clearance, 5in unladen.

**SADDLE :** Lycett. Unladen height, 30½in.

**WEIGHT ·** Complete outfit, 616 lb fully equipped and with full tank.

**PRICE :** Machine only, £142, plus Purchase Tax (in Britain only), £38 6s 10d.

**ROAD TAX :** £5 a year ; £1 7s 6d a quarter. Half-duty if only standard ration is used.

**MAKERS :** Norton Motors, Ltd., Bracebridge Street, Birmingham, 6.

**DESCRIPTION :** *The Motor Cycle*, 30 October, 1947.

### SIDECAR

**MODEL :** Swallow. Single-seater.

**CHASSIS :** Norton Model G. Double triangulated steel chassis with cee-springs at rear and laminated leaf springs at front.

**BODY :** All-welded steel construction. Overall length, 79in. Width, 22in. Squab to toe plate, 40in. Height inside when the hood is raised, 33in. Windscreen measures 21½in x 11in deep. Squab measure

23in x 18½in wide. Seat cushion, 19½in long x 16½in wide. Locker dimensions, 17¼in wide x 18in long x 14in high.

**PRICE :** £57, plus Purchase Tax, £15 4s.

### PERFORMANCE DATA

**MEAN MAXIMUM SPEED** Bottom :* 27 m.p.h.
Second :* 41 m.p.h.
Third : 53 m.p.h.
Top : 55 m.p.h.
* Valve float occurring.

| **MEAN ACCELERATION** | 10-30 m.p.h. | 20-40 m.p.h. | 30-50 m.p.h. |
|---|---|---|---|
| Bottom : | — | — | — |
| Second : | 5.8 secs. | 8.8 secs. | — |
| Third : | 8.8 secs | 8.6 secs | 13.4 secs |
| Top : | — | 11.4 secs | 16.4 secs |

Mean speed at end of quarter-mile from rest : 51 m.p.h.
Mean time to cover standing quarter-mile : 24.2 secs.

**PETROL CONSUMPTION :** At 30 m.p.h., 59 m.p.g. At 40 m.p.h., 48 m.p.g. At 50 m.p.h., 36 m.p.g.

**BRAKING :** From 30 m.p.h. to rest. 45ft 6in.

**TURNING CIRCLE :** 16ft 8in.

**MINIMUM NON-SNATCH SPEED :** 15 m.p.h. in top gear, with ignition fully retarded.

**WEIGHT PER C.C. ·** 1.03 lb.

## How It Is Done at
## the Factories—No. 3

# Norton

### Third of a Helpful Series of Arti
### By

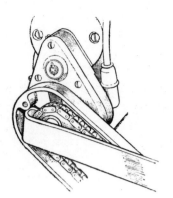

*An unusually simple sprocket drawing tool. The loosened retaining unit on the end of the tapered shaft is used as a fulcrum, and pressure is exerted towards the engine*

SO simple are the Norton single-cylinder engines — the overhead-camshaft International and Manx engines included—that there are no special servicing wrinkles that apply to removal of the heads and barrels. In each case the job is perfectly straightforward. Pistons can be removed easily and the gudgeon pin is (or should be) no more than an easy push fit in the piston bosses and small-end bush.

Before refitting pistons, Norton service people usually make a point of running a reamer through the gudgeon pin bosses; or, if a reamer were not available, they would run the blade of a pocket knife round the outer edge of each boss to ensure that there was no burr that might interfere with the fit of the pin.

During, say, a decoke in the Service Department, piston rings are generally left in position on the piston and new rings are only fitted after an engine has been rebored—unless, of course, a ring

happens to be found broken or its outer surface is discoloured. The reason given for this is a multiple one. First of all, if there is carbon behind a ring, it is best to leave it there, since it is helping to provide a good gas seal. To fit new rings in a partly worn barrel, the Service personnel say, can never be a successful work, since cylinder wear is not equal " all the way round "—in other words, because a barrel wears oval. And, of course, lapping-in a new ring in a worn bore is the devil's own job. In the event of replacing a broken ring with a new one, the carbon must be carefully removed from the groove and the fact that the ring is completely free in its groove ascertained before the ring is fitted.

A " peeling " method for removing piston rings is employed. The tool used is an old hack-saw blade, ground to the shape of a pen-knife blade, but with no cutting edge to it. The mechanic I watched did not, incidentally, recommend using new circlips after each gudgeon pin removal; his opinion was that they may be used over and over again.

### Valve-guide Removal

Cylinder heads are condemned to the scrap heap when the valve seats become too deeply pocketed and further cutting of the seat will tend to cause alteration of the striking angle of the rocker. Worn guides are determined by testing for shape by moving the end of the valve stem in the guide. If the guides are badly worn, of course, one of the consequences is that the valve is allowed to " rock " slightly, and " spreading " of the valve seats will quickly occur. Old guides are merely knocked out with a two-diameter drift, and only in the case of the alloy-engined trials model is it recommended that the head be heated for the removal or fitting of guides.

The method adopted for guide removal by the Service people is to stand the head with, say, the exhaust port down, on the bench, and drive the inlet guide out, driving it from outside into the combustion chamber. Then the head can be reversed and the procedure adopted for the exhaust guide.

During replacement, great care is taken to ensure that the guide being fitted is not too tight in the housing nor, of course, too loose. If it is too tight, there is danger of the housing being fractured— which means that the head immediately becomes scrap—or, if it is not quite so tight as all that, the guide, being " squeezed " excessively, will bind on the valve stem. If a guide is too big, the fact is evident as soon as one starts to drive it in; conversely, if it can be pushed in easily, it is obvious that it is too loose. While I was at the works I saw a guide removed from a 1939 Manx head. It was a home-made guide and much too tight. The correct interference—home tuners, please note !—should be 1-1½ thou.

On that quite awkward job of com-

pressing valve springs to remove or replace the cotters—awkward if, like me, you use two hammer shafts to compress the springs and have your wife or a friend lift out the cotters with the aid of a knitting needle !—the Norton people had quite a lot to say and show me. How simple it all is if one uses a little forethought !

The valve-spring compressor used for the o.h.v. engines is so simple that anyone with a few hand tools and odd pieces of scrap material could knock up a similar arrangement in an hour. It consists simply of a square flat board, fitted in the appropriate place, with a hemispherical block to locate inside the head. On one side there is a lever working on a raised fulcrum, as shown in the illustration. The lever is " divided " so that each of the two edges bears on the sides of the valve collar. A significant and very important point made by a works' mechanic was that he always gives the valve collar a smart tap with a hammer before attempting to compress the springs. This is an old dodge, not known by all, and in many cases forgotten by those who do the job only once every five years. It is done to jar the collets, which in nearly every case will be sticking to the spring collars.

### Side-valve Engines

The tool used for compressing the valve-springs on the side-valve engines was even more simple. An old piston with a domed crown is bolted to the bench. Behind it, about a foot away, is a vertical ⅜in bolt some 10in long, inserted through the bench from the underside. The bolt is threaded at the top to take a nut. The lever part of the tool is a massive, car-type tyre lever. This is drilled at one end with a ⅜in hole, fitted over the ⅜in vertical bolt, and the nut is

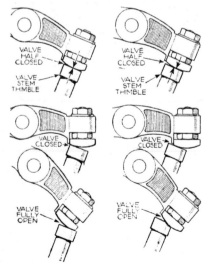

*Diagram showing the importance of " straight-line " rocker operation ; the correct action is shown on the left. Incorrect positions (on the right) are exaggerated for clarity*

VALVE HALF CLOSED
VALVE HALF CLOSED
VALVE STEM THIMBLE
VALVE STEM THIMBLE
VALVE CLOSED
VALVE CLOSED
VALVE FULLY OPEN
VALVE FULLY OPEN

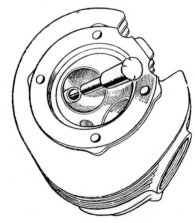

*A two-diameter drift is used to drive out worn valve-guides. Usually the Service staff drive the guides inward*

# Servicing Wrinkles

## Giving Details of the Methods Used by Works' Service Departments

GEORGE WILSON

screwed on after it. About 9in away from the hole, the lever is drilled and tapped and a $\frac{1}{4}$in screw inserted in the top so that it projects about $\frac{1}{4}$in through the underside. This is to act as a guide for a $3\frac{1}{2}$in length of $\frac{3}{8}$in o.d. mild-steel tube with, at one end, the sides cut away, leaving two projecting tails, each $\frac{1}{4}$in wide and $\frac{3}{4}$in long, situated diametrically opposite to one another.

In order to remove the valves, the cylinder barrel is placed upside down on the bench, and located by the old piston crown. A wooden stock is placed under the valve heads and between the head studs to keep the valves from dropping. The valve collars are given a smart tap with a hammer. Then the tails forming one end of the short piece of tube are placed vertically on the valve collar, the tyre lever is brought down, the $\frac{1}{4}$in screw goes into the top end of the tube, and pressure is applied to the lever.

### Both Hands Free

Then comes the real *pièce de résistance* of the whole job. On a screw on the front edge of the bench is a pivoting $\frac{1}{4}$in-dia. rod with a hook at one end. When the spring is compressed the rod is swung up and the hook slipped over the end of the lever. You then have both hands free for removing the collets and, furthermore, you have all the time in the world in which to do the job!

Hairpin springs on the camshaft engines? The tool for dealing with those is perhaps the simplest of all. It consists of an easily made pincer, made, in fact, from an old pair of pliers. In order to gain the leverage necessary, 10in lengths of $\frac{1}{2}$in electrician's tubing are pushed over the normal handles. To one jaw is welded a 2in×1in piece of flat, $\frac{1}{8}$in mild-steel sheet. The opposite jaw is cut off near the pivot and to the root remaining is welded a similar piece of mild steel, which is curved to clear the circular part of the valve spring. And that's it.

Loosening timing sprockets on their tapers has always presented me with a problem since, usually, they are (a) "up good and tight" and (b) there is seldom sufficient space between the outside of the timing chain and the edge of the case to accommodate the legs of a sprocket drawer. On one occasion when I made a sprocket drawer for this particular work, so light had the legs of the drawer to be, because of the space question, that I bent the legs. Then, after hardening the legs, the centre bolt in the drawer bent!

If I had been able to have a chat with the gen man at Nortons first, I could have saved myself a lot of trouble. His tool consists of a tyre lever ground at one end to a chisel-like (though not sharp) edge and with about 2in of the same end turned over to form a U. To slacken a sprocket he unscrews the nut two or three turns until it projects a thread or two beyond the end of the shaft. The looped end of the lever is then slipped behind the sprocket, where it passes easily between the runs of the chain. This done, the inside face of the outer part of the lever comes into contact with the outer face of the nut on the shaft.

The lever is held inward with hand pressure, and then, with a hammer, given a smart tap in the same direction. In numerous cases when this demonstration was being given to me the sprockets eased immediately. The scheme is indubitably the best for this particular job that I, personally, have ever come across.

To remove the inlet valves on the Dominator Twin it is necessary first to pull out the rocker spindles and take the rockers out of the way. The spindle ends are screwed with a female thread to facilitate withdrawal. A 5/16in B.S.F. bolt screwed in gives one something to pull on, but the works' people use a 9in long rod with a right-angle turn at one end, and they tap the tail formed by the bent end with a hammer. The rocker spindles, incidentally, have a spring washer at one end and a shim at the other. Exhaust valves can be fetched out without removing the rockers. The valve-spring compressor used is a very special job made for the twin cylinder-head, but I was told that the Terry spring compressor does the job admirably. Before a Service mechanic lifted a twin head off, he marked one side of the head and the pair of valves fitted in that side so that there would be no confusion during reassembly.

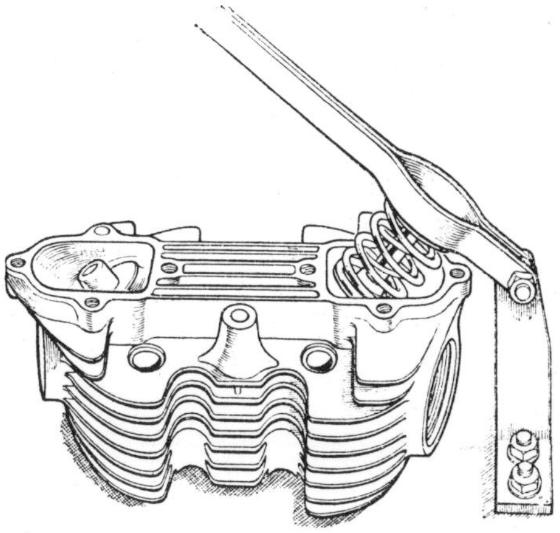

*The valve-spring compressor for overhead-valve engines is simple and easily made up*

### Refitting the Head

Refitting the head of a twin while the engine is on the bench is a quite straightforward one-man job. However, for doing the job while the engine is still in the frame it is almost certain that two pairs of hands would be required. The procedure is first of all to place the head upside down on the bench and slip the push-rods into their tunnels. The inlet rods are longer and go to the inside.

When the head is turned right-way up, and placed on the cylinder block, the push-rods drop down the tunnels in the block and on to the large-area cam followers. The inlet rods are easily located on the rockers—they simply fall

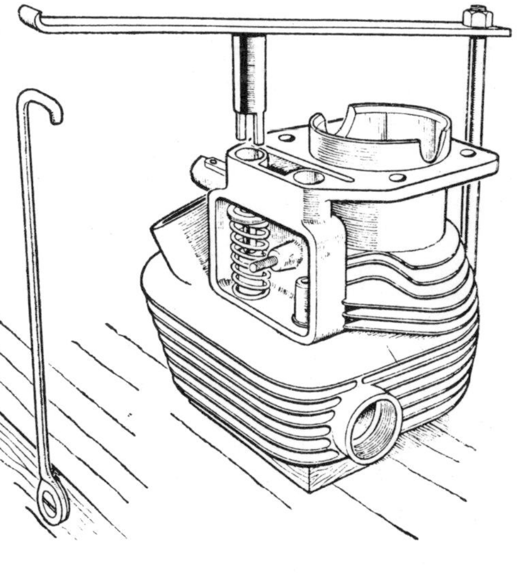

*Right: Simple tool used for compressing the valve-springs on the side-valve engines. An old piston is used to locate the barrel*

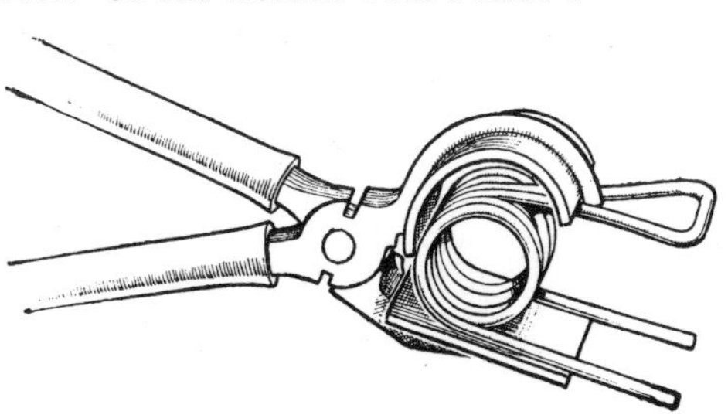

*Left: An easily made pincer for dealing with hairpin valve-springs on the overhead-camshaft engines*

## Norton Servicing Wrinkles . .

into place. By this time, however, the exhaust rods have dropped to the bottom side of the tunnels. To raise them, the Service boffin I watched used a piece of bent wire, which he hooked under the rod and raised it till he could locate the rod on the rocker.

When fitting new shock-absorber rubbers to clutches, the Norton people generally remove the clutch and do the job in a special rig. I was shown how the job can be done, however, by using the special tool available from Taylor Matterson, of London, or by means of a tool made up by a pair of clutch plates riveted together and fitted with a lever. The tool required is, in fact, identical to one illustrated in the first article in this particular series. The object is to compress one set of rubbers while the second set is being inserted, and the job can only be done with considerable leverage applied to the clutch centre.

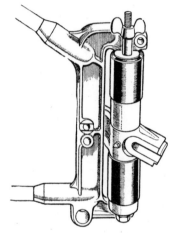

*Effective use of a rear-brake rod for dismantling and reassembling the rear-springing plunger unit*

To withdraw the gear-box mainshaft or the clutch for any reason, special works' withdrawal tools are essential. These can be bought from Nortons, however, or they can be borrowed for a few days from the Service Department.

On the old-type gear box (as distinct from that now used on the twin and several other models) the kick-starter spring is fitted externally and enclosed in a stub-fitting cover. In order to gain access to the spring, a Service mechanic, after taking off the kick-starter crank, placed a foot-long length of an old exhaust pipe over the cover and, using the pipe as a lever, worked it this way and that. The inside diameter of the exhaust pipe was just right for the job, being a tight push-fit over the tapering cover. Pulling the pipe to and fro quickly loosened the cover, allowing it to be drawn off.

The broken spring removed, a new one was slipped into position. Loading it? Easy! The outer end of the spring was slipped into its hole in the kick-starter shaft. Then a piece of string was

looped round the other end and with a quick pull, the end of the spring was located in its slot in the main, kick-starter axle bush. It was as easy as that !

Everything so far had been plain sailing. But what about cycle parts? What, for instance, about dismantling and reassembly of the rear-springing plunger units in the event of its becoming necessary to grease, or even to change the springs ?

The mechanic carrying out the job had handy a rear-brake rod fitted at one end with a nut and lock-nut. Slipped over the rod was a pair of steel tank washers, with a segment filed off each of them. Then there was a 2in long distance-piece and, lastly, on the end opposite to that with the two hexagons, was the wing-nut adjuster fitted to the rod normally.

### Simple Dodges

First step was to remove the wheel. This done, the pinch bolts on the centre post were loosened, the nut on the bottom end of the post was unscrewed, and the post knocked upward until it could be pulled out altogether. Then the spring boxes were tapped gently sideways until part of the holes in the top and bottom outer covers projected beyond the edges of the frame lugs.

This is where the brake rod came into account. With the wing-nut, distance-piece and one of the tank washers removed, the rod was inserted from the bottom and the washer turned so that the flat was adjacent to the frame lug. Then the second washer was slipped on the rod; this was followed by the distance-piece and the wing-nut was

fitted. The purpose of the rod now becomes apparent. The wing-nut was screwed right up until it was compressing slightly the springs in the boxes. This took the strain from between the frame lugs, and the boxes were lifted easily out and placed on the bench. With the wing-nut unscrewed, the whole of the spring box came easily apart. Re-assembly was merely the reverse of what I have just described.

Front fork dismantling and assembly on the Nortons is quite straightforward. The only point to be watched is that, after reassembly, and when the wheel is in position, the machine should be bounced a few times to centralize the legs, before the pinch bolt adjacent to the spindle is tightened. In any case, the pinch bolt should be absolutely the last to be tightened—otherwise binding of the legs might conceivably occur.

Here are details of a few simple Norton dodges : Cables are lubricated by a mixture of petrol and oil. The mixture is contained in an oil can and squirted down a cable held between the mechanic's forefinger and thumb in such a way that the fingers form a cup. The petrol washes the grit away and then evaporates, leaving the oil.

When replacing the tank, be sure that the top collar is in position above the top rubber—otherwise the tank bolt is liable to go through the tank. To loosen or tighten the gear-box main-shaft nut at the clutch end of the shaft, use a box spanner, leave the rear chain in position, and have someone hold the rear wheel, to prevent it, and consequently the mainshaft, from turning. To replace awkward screws, such as those holding the top spring covers on the fork, use a magnetized screwdriver.

# "Featherbed" Dominator Makes Its Bow

## Nortons Eve-of-Show Surprise : The Dominator 497 c.c. Parallel-twin Engine in the "Featherbed" Racing Frame

*Three-quarter view of the Dominator de luxe, which incorporates the famous T.T. frame*

A NEW Dominator will be exhibited at Earls Court. It will be on the Norton stand—in company with the T.T. winners from which it was developed, and which it so strongly resembles. The new mount, the Dominator de luxe, incorporates the T.T.—or "featherbed"—frame, the Norton twin-cylinder engine and gear box, and a host of novel features.

Production will start soon, and eventually the model will be available in quantity on the home market. For the time being, however, the entire production will be exported.

It will be remembered that the frame consists of a pair of tubes bent roughly to rectangular shape and braced by cross-members. For the production frames, the tube will be of 14-gauge and of the cold-drawn, weldless steel type. From the rear of the bottom of the steering-head the twin tubes mentioned earlier run rearward and outward, sweeping downward at a point just to the rear of the tank, forward again just behind the gear box, and then they return to the top of the steering head.

Forming the steering head is a short length of heavy-gauge plain tube. Heavy gauge is employed so that recesses can be turned in each end to accommodate the head bearings. These are robust, angular-contact ball-journal bearings—which are capable of taking both axial and radial thrust—instead of the more usual, loose ball races. Dimensions of the bearings are 25mm bore, 52mm outside diameter, and 15mm deep.

Arc welding is used throughout in the construction of the frame since it is a better production proposition than sift-bronze welding. Extending from roughly half-way down the vertical rear-frame members to beyond the bottom bend are two stout, mild-steel gusset plates, forming locations for a cross-tube, which carries the top-rear engine bolts, and for the pivot rod of the rear fork. This fork is manufactured from parallel $1\frac{1}{4}$in × 10-gauge tube, and is bridged at its forward end by means of a $1\frac{7}{16}$in × 10-gauge cross-tube which houses the Silentbloc bushes.

Each of the bushes is 3in in length and,

fitted into the pivot tube from each end, they are separated by a short length of plain tube. The "inners," or inner tubes of the bushes, are of a carefully calculated length and, when in position, they are locked up by the $\frac{1}{2}$in diameter through rod between the frame gussets. No lubrication or other form of maintenance is required by this type of bearing; it is absolutely silent in operation, has a long life and is, of course, replaceable. Rear fork-ends are formed by linering the ends of the tube and then trapping them.

Controlling the rear fork are a pair of near-vertical plunger units which provide for a total up-and-down movement of approximately 3in. In design and construction these plunger units, for which there is a provisional patent specification, appear at first sight to be complicated; so they are, but it is Norton's claim that they are the best shock-absorber units that have ever appeared on a production machine.

### Flap Valve

Each assembly is as follows: at the bottom there is a malleable iron end-cap incorporating the Clayflex-bushed eye for fitting to the fork-end. Copper brazed to the cap is a steel tube which forms the outer oil cylinder of the unit. Clamped to the "floor" of the unit—in the centre of the base of the outer cylinder—there is a spring-loaded flap valve, and fitting over a spigot on the valve is another vertical tube which acts as a cylinder, or inner oil chamber.

*The new Norton has a "greyhound straining at the leash" appearance—in keeping with its illustrious ancestry*

*Nearside view of the new Dominator*

Inserted into the top of this cylinder, and attached to the lower end of a $\frac{3}{8}$in-diameter steel rod, is a piston incorporating a second spring-loaded flap valve. At its top end the piston rod is anchored to the top cap of the leg which, of course, also incorporates an eye, is also fitted with a Clayflex bearing, and anchors to the sub-frame of the machine.

A light-alloy bush, spigoted into the top end of the inner cylinder, forms a guide for the piston rod. And so that oil may not escape up the rod through the guide and cause loss of efficiency or external messiness, there is, housed in the guide, a spring-gartered, synthetic-rubber oil seal with a downwardly extending lip. To avoid fluid pressure on the seal, there is a recess below it, connecting, by means

of a downwardly sloping oil-way, to the outer cylinder of the leg.

Immediately above is a second seal, the lip of which extends upward. Its purpose will be appreciated when it is understood that above it there is an oil-impregnated felt bush which, in turn, is topped by an Oil-ite bush.

The reason for the use of an upper oil seal, then, is to retain the oil soaked into the close-fitting felt bush, since the tendency of the oil would be to run down the piston rod and thus be lost.

Clamping down on top of the light-alloy guide mentioned earlier (and therefore securing the piston cylinder and lower flap valve) is a pillar-shape plug. Also in light-alloy, this plug houses the felt and Oilite bushes, and screws finally into the top of the outer cylinder. Below the outer circumference of its base, there is a third oil seal to prevent loss of oil from the outer cylinder.

Clamped between the top edge of the inner cylinder and the piston-rod guide is a closely fitting shroud

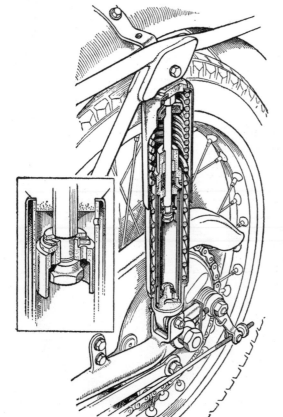

*Left: Section through the rear - suspension leg. The lower valve is similar in principle to the upper valve, shown enlarged*

*Right: The cylinder head stay is carried up to the steering head and is used to mount the horn. The part-section shows the combined radial and thrust head bearings*

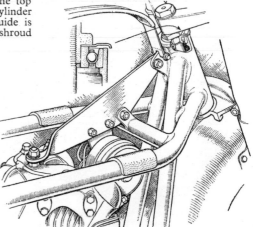

The new Norton front fork, with inset of the hydraulic valve

tube—the purpose of which will be apparent when the working of the unit is discussed. Surrounding the unit, as described, is a two-rate spring. Cylindrical covers are fitted.

The oil used is Castrol Shockol, 70 c.c. of which is inserted into the inner cylinder of each leg. When under load, the unit

# "Featherbed" Dominator Makes Its Bow

telescopes and the inner cylinder moves up the piston. This causes an increased pressure below the piston and a decrease above it, forcing the piston flap-valve to open, and allowing oil to flow into the upper part of the cylinder.

On reaction, the piston flap-valve closes, and the oil trapped above it is forced through a metering hole in the upper end of the piston cylinder. Thus, damping is provided. As the oil flows out of the inner cylinder it is retained within the tiny annular space between the outside of the piston cylinder and the shroud tube which extends downward until its open end is below the minimum oil level.

In this manner, oil returning from the inner cylinder by way of the outer one—to recuperate the chamber beneath the piston—is kept out of contact with the air which could aerate it and upset the working of the leg. Oil returns to the piston cylinder through oilways in the lower flap valve which are, of course, open when the leg is on "recoil."

Since the frame was designed primarily for racing, the steering head was kept as low as possible in the interests of reducing frontal area. While this is not an important aspect of a road machine, it has the advantage that the fork is shorter and the cantilever effect between the steering head and front-wheel spindle is therefore reduced.

### Positive Hydraulic Control

The front fork used is also identical with that employed on racing models. It differs from the fork fitted to the other standard Nortons in that there is positive, hydraulic control throughout the entire fork movement. In the standard fork there is simply a solid damper peg at the lower end of the fork slider. This gives progressive downward damping by passing oil through a gradually decreasing orifice between the main stanchion and the taper damper peg.

In the racing fork, there is a damper cylinder instead of the damper peg. Working in conjunction with the cylinder is a piston-controlled valve fitted to the lower end of a piston rod passing from the top plug down the middle of the stanchion. Comprising the valve is a steel "bucket" which is free to oscillate slightly in a vertical direction on the rod. Its upward movement is controlled by a small cross-pin in the rod. Below it is a steel star-washer.

### Negative Pressure

In the static position, the oil—Castrolite—is contained within the fork slider. On impact, the sliding member telescopes into the fixed one. Negative pressure is created on the upper side of the inverted piston-valve and oil flows from the main chamber into the annulus formed between the rod and damper cylinder above the piston.

Damping on impact is not great, because the restriction as oil flows through the piston is almost negligible. On rebound, the oil trapped above the piston is forced back through the carefully controlled clearance between the "walls" of the piston and the cylinder. Obviously,

because of the pressure above the piston, a seal is provided between the piston and the star washer.

The fork slider is a light-alloy forging and the top bush, which it carries, is of sintered bronze and fitted with a gartered synthetic-rubber oil seal. The lower bush is in steel. Another difference between this and the standard fork is that, whereas in the former the spring is fitted outside the stanchion, in the fork of the new Dominator the spring is fitted between the top of the damper cylinder and the top plug. Total movement is approximately 4½in—3in on impact and 1½in on rebound. No steering damper is fitted.

As on the racing Nortons, a strap fixing for the fuel tank is employed. Sitting on rubber pads on the top frame rails, the fuel tank is a sleek, steel design with a capacity of 3½ gallons. It is fitted with one tap which provides for reserve.

### Valanced Mudguards

It has been mentioned that the gear box is identical with that on the standard Dominator. The gear ratios are higher, however, and are 4.64, 5.61, 8.2 and 13.8 to 1. It will be noted that third and top are very close. As usual, the clutch incorporates a rubber vane-type shock-absorber. There is a folding kick-starter.

Total weight of the new machine is given as approximately 380lb. Wheelbase is 55in; width over the tank top in the region of the rider's knees is 12in. There are no knee grips—just a plain, smooth, enamel surface. Ground clearance is roughly 5⅜in when the machine is unladen.

Both mudguards are valanced; the front mudguard is fitted to the sprung part of the fork. This method of attachment has

*A 7in-diameter headlamp is fitted. On top of the front fork there is a facia containing speedometer, light switch and ammeter*

the great advantage of reducing unsprung weight. On the tip of the front guard there is a reverse lip, and there are channels on the edges so that water is led back to the bottom of the blade. There is, already, a provisional patent on this design. Both brakes are 7in diameter by 1⅛in wide. Tyres are Avons, size 3.25 × 19in front, and 3.50 × 19in rear.

The dualseat is of orthodox construction. That is to say, it has a sheet-metal base, foam-rubber padding, and a Vynide covering. It is secured by two wing nuts underneath and, when removed, reveals the rectangular tool-box—placed there because one normally lays one's tools on the seat anyway! On the side of the tool-box are carried the air lever and ignition cut-out button, and on the front of it is the voltage-control regulator.

There is a 7in-diameter headlamp with an underslung pilot light, and on top of the front fork there is a facia containing the speedometer, light switch, and ammeter. Two stands, one a centre type and the other a prop, are provided. Finish is lustrous polychromatic grey.

The Norton Dominator o.h.v. vertical-twin engine is too well known to warrant detail description; but, for the benefit of those to whom the unit may be unfamiliar, an outline specification is given.

### Excellent Cooling

The capacity is 497 c.c. (66 × 72.6 mm bore and stroke) and the valve-gear is totally enclosed and operated from a single camshaft in front of the crankcase. Widely spaced exhaust ports ensure excellent cylinder-head cooling. Inlet ports are set closely together and fed through a light-alloy manifold from a single Amal carburettor. Chain drive is employed for the magneto and camshaft. Large main bearings, roller on the driving side and ball on the timing side, carry the built-up crankshaft.

Connecting rods are forgings in R.R.56 and the big-end bearings are of the steel-back, shell type. Pistons are of Lo-Ex aluminium-alloy, and they give a compression ratio of 6.7 to 1. Ignition and lighting are by separate magneto and dynamo.

### Road Experience

A member of the Staff of *The Motor Cycle* who has had road experience with the prototype Dominator de luxe, covered, on one occasion, 69 miles in one hour and five minutes, without having the impression that he was hurrying unduly. This exceptionally high average was achieved because of a combination of five factors: impeccable steering and road-holding—which is the equal (except for the increased top hamper) of that possessed by the works' racing machines; excellent all-round engine performance; a first-class gear change; above-average braking power; and a riding position that was not only very comfortable, but which also furnished perfect control. Mudguarding is good enough to allow speeds of 30 m.p.h. on wet roads without the rider's legs becoming damp from spray off the wheels of the machine.

Makers of the Dominator de luxe are Norton Motors, Ltd., Bracebridge Street, Aston, Birmingham, 6. The price has not yet been announced.

# 499 and 348 c.c. Manx Nortons

## Most Famous Racing Manager in the World, JOE CRAIG, M.I.Mech.E., M.S.A.E. and GEORGE WILSON Discuss Two Famous Production Racing Engines

IT is fitting that the words "Manx" and "Norton" should combine to name what are probably the most widely renowned racing machines in the world. In a thousand exploits, Manx Nortons have earned for themselves, and for the entire British motor cycle manufacturing industry, enviable fame. Based on the design of the famous factory power units, the Manx engines are magnificent, high-performance examples of their type. But high performance is not in itself the sole requirement for racing. It is a truism that a machine cannot win a race unless it finishes. Hence, allied with high performance, there must be absolute reliability. Therefore, at the beginning of my discussion with Joe Craig I said: "To be successful, any racing machine must have two attributes: reliability and high power output. Will you be so kind as to explain in general terms the broad principles by which you achieve such high performance and such a high standard of reliability?"

*Answer:* "As you imply, reliability and high power output are entirely interdependent and both must be continuously available throughout a race. Reliability is ensured mainly by thorough observations of the engines in use during a racing season. Components which give trouble are subjected to a careful post-mortem ex-

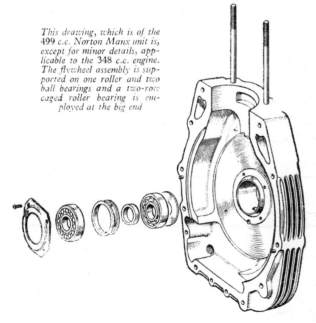

*This drawing, which is of the 499 c.c. Norton Manx unit is, except for minor details, applicable to the 348 c.c. engine. The flywheel assembly is supported on one roller and two ball bearings and a two-row caged roller bearing is employed at the big end*

amination. Entire winters are spent investigating means of increasing reliability and performance. Changes are made after test and retest, and then only when it is definitely established that a gain will result. Every care is taken to ensure that the engine will not wreck itself be-

cause of the high inertia forces. These, as you may know, increase as the square of the speed, and assume tremendous proportions in an engine tuned for ultimate efficiency.

"High performance is achieved chiefly by admitting the greatest weight of charge per induction stroke (at high piston speeds) and burning it efficiently. The highest possible weight of charge is obtained through having a long induction period and by making maximum use of the kinetic energy of the exhaust gases from the previous stroke. The pressure difference across the exhaust valve encourages the new charge to flow readily into the cylinder. Engine torque is of prime importance, and although an increase in b.h.p. may be possible between, say, 6,000 and 7,000 r.p.m., the torque at this speed may be decreasing. Briefly, we aim at the highest torque at the highest possible engine speed while ensuring that the torque at low r.p.m. does not suffer unduly in consequence.

### Heat Retained

"When the best compromise of inlet and exhaust port shape has been established in conjunction with the length of valve opening period, diameter of valve head, and the displacement curve of the valves dictated by the shape of the cams and the required 'overlap,' work begins on improving the combustion of the charge. The aim is to provide the optimum amount of 'swirl'—agitation of the mixture—and so improve the evenness of the burning. Swirl is influenced by port shape, diameter and angle, valve diameters, and the configurations under the valve head. Governed in this way by compromise, the best set of conditions is established. The combustion-chamber shape then receives attention so that the fuel is burned as efficiently as possible. It is of the utmost importance that the surface-area-to-volume ratio is as low as possible, for it is this ratio which decides the proportion of heat that will be retained in the charge and the amount which will be dissipated through the cylinder head, barrel and valves. Heat retained is capable of being converted into useful work, but heat dissipated is responsible for many of the troubles associated with the internal-combustion engine."

*Question:* "I believe that some amateur racing men are inclined to over-rev their engines, sometimes before the oil is properly on the job. This misuse often brings about inertia failures at the big-end, and valve and valve-spring troubles. Are any steps taken in the Manx engine to prevent bothers of this sort arising?"

*Answer:* "No advantage is to be gained by allowing a Manx engine to turn over at speeds in excess of 6,200 r.p.m. for the 500 c.c. and 7,200 r.p.m. for the 350 c.c. Engines will usually withstand a sudden increase of, say, 500 r.p.m. momentarily, as for instance when a gear is missed or a chain breaks; but when an engine is over-revved the big-end bearing, gudgeon pin and piston bosses are subject to excessive overloading. It is difficult to take any steps to prevent this occurring, apart from impressing upon the rider how harmful and expensive the practice of over-revving can be."

*Question:* "Bore and stroke dimensions for the 350 and 500 c.c. engines respectively are 71 × 88mm and 79.62 × 100mm. These stroke dimensions are relatively long for modern racing engines in view of the present-day high power outputs. Will you explain, please, the requirements governing the Manx bore and stroke dimensions? Is it not a fact that the use of a long stroke puts a limit on r.p.m. because of piston speed and inertia loading considerations?"

### Power and R.p.m

*Answer:* "While there is at present a tendency towards 'squarer' engines, we feel that our 71 × 88mm and 79.62 × 100mm power units have been—and are —quite successful in the hands of the general racing public. Although we agree that the squarer engine may have the ability to rev more for similar piston speed and inertia loading, one should not overlook the important point that higher engine speed is of no merit unless accompanied by a substantial gain in power."

*Question:* "One of the most prominent features of the Manx engines is the large, square cylinder head. What is the reason for the use of square-profiled finning?"

*Answer:* "Large fins are employed on the cylinder head in an endeavour to get a substantial cooling surface out into the air stream, and not rely entirely on the air that might pass the fork, mudguard and frame tubes. The square shape is employed so that the passing air makes contact with the fin surface for the entire length of the head, thus making greater use of the available fin-tip area."

*Question:* "I believe that the original Manx cylinder head comprised a bronze skull, with the light-alloy fins cast on it. Why did you make the change-over to the present type of all light-alloy head with inserted valve seats?"

*Answer:* "In the years before the war

# MODERN ENGINES

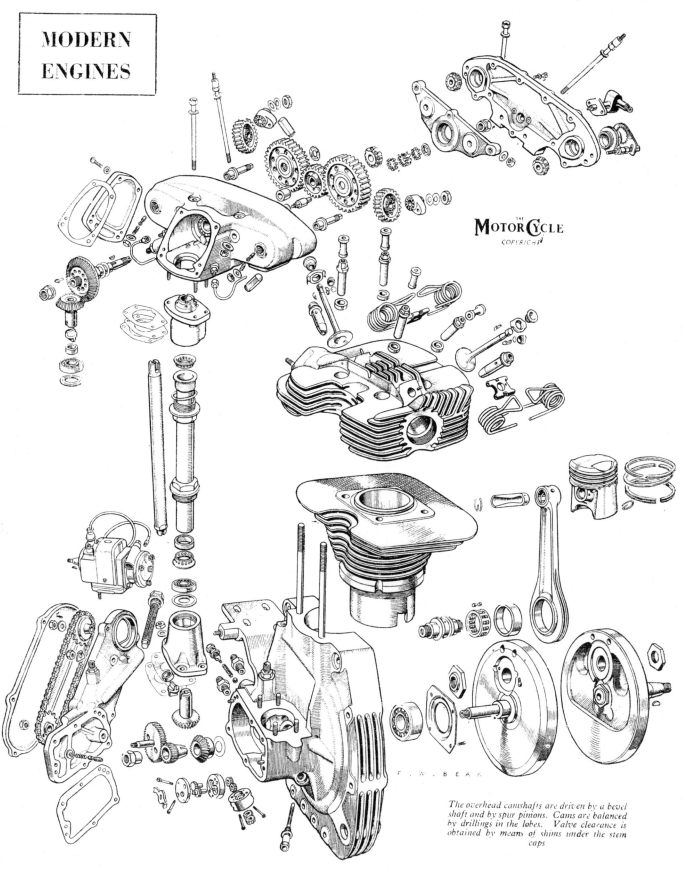

*The overhead camshafts are driven by a bevel shaft and by spur pinions. Cams are balanced by drillings in the lobes. Valve clearance is obtained by means of shims under the stem caps*

# Modern Engines.. Manx Nortons

when petrol-benzole fuel was used, the composite-type head was most satisfactory. Since the war, however, the available fuel has tended to create higher combustion-chamber surface temperatures. The thermal conductivity of the aluminium-alloy head is superior to that of a composite aluminium-bronze unit, and lower combustion-chamber temperatures, therefore, result."

*Question:* "What is the material used for the cylinder head?"

*Answer:* "We use a special, low-expansion, high-silicon alloy which, among its other virtues, has good thermal conductivity at elevated temperatures."

*Question:* "What material is employed for the valve guides?"

*Answer:* "The material for the inlet guide is phosphor bronze and for the exhaust, chromium bronze. The high thermal conductivity of chromium bronze enables full use to be made of sodium-cooled type exhaust valves. In other words, the hot stem of the exhaust valve is able to lose its heat rapidly through such a guide, thereby lowering the temperature of the exhaust-valve head."

*Question:* "How are the guides inserted and how is concentricity ensured between their bores and the guide housings?"

*Answer:* "The guides are arranged to have an interference fit to the cylinder head. Every care is taken to ensure concentricity of the valve-guide bore to its outside diameter during manufacture, but, to provide absolute concentricity, the valve seats are cut and the valves ground after the guides have been fitted. The actual guide bore is used as a location for these operations."

## Combustion-chamber Shape

*Question:* "Is there anything unusual about the cylinder-head combustion-chamber shape?"

*Answer:* "No; the combustion chamber is nearly hemispherical. This shape has always been found to be very good, both volumetrically and thermally. The fact that it is also readily machineable ensures good 'reproduceability.'"

*Question:* "Are the valve seats pressed, or cast into position?"

*Answer:* "The valve seats are shrunk into the cylinder head with approximately 0.003in interference. This operation is carried out by heating the cylinder head to a predetermined, controlled temperature, until the degree of expansion enables the seats to be readily inserted."

*Question:* "What are the valve seat materials and why are they used?"

*Answer:* "The valve seat inserts are made from an austenitic cast iron—a material with approximately the same coefficient of expansion as that of the cylinder head, and possessing qualities which render it comparatively free from distortion. Long seat life is thus assured."

*Question:* "Will you explain, briefly and in as non-technical a manner as possible, how the Manx system of megaphone exhausting affects power output?"

*Answer:* "In an exhaust system for a racing engine, the gases must be discharged so that the piston works against the minimum possible gas pressure. The kinetic energy of the gas must be utilized in such a manner as to produce the maximum negative pressure in the cylinder towards and at the end of the exhaust stroke. Use can thus be made of a large valve overlap to get the inlet gas column moving in readiness for the next filling stroke. It has been established that the combination of exhaust pipe length and diameter is important in achieving the best possible results, and that no one combination is equally efficient over the whole speed range of the engine.

"Usually a long pipe of small diameter is good for power at low r.p.m., while a short pipe of larger diameter is better for power at high r.p.m. It is necessary to compromise with a pipe diameter and length that will give the best results at the most used part of the engine-speed range. The length is often less than the regulation requirements for racing, and in the early days the megaphone was introduced to bring the length of the exhaust pipe to that required by the regulations. In later years, however, the exhaust pipe has been subjected to intensive investigation, and the angle of taper and length of megaphone have been found to be important in achieving the greatest possible extractor effect and the consequent beneficial influence on top-end performance."

### A Compromise Length

*Question:* "Is it not true that considerable induction pipe length and long valve opening periods are necessary in order to make full use of the phenomenon you have described? What are the length and diameter of the 348 and 499 c.c. induction pipes respectively, and how were the dimensions arrived at?"

*Answer:* "In the 499 c.c. Manx engine, the diameter of the inlet port is $1\frac{7}{32}$in, and the distance from the end of the carburettor trumpet to the inlet-valve head is approximately $10\frac{3}{8}$in. The 348 c.c. Manx engine has a $1\frac{1}{8}$in-diameter port, and the tract measures $10\frac{3}{8}$in from the end of carburettor trumpet to the inlet-valve head. Disregarding all the complex problems associated with the kinetic energy of the inlet charge, it may be said that the indicated mean effective pressure could be raised considerably at any one engine speed by the use of a longer induction tract. In the case of the Manx racing engine, we are forced to use a certain compromise length in order to accommodate the widest possible speed range. It may be said

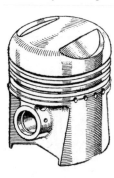

*Piston for the 348 c.c. engine has a flat top and is very deep between the crown and the gudgeon-pin bosses*

that, generally speaking, the greater the length or the smaller the diameter of the tract, the greater is the amplitude of the pressure waves and the later is the arrival of the pressure peak near the time of closing of the inlet valve."

*Question:* "What is the reason for the centres of the inlet and exhaust ports being offset in plan as they are? If the ports were truly aligned, would there not be greater advantage from the extractor effect of the megaphone?"

*Answer:* "The offset inlet port helps to impart the necessary swirl (or agitation) to the ingoing charge, thus ensuring an acceptable rate of flame travel through it. The offset exhaust port is necessary to allow the exhaust pipe to clear the frame tubes. The offset also helps to direct the hot gases away from the valve stem. The advantage gained in promoting turbulence to the ingoing charge is far more important than any possible advantage to be had from straight-through ports and the assumed microscopically greater extractor effect of the megaphone."

*Question:* "Since the speed of the pressure waves in the induction pipe varies with temperature changes, does not the brake mean effective pressure vary considerably with altitude and geographical locations of various race meetings?"

*Answer:* "Yes, the speed of the pressure waves in the induction pipe varies slightly with changes of temperature which, theoretically, have their effect upon the kinetic energy of the inlet charge. In practice, however, this amounts to very little, and the variations of atmospheric pressure due to altitude have a much greater effect than temperature changes. These variations affect the specific weight of the air and consequently the b.m.e.p. As I said earlier, it is the weight of the inlet charge that is important for high power output, not necessarily the volume."

### Cylinder Charging

*Question:* "According to the data in the information panel, the inlet valve opening period is 307.5 degrees. Is there any direct relationship between the length of the induction pipe, the r.p.m. and the inlet opening period?"

*Answer:* "In a naturally aspirated engine, the ingoing air has imparted to it a velocity sufficiently high at the carburettor jet to raise petrol and to continue at an increasing velocity along the port until it enters the cylinder. The force mainly responsible for this velocity is the negative pressure created by the descending piston. This negative pressure occurs only for 180 degrees of crankshaft movement and at, say, 6,000 r.p.m., precious little time is afforded to this cylinder-filling period. However, because the gas column is travelling at such high velocity, cylinder charging continues until the pressure created in the cylinder by the rising piston is equal to the pressure exerted by the gas column. In the case of the Manx engines, this pressure balance takes place some $67\frac{1}{2}$ degrees after bottom dead centre. This ramming effect occurs as a result of high engine r.p.m., the shape of the valve-lift curve and the length, diameter and shape of the inlet tract. As I have mentioned, the kinetic energy of the exhaust gases helps the inlet charge provided, in the case of the Manx engine, the inlet valve is open some 60 degrees before top centre."

*Question* : "Obstructions in the inlet pipe. I believe, set up turbulent pockets which result in a falling-off in the size of the pressure waves. In the Manx engines, the inlet-valve guide protrudes well into the port. Is this not a disadvantage in a high-performance engine? "

*Answer* : "Even in racing engine design a certain amount of compromise has to be faced. In this instance, the guide does protrude a short distance into the port, but this is necessary to provide sufficient guide length for supporting the valve. The guide is, however, fairly well tapered to offer a minimum restriction to the inlet charge and, furthermore, care is taken to see that there is no reduction in cross-sectional area of the port. As a matter of interest, I might add that it has been found that when an inlet port was very large, a gain in power could be obtained by extending the inlet guide farther into the port."

*Question* : "What is the reason for double overhead-camshaft operation of the valves? "

*Answer* : "The reciprocating mass of each valve and its attendant mechanism can be kept to a minimum consistent with reliability. This low inertia of the reciprocating mass facilitates high-speed valve operation in conjunction with the cam profile necessary for high power output."

### Why a Vertical Shaft ?

*Question* : "Some successful racing engines with o.h.c. operation of the valves employ chain or spur gears to transmit the drive from the crankshaft up to the cylinder head. Why do you favour the use of a tubular coupling and two sets of bevels? "

*Answer* : "The use of a vertical shaft and bevels for the camshaft drive reduces the possibility of cyclic variations in the system. It simplifies compression ratio changes, which, in the case of spur-gear drive with fixed gear centres, have usually to be made by alterations to the piston-crown height and shape."

*Question* : "How is balancing of the cam lobes effected? "

*Answer* : "Balancing is by means of a suitable hole drilled through the cam lobe. However, as the cams run at only half engine speed, balance is of secondary importance."

*Question* : "What is the reason for the Oldham couplings at the top and bottom of the vertical shaft? "

*Answer* : "These couplings are employed principally to take care of shaft-length variations caused by expansion and contraction. Compression ratio changes, too, are simplified; the couplings can also accommodate slight malalignment between the bevel gears and the vertical shaft."

*Question* : "Why do you favour the use of separate caps on the tips of the valve stems? Is it not preferable, with racing engines, to harden the tips? "

*Answer* : "The type of steel used for the manufacture of racing valves is not easy to harden. But as there is no rubbing motion on the ends of the valves, the caps are not hardened either, but heat treated to ensure toughness. Caps are used, too, for convenience—because the method of adjusting the valve clearance is by the use of shims under the caps. The virtue of this method is that it keeps the reciprocating weight at this critical point to a minimum consistent with the provision of some adjustment."

*Question* : "Valve timing is, presumably, rough set by means of meshing the pinions in the cam box in their appropriate positions to one another. How is fine adjustment achieved? "

*Answer* : "Valve timing is rough set in the first instance as you suggest, and finer adjustments are effected at two points: a removable peg locating one of the 12 holes in the cam-box bevel gear to one of the 11 holes in the cam-box bevel shaft, provides for approximately $2\frac{3}{4}$ degrees angular adjustment, representing approximately $5\frac{1}{2}$ degrees at the engine shaft. In the second case, the same principle is applied to the cam and its pinion: i.e., the cam has 11 equally spaced holes and the pinion 12 holes."

*Question* : "What material is used for the cam-box pinions and for what reasons is it suitable? "

*Answer* : "The material used is EN.36V. It is used because it gives a very hard case with a strong core, while retaining a high degree of toughness."

*Question* : "I note that the idler pinions in the cam box have 33 teeth and those of the cam pinions only 21 teeth."

*Answer* : "This particular train of gears has been arranged to work in with the overall geometrical requirements dictated

---

### TECHNICAL DATA

**CAPACITY** : 499 c.c. (343 c.c.).

**BORE** : 79.62 mm (348 c.c., 71 mm).

**STROKE** : 100 mm (348 c.c., 88 mm).

**COMPRESSION RATIO** (for 80-octane fuel) : 8.6 to 1 (348 c.c., 9 to 1).

**PISTON RING END-GAP** (499 and 348 c.c.) : compression rings, 0.015-0.020in ; side-clearance, 0.002in ; scraper rings, 0.008in ; side-clearance. 0.002in.

**VALVE CLEARANCE** (499 and 348 c.c.) : inlet, 0.012in ; exhaust, 0.024in (when cold).

**VALVE TIMING** (499 and 348 c.c. set with 0.007in inlet clearance and 0.019in exhaust clearance) : inlet valve begins to open 60 degrees before top dead centre and closes $67\frac{1}{4}$ degrees after bottom dead centre ; exhaust valve begins to open 85 degrees before bottom dead centre and closes 45 degrees after top dead centre.

**IGNITION TIMING** (499 and 348 c.c.) : 36 degrees on full advance.

**ENGINE DIMENSIONS** (499 and 348 c.c.): drive-side crankshaft roller and ball bearings, $1\frac{1}{4}$in bore, $2\frac{1}{2}$in outside diameter x $\frac{5}{8}$in wide ; timing-side crankshaft double-row ball bearing, 25 mm bore, 62 mm outside diameter x 24 mm wide ; crankpin diameter, 1.436in ; gudgeon pin diameter, $\frac{7}{8}$in (−0.0007−0.0010in) ; small-end bush bore diameter $\frac{7}{8}$in (+ 0.0005+0.0010in). 499 c.c. big-end to small-end centres, 7.5in (348 c.c., 6.5in) ; inlet valve head diameter, 1.844in (348 c.c., 1.64in) ; exhaust-valve head diameter, 1.734in (348 c.c., 1.531in); seat angle, 45 degrees ; valve lift, inlet and exhaust. 0.4463in (348 c.c., inlet, 0.446in, exhaust, 0.422in).

**CARBURETTOR** (499 and 348 c.c.) : Amal type 10 G.P. 499 c.c., $1\frac{5}{32}$in choke diameter (348 c.c., 1in). No. 5 throttle slide, needle No. GP6, 0.109 needle jet, needle position No. 3. 260 main jet for 80-octane fuel (348 c.c., 230). $\frac{5}{8}$in air jet (348 c.c., $\frac{1}{16}$in).

---

by the distance across the valve tips. This in turn is controlled by the valve angle and length, and by the relative vertical position of the cam box to the cylinder head."

*Question* : "What is the reason for supporting all the cam-box spindles on these expensive-looking ball and roller bearings? "

*Answer* : "The camshafts are each supported on a roller bearing at one end and a ball bearing at the other. The idler gears run on standard $\frac{3}{16}$in-diameter × $\frac{7}{16}$in-long rollers suitably caged about a fixed spindle. The bevel shaft, as you can see, is mounted on a ball bearing at the bevel gear end and a roller bearing at the other end; the whole provides an arrangement that offers very little frictional loss and does not require pressure lubrication."

*Question* : "Oil-pump drive is by means of spur gears from the timing-side mainshaft. What is the reason for the driven 44-tooth pinion being so much narrower than the 22-tooth driving pinion? I note that the larger is $\frac{5}{16}$in wide and the smaller $\frac{1}{2}$in wide."

*Answer* : "A certain amount of end adjustment is required for both gears, and the position of the timing pinion on its shaft is dictated by a 30-degree, included-angle taper. The difference in gear widths ensures full tooth contact."

### Extra Rigidity

*Question* : "I note that the mainshafts are separate from the flywheels and pressed in. Would not the assembly be more rigid if the units were forged integral with one another? "

*Answer* : "We like to case-harden our flywheel shafts so that a tough core is obtained, and also to eliminate the danger of seizure of the bearing inner race to the shaft. To produce hardened shafts and soft flywheels with an integral design would be extremely difficult. In our arrangement, the shafts are of $1\frac{1}{8}$in diameter where they enter the flywheels, to which they are force-fitted, keyed, and nutted up against a large flange formed on the shaft. A very rigid assembly results."

*Question* : "The crankpin, I note, is made from the solid. Some racing crankpins are in two parts, a separate roller track being pressed on the pin proper. What are the advantages of your system? "

*Answer* : "Although the one-piece crankpin is more costly to produce, we feel that it is worthwhile because of its extra rigidity. In addition, much greater accuracy is always possible where the number of parts demanding concentric accuracy is kept to a minimum."

*Question* : "The big-end eye of the connecting rod is $2\frac{5}{16}$in in diameter and the small-end bush bore diameter is $\frac{7}{8}$in. The rod is no less than $1\frac{1}{4}$in wide at the small end and $1\frac{1}{2}$in wide where the big-end webs blend to the general rod section. The webs around the big-end eye are on the rod's outer edges. What is the advantage of this design over the more common one of having a single web running round the big-end eye ? "

*Answer* : "There is less tendency for the outer edges of the big-end eye to become 'bell-mouthed' and there is a web supporting the track under each set of the

## Modern Engines .. Manx Nortons

two rows of rollers in the big end. While this form of construction is costly, we have found it to be worth while."

*Question:* "Obviously, the Manx connecting rod must be able to withstand very severe bending loads. What is the material used and what are its properties? "

*Answer:* "The connecting rod material is KE805 which is a nickel-chrome, molybdenum seel suitably heat-treated to give a high tensile strength, good fatigue qualities and high resistance to shock loading."

*Question:* "Pistons for both 499 and 348 c.c. engines are of slipper design, but the 499 c.c. piston has a dome top and the 348 c.c. piston a flat crown with a markedly prominent radius between the top land and the crown. Also, with the 348 c.c. piston, there is more land above the gudgeon-pin bosses than there is with the bigger one. Will you explain the reasons for these differences? "

*Answer:* "As I mentioned earlier, the best thermal conditions in a combustion chamber are obtained when the surface-area-to-volume ratio is as small as possible. A flat-top piston offers the least surface area of any, and although the 499 c.c. piston has a slight curvature, for all practical purposes it could be considered flat. This slight curvature and any other discrepancies between the crowns of the two sizes of piston have been necessary to obtain the desired compression ratio in conjunction with the combustion-chamber shape."

*Question:* "What is the piston material? "

*Answer:* "The pistons are forged from Hiduminium RR59 which, when heat-treated, possesses excellent mechanical properties at elevated temperatures, high thermal conductivity and a low friction coefficient."

*Question:* "I note that the big-end bearing has a Duralumin cage while the main bearings have bronze cages. Why is there this difference? "

*Answer:* "A main bearing cage, unlike that for the crankpin, does not impart centrifugal loading to the bearing. Hence, bronze can be employed for the main-bearing cage."

### Power Outputs

*Question:* "What is the reason for the very tall crankcase? "

*Answer:* "It enables the cylinder barrel to be deeply sunk into the crankcase and, by keeping the joint between crankcase and cylinder barrel as high as possible, the whole engine structure is extremely rigid."

*Question:* "Is a bonded liner used in the composite cylinder? "

*Answer:* "No. The close-grained, cast-iron liner, which has a corrugated outer surface for keying purposes, is cast into the light-alloy finned muff."

*Question:* "What is the recommended r.p.m. range of each of the engines? "

*Answer:* "Up to 6,000 r.p.m. for the 499 c.c. and 7,000 for the 348 c.c."

*Question:* "What are the respective power outputs? "

*Answer:* "Approximately 37.5 b.h.p. at 6,000 r.p.m. for the 499 c.c. engine and 29.5 b.h.p. at 7,000 r.p.m. for the 348 c.c. These figures are for 80-octane fuel, and assuming normal barometric pressure and temperature conditions."

*Question:* "Will you explain briefly at what part of the torque curve a rider should change gear when racing, and why? "

*Answer:* "Generally speaking, the torque curve of a racing engine over its useful revolution range is more or less flat, with a pronounced dip at the ends, i.e., at low r.p.m. and at the highest r.p.m. In order to make full use of the engine torque in travelling from A to B in the shortest possible time, a higher gear should be selected at the engine speed at which the torque (*not the h.p.*), has just begun to 'fall off' from peak. By so doing, one not only has the maximum effort the engine can exert available for acceleration, but any tendency for the engine r.p.m. to decrease (because of gradient, or headwind) is overcome by the torque increase accompanying this slight falling off in r.p.m. The engine should be taken up to this predetermined r.p.m. in every gear until top gear is engaged, and in top only should the engine be allowed to reach peak revs. The time taken to reach peak revs after maximum torque has begun to fall off can usefully be employed in accelerating in the next gear. For example, the 499 c.c. Manx engine develops its maximum torque between 4,500 and 5,500 r.p.m., with a slight 'falling off' up to 6,200 r.p.m. The time to change gear, therefore, is when the engine revs have reached, say, 5,600 r.p.m."

# New Norton
# Rear Springing

### Pivoted-fork Suspension for Dominator Twin and ES2 Models
### Dual-seats Standardized : Many Other Detail Improvements

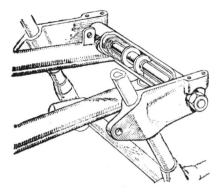

*Silentbloc bushes are employed for the new rear fork pivot bearing*

RACE breeding is no idle term as applied to Nortons. For a quarter of a century the marque has held a leading position in road racing throughout the world, and the vast experience gained in this most searching of all fields of test has borne fruit in the production models—not only in the over-the-counter Manx racers but also in the normal road machines, including the side-valve models. For more years than many present owners can remember, Nortons have had a reputation for being, if anything, ahead of contemporary progress in the matter of first-class steering, roadholding, and high-speed reliability—in fact, in the ability of engine and machine as a whole to take sustained punishment and ask for more.

In the 1953 Nortons, this reputation is upheld and enhanced. Two years ago, plunger-type rear springing gave place to pivoted-fork suspension on the factory racers. For 1953, the Dominator twin Model 7 and the ES2 have entirely new pivoted-fork rear springing in place of the plunger-type suspension. All models in the range except the 500 T trials mount are equipped with Norton dual-seats and built-in pillion footrests. The new Lucas stop- and tail-lamp unit is fitted to all models equipped with lighting. An improved silencer is featured on the ES2 and Dominator 7 and 88 (de Luxe) machines. There is more efficient lubrication of the twin-cylinder engine. Several modifications appear on the Dominator

de Luxe. Only the 490 c.c. overhead-valve 500T trials model remains unaltered. Price reductions have been made possible by economies in production.

Most important change in the 490 c.c. o.h.v. ES2 and 497 c.c. o.h.v. Dominator Model 7 is the new rear suspension. To accommodate it, the rear portion of the standard cradle frame has been redesigned. From the lug at the top of the seat pillar, two tubular stays extend to the rear for a short distance, then curve downward, substantially parallel with the seat tube, to meet the frame members which provide the bottom anchorage for the gear box. Located near the bottom of the rear stays are forwardly projecting lugs which carry the pivot bearings for the fork. Bolted to the lugs is a fabricated steel bracket which links the lugs to the gear-box plates.

Of welded tubular construction and

similar to that employed for the "featherbed" frame, the rear fork pivots on Silentbloc bushes; these, of course, require no maintenance. Fork movement is controlled by hydraulically damped, telescopic spring legs which, at the top, are pivotally attached to brackets welded to the rear stays.

The new suspension permits, of course, appreciably greater wheel movement (3½in) than was possible with the plunger springing. Further, the pivot centre is less than 3in behind the final-drive sprocket centre; hence the variation in chain tension is microscopic. The chain is, of course, in normal adjustment at the mid position of the springing, and the tension slackens slightly at extremes of wheel movement. The wheelbase is the same as it was with plunger springing, namely, 54½in.

In conjunction with the new spring

*Popular sidecar mount—the 596 c.c. side-valve Big 4*

*Striking single—the 490 c.c. o.h.v. ES2 with the new rear springing*

frame, a very wide (approximately 7½in) and deeply valanced rear mudguard is fitted. Indeed, the proportions of the guard are such that it is said to be self-supporting. The tail end of the guard is hinged, and stability of the hinged portion is ensured by the fitting of two tubular lifting handles, one on each side of the guard. Forward end of each handle is anchored at the spring-unit top-pivot bolt, and the rear end is drilled to receive two bolts; these latter screw into captive nuts positioned under the guard —one on the fixed portion and one on the hinged portion. Raising of the hinged portion for wheel removal therefore entails merely the withdrawal of two bolts.

The new suspension has also permitted the

fitting of a quickly detachable rear wheel, which is identical with the type employed on the solid-frame models. Removal of three sleeve nuts and the spindle allows the wheel to be withdrawn without disturbing the rear chain and brake.

A new tool box of pleasing shape is fitted neatly into the angle of the rear stay on the left side of the Model 7 and ES2. The lid is secured by a captive screw which has a half-wing head, i.e., a wing projecting to one side only. The scheme (which was employed during the war) is ingenious since, if the screw is not adequately tightened and therefore tends to loosen, the weight of the wing when it reaches "bottom dead centre" prevents further spontaneous unscrewing. The electric horn is mounted on the right-hand side and, also on the right, the tyre pump is clipped to the rear stay.

The new silencer on the Models 7 and 88 Dominators and the ES2 looks, in side elevation, somewhat like an elongated pear—albeit a flattened pear! The silencer is deeper as regards maximum height, but shallower as regards width, than the former round pattern. Internally, the new silencer is divided into three compartments by means of two perforated plates. The integral outlet pipe extends forward to meet the foremost plate, and it has two sets of holes—one set on each side of the second plate. Hence three compartments communicate with the outlet pipe through a multiplicity of holes. This arrangement is claimed to give more efficient silencing with slightly less absorption of engine power.

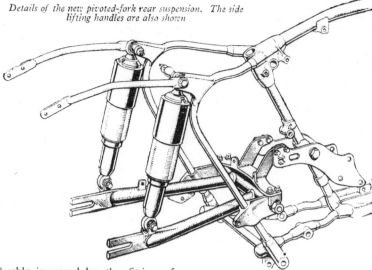

*Details of the new pivoted-fork rear suspension. The side lifting handles are also shown*

siderably improved by the fitting of a normal type of front mudguard to the unsprung portion of the fork legs; hence the guard moves up and down with the wheel, and the gap between tyre and guard is eliminated. In the light of further experience with this model, the factory has found it desirable to revert to the standard Dominator gear ratios (of 5, 6.05, 8.85 and 14.88 to 1) in order to provide optimum performance.

Other improvements to the de Luxe model are a rubber-mounted handlebar and the addition of thin kneegrips to the petrol tank. Sad news for enthusiasts in

this country is that the Dominator de Luxe is still for export only.

Solid-frame models in the range—the No. 1 Big 4 and 16H side-valve machines of 490 c.c. and 596 c.c. capacity respectively, and the 490 c.c. overhead-valve Model 18—remain unaltered except for the standardization of Norton dual-seats, built-in pillion footrests and the new rear-light unit. Incidentally, a big advantage of the light unit is that it is blatantly visible from the side as well as from the rear.

The range is completed by the famous overhead-camshaft Nortons of 500 c.c. (Models 30 International and 30 Manx) and 350 c.c. (Models 40 International and 40 Manx). The specifications and prices of these machines are not yet available.

The makers are Norton Motors, Ltd., Bracebridge Street, Birmingham, 6. Prices of the models described (in which total price includes Purchase Tax, payable in Great Britain only) are as follows:—

*Still for export only—the 497 c.c. Dominator 88 with racing frame*

|  | Basic Price | Total Price |  |  |
|---|---|---|---|---|
|  | £ | £ | s | d |
| Model 18, 490 c.c. o.h.v. ... | 150 | 191 | 13 | 4 |
| ES2, 490 c.c. o.h.v. ........ | 164 | 209 | 11 | 1 |
| 16H, 490 c.c. s.v. .......... | 146 | 186 | 11 | 1 |
| No. 1 Big 4, 596 c.c. s.v. ... | 149 | 190 | 7 | 9 |
| No. 7 Dominator, 497 c.c. o.h.v. twin ............. | 187 | 238 | 18 | 11 |
| No. 88 Dominator de Luxe, 497 c.c. o.h.v. twin ...... | 208 | 265 | 15 | 7 |
| 500T, 490 c.c. o.h.v. ... | 156 | 199 | 6 | 8 |
| Model G sidecar ......... | 66 | 83 | 12 | 0 |

Another modification to the exhaust system of the ES2 is the fitting of an exhaust pipe of smaller diameter—1⅛in instead of 1¾in. This is said to give slightly improved power at low speeds. Also on the ES2 a 43-tooth rear-wheel sprocket is fitted; it gives overall gear ratios of 4.75, 5.75, 8.4 and 14.2 to 1.

On the twin-cylinder engines, the rocker-box lubrication is improved. A spring-loaded ball valve is arranged in the oil return line to ensure an adequate supply of oil to the rocker gear. It will be recalled that the Model 88 Dominator de Luxe has no oil-pressure gauge. This lead is followed on the Model 7 Dominator; it also has no pressure gauge for 1953.

Front-end appearance of the featherbed-frame Dominator de Luxe has been con-

*More handsome than ever with the new springing—the Model 7 Dominator twin*

# "Is There a Better 'Bigger Banger'?"

*Setting out for its first I.S.D.T., Quantrill's Norton leaves Bowling Green Lane, en route for Italy.*

*In a snowstorm at the top of the Julier Pass, the same machine on the same mission four years later.*

IF only the speedometer would refrain from going out of action the moment I head for home from abroad, I should know how many miles the "Bigger Banger" has covered. Certainly more than 50,000, probably nearer 60,000 since I called at the Norton factory to collect the 596 c.c. "International" that I had persuaded gaffer C. Gilbert Smith to let me have.

Persuaded? Perhaps not; you can't persuade Gilbert. No "flannelling" with him: he's a yes or no man.

I'd been trying to approach the subject, over lunch in the "Midland" with the late Charlie Markham, then our Midlands man. "Come on," said Gilbert, "let's have it. What're you after?"

Because I'd set my heart on a "596" for years, and because I knew that the factory hadn't made one since before the war, and because it was little more than a year since they'd supplied me with a very nice push-rod Model 19, and because I knew that if C.G.S. said "can't be done" then I'd had it, it was in a very small voice that I said, "I'd like a camshaft job . . . a big one . . . you know, a 600 Inter."

"Oh," said Gilbert, "you would, eh?" Tilting right back in his chair he looked at me, straight, from beneath his spectacles, and, for a while, didn't say anything. "Ar . . ," and eventually, "right! If we can find the bits we'll do it."

Weeks passed. Then a message came over the teleprinter from Charles in the Birmingham office. "FLOG MODEL 19," it read, "AT BRACEBRIDGE STREET THIS AFTERNOON SEEN BIGGER BANGER NEARING COMPLETION. LOOKS A BEAUTY."

"Bigger Banger!" One of Charlie's inventions, like "Gunga Din" for the gran'daddy of all "Black Lightnings" and "The Gent" for the most luxurious of all "Square 4s." And an apt label, too, for a machine which has a 113 mm. stroke engine and thumps out around 35 b.h.p. (real Shire horses, not the racehorse type that get tired if they have to pull a sidecar), and one which has stuck.

I took delivery in time for one short Continental canter before going to the 1948 T.T., and attached the Norton to "H.M.S. Insufferable." A vintage Hughes racing sidecar that was—for the benefit of our youngest readers—and I had inherited it from Alec Menhinick, who inherited it from Harvey Pascoe, who inherited it from Denis May, who . . . discovered it, I think, in some junk-yard.

The "Banger" was the object of much jealous admiration as it stood, in all its gleaming newness, on the forecourt of the "Castle Mona," and I was the proudest of all proud owners in the Isle of Man in June, '48. And with good reason, too, for it isn't every sidecar outfit that will better 70 m.p.h. on "Pool." I was pleased with its performance, but at that stage I had still to learn about the big Norton's most endearing characteristic.

It took me to the Belgian Grand Prix. In those days the road from the coast, through Brussels and Liège, consisted mostly of steeply cambered pavé, with moss growing between the stones. I remember coming back from Spa, with five hours in which to catch the midnight boat from Dunkirk, nearly 200 miles away, sitting on the sidecar cross-bar to keep the empty "chair" down and with the handlebars on permanent right lock, as the back wheel slid down the greasy camber in an endeavour to overtake the front. At Bruges I stopped to remedy a headlamp short and the garage folk were so friendly—with memories of liberation still fresh—that they wouldn't let me do the job myself, and promptly dropped the little switch spring down the drain. Oh, well!

At Adinkirk there was one of the first of what has now become a regular series of encounters with the jocular French frontier official (he must be on permanent night duty) who thinks I'm mad to ride a motorcycle in the rain and who invariably, at a few minutes to zero hour, wags his finger and—in the leisurely manner in which Frenchmen love to conduct a "discussion"—tells me that it is "inutile" to carry on for the last few kilometres to the dock. "Certainement, m'sieu, the ferry-boat she is taken the depart."

Certainement, she hasn't; I've been last aboard before. But, bless him, he's a dear old chap—the sort of gentlemanly official that, for some reason, you find only in the French and Belgian Customs services.

A week or so later, we went that way again—the "Banger" and I, en route for the Moto-Cross des Nations—but this time the sidecar was discarded and the 19-tooth engine sprocket replaced by a 22-tooth soup-plate. On the return journey I took the road through Tielt and Dixsmude. It is a good route, with stretches of really smooth pavé and a certain amount of concrete, and has the advantage of being utterly deserted at night. The moon was up,

## CYRIL QUANTRILL

### RECALLS SOME OF THE MANY MILES HE HAS COVERED ON HIS SPECIAL 596 c.c. " INTERNATIONAL " NORTON COMBINATION

*(Right) Less than two hours after the picture on the left was taken, the Norton was in sunny Italy, alongside the shores of Lake Como.*

*(Below) When the outfit was new. Charlie Markham watching Quantrill trying the paces of his Norton-Hughes combination over the measured "quarter."*

it was dry, and for mile after mile, between villages, the Norton's speedo. sat around the " 100 " mark. I was almost too early for the boat on that occasion and, four years later, it still remains one of my happiest motorcycling memories.

Then to San Remo, for the most enjoyable of all post-war " Internationals," with a good passenger, new type " Manx " front forks and a conical-hub " Manx " front wheel. I went touring on the way out, visiting the beautiful little Grand Duchy of Luxembourg for the first time. As thousands of others have done I got a big surprise when, sitting drinking beer in a pavement café, I suddenly found myself enveloped in steam and showered with sparks, as a train—as bizarre as one of Emett's creations—came clanking and hissing along the tramlines, in the heart of Luxembourg city. In every way Luxembourg is a city of contrasts, with German sausage-shops bearings names like " Schmidt Frères " and " Guggleheim et Cie "—Francized since the war but still inscribed in Gothic charac-ters—and an American bar in which you will hear the English and trans-atlantic accents of the radio station staff.

The countryside through which the 1948 I.S.D.T. ran is the loveliest—with the possible exception of the Lebanese slopes above Beirut—of any I have seen. Over the first range of hills from the modern pleasure resorts, and one is in a land which has changed little in centuries.

With the photographer, Alf Long, in the " chair," we'd go dicing up the rough mountain roads, early in the morning, following the trial. He had to work hard as a passenger, too, for with high " Clubman's " gear ratios I had to take the corners smartly on the climbs, in order to keep the revs. up. We'd get our day's " bag " of pictures and notes, then rein up somewhere, to take in the beauty of the scene.

It was so quiet, in those Ligurian Alps, that the chirp of a cricket

sounded loud. Below, in the valley, there would be tiny green fields, a fast-flowing stream and farmsteads, and occasionally the clink of a cow-bell or the laughing voice of a woman would rise clearly through the still air. Vineyards climbed the lower slopes and there were chestnut groves and pine forests, and high up, where the narrow, military roads ran, the ground was rocky.

Across the valley there would be three, four, or more little towns, perched atop a hill or on some crag lower down, each with tall, white-walled houses, pink-roofed and with blue or green painted verandahs, and each dominated by a great Byzantine church, seemingly much too large for the congrega-tion it served. With a fine disregard for modern ways, the church bells chimed sweetly, or clanked in ancient cracked tones, their individual reckoning of the hours of each day. What matter, in 500 years, if a few minutes had been lost?

The return from Italy, through Burgundy where the precious grapes from which life-making wine would shortly be pressed were being harvested, and into the rolling downland and plains of northern France—where ploughing was in progress and leaves, torn from the tall poplars by the first autumn gales, were already dancing along the broad Routes Nationales—were made in a hurry. And it was then that I really discovered the Norton's finest characteristic, an ability to do 200, 300 or 400 miles straight off the reel, at a sustained 60 m.p.h. or more.

During the next year the Hughes gave way to a modern Watsonian " Avon "—my wife never *did* like the Hughes—and a 4-in. by 19-in. rear tyre replaced a long line of 3.50-in. by 20-in. covers, which had been scrubbed out in the course of cornering on the Continent. The " Banger " did less foreign touring—I took a proto-type " alloy " Ariel across on one occasion, and used a Vincent outfit for the Belgian and Dutch round trip—but, in addition to routine motoring to and from the office and to sporting events at the week-ends, there was the I.S.D.T. in Wales.

It is all too well known that the " Six Days " is a tough ordeal for competitors' machines. Believe me, it is almost equally hard on the mounts used by Pressmen. Having seen the last man away from the start, you have to catch up with the runners somewhere out on the day's route, try to check up on progress at the lunch stop, then get back in time to see them all in at night. Before you know where you are you've done 300 miles, including a lot of rough-stuff that you'd never dream of hammering the outfit over at other times. Your passenger has broken the sidecar windscreen or sat on the lamp, you've missed your lunch, you've got wet through and you've torn your waders. But you have had a wonderful day. The I.S.D.T. is

## "Is There a Better 'Bigger Banger'?"    -    -

like that! Year after year, you loathe it and love it.

In 1950 the Norton suffered the indignity of being hitched to a vast two-seater sidecar, in order to transport my family to Belgium for their summer holidays. While Pat and Jean were paddling at Coq-sur-Mer and their mother was enjoying the good food at the Hotel Beau-Rivage, their dad, again teamed with Alf Long, was busy at the Belgian and Dutch races.

Another Welsh I.S.D.T. in 1950—the wet one—and Continental journeys to Florelle and the Belgian and Dutch Grands Prix and then, right at the end of the year, that fantastic winter ride to Italy. Rain and snow all the way there and all the way back. What an experience it was! One I wouldn't have missed for anything—now it's over—but one which was certainly the toughest I have ever had. Had I been on any machine other than the Norton, I think I'd have jacked in before the end of the second day. But the "Banger" didn't miss a beat, so why should I?

The longest outing last year was the Belgian-Dutch-French Grands Prix dice. Three races in three week-ends, and hundreds of miles to be covered in between. London to Spa, in the south of Belgium; Spa to Assen, in the north of Holland; Assen to Albi, in the far south-west of France; then back home again. How the trade reps. managed it, with their mobile workshops, beats me. But they did. They always do.

With the Norton, the whole journey was a delightful experience. Earlier in the year it had done a mere 300-mile round trip from Dunkirk to Mettet, then polished off the 430 miles each way to Berne, for the Swiss Grand Prix, in single days; now it had something to get its teeth into. I finished up by doing the 700-odd miles from Albi to the coast virtually non-stop.

Later came the Italian Grand Prix at Monza, and the "International," at Varese. More pass-storming for the "Banger," more over-revving in bottom gear, and more dust to be swallowed. Then another quick-as-possible return journey. At the end of it the model was in sore need of an overhaul—and it got one. One item that had to be attended to was the petrol tank which, after three years' hard use, suddenly decided it had had enough and opened up, as if a fastener had been zipped undone, along its bottom seam. I hadn't noticed anything untoward, apart from feeling that I'd had to switch on to reserve before it should have been necessary—until I stopped at a petrol station in St. Dizier.

Mon Dieu! Alors! and S'trewth! The petrol-peddler went "spare"! Precious "Super-carburant" was sizzling all over the hot engine like water does when you put a frying-pan under the tap.

I don't know a lot of French, but it was apparent that he thought I should take my departure from his establishment. Perhaps he hadn't paid his fire insurance.

So there I was, on that long, straight road between St. Dizier and Vitry-le-François and with little hope of getting much farther. But, by the most extraordinary good fortune, within ten minutes, a van, with English registration plates, came trundling along, stopped, and Dick Clayton got out.

"In trouble?"

Trouble? Ha-ha! Funny man! But Dick that day saved the ship for me. "Got a tin of some stuff they gave us in Italy," he said, "'Loy' plastic metal. It's supposed to cope with split tanks." And he rummaged in the back of the wagon and produced a little blue tin.

It was incredible. There is no other word for it. Not only did the "Loy" seal the leak so that I was able to get home, but it

was not until some weeks later that I found time to have the tank welded. I have that tin on my desk to this day, as a souvenir.

And so to 1952. Mettet again, and the Swiss Grand Prix—and all the time, the ordinary day-to-day journeys.

"Getting a bit long in the tooth, that bike of yours, isn't it?" said the Editor. "Thought about what you'll get next?"

Thought about it! Of course I had. After the "Belgian," perhaps; I'd see what I could replace it with then. Or after the Italian Grand Prix and the I.S.D.T. That, after all, was going to be a *very* steady outing and, even if the Norton was getting old, it was at least known to be reliable. Yes, I'd hang on to it until the winter. In the meantime the outfit was placed in the careful hands of Jim Pocock, works manager of the Taylor-Matterson establishment, for attention to all the minor items that get frayed after four years' continuous use.

Apart from thoroughly overhauling the cycle parts there was not much of a serious nature to be done. In fact, the major replacements consisted of a set of new tyres and tubes all round.

Now I'm back from Italy and Austria. The trip has put another 2,500-odd miles on the "clock." At least I've *covered* that mileage, although it isn't all recorded. On the Continent it is always a toss-up whether the pavé will wreck my wrist-watch or the speedometer first, and although the watch won the race by a short head—is there *really* such a thing as a shockproof watch?—the speedo. soon followed suit. The "Banger" ran perfectly and, thanks to the autobahn in Germany, I managed to crowd more miles into nine hours' motoring than ever before—to Cologne in one hop from the Austrian frontier—and at the end of it all, the motor stood up to covering the 50-kilometre length of the Aalter-Jabbeke autostrade with the twistgrip wound hard against the stop.

Swop it? O.K.—but for what?

**ROAD TESTS OF
NEW MODELS**

# 490 c.c. Model

### All-purpose Overhead-valve Single Capa

IT is over a quarter of a century since the Model ES2 was introduced into the Norton range. Throughout that time it has retained its basic design characteristics and has achieved popularity as a reliable, pushrod-operated, overhead-valve, single-cylinder five-hundred with a full cradle frame. Now, with the adoption of pivoted-fork rear springing in addition to its telescopic front fork, it combines the traditional performance of the long-stroke big single with modern trends in wheel suspension.

*In appearance the ES2 is well proportioned. Engine and gear box remained commendably oiltight*

The riding position is good, though the reach from seat to handlebar is long for a rider of average build. The resultant extended-arm posture caused the rider's shoulders to ache on a long run. The most comfortable leg angle was achieved with the footrest hangers mounted one serration below the horizontal position. When the machine carried a pillion passenger, the rider's footrests could be made to ground fairly easily at this setting. Both brake and gear pedals could be ideally adjusted to suit the footrest position.

A standard fitment, the 25in-long dual-seat was comfortable

and very well placed on the machine. It was found that the rider's natural seating position was at the front of the seat; hence there was ample room for rider and passenger, both wearing bulky winter riding kit. Owing to the combination of front-brake and air levers and clutch and ignition levers, it was not possible to arrange the horn button and dipswitch as closely to the grips as was desired for convenient operation. The speedometer registered four to five per cent fast throughout its range; both mileage recorders were inconsistent.

Engine starting from cold was normally effected at the first kick, provided that care was taken to depress the carburettor tickler only momentarily, and the throttle was opened no more than a sixteenth of an inch. An accessible throttle-stop adjuster on the carburettor obviates the need for fine judgment in this respect. When hot, the engine was more sensitive to fuel level and throttle opening. If it failed to respond at the second kick, a wide-open throttle could be relied upon to evoke a start. The tick-over was completely reliable, and retarding the ignition one-third eliminated a slight tendency for it to be erratic.

At the lower end of the r.p.m. scale, the engine responds to an unusual degree to the use of the ignition control. By this means considerable flexibility under traffic conditions could be achieved. There was no undue tendency to pinking, even on Pool petrol. Thus the use of 80-octane fuel produced no marked difference in acceleration and speed performance unless the engine was deliberately abused. Compression ratio of the model tested was 6.16 to 1. Piston slap was pronounced when the engine was cold; otherwise the engine was reasonably quiet mechanically.

In town, the Norton would tick along smoothly at 30 m.p.h. in top gear on full advance, though lusty acceleration from that speed necessitated use of the ignition control if some pinking was not to be heard. The charm of the engine lay in its lusty pulling power at low and moderate r.p.m., and its immediate response to throttle opening. Because of these characteristics, allied to its high gearing and the positive manner in which the clutch takes up the drive, the ES2's getaway is deceptively good.

It is difficult to define the most comfortable top-gear cruising speed. At 50 m.p.h. the machine lopes along lazily at a fast tick-over; at sixty, the engine still turns over freely and effortlessly. It is not until 70 m.p.h. is reached that the engine appears to be really working. This speed can be maintained indefinitely; indeed, the Norton never showed the slightest objection to the prolonged use of maximum performance. Engine vibration was negligible in the lower and middle speed ranges, but became more noticeable from just below 70 m.p.h. to the maximum, and was the chief factor in determining the highest indefinite cruising speed.

A characteristic which contributed to the achievement of 50 m.p.h. averages is the way in which the engine maintains a set cruising speed up long gradients without an increase in throttle

*Latest ES2 rear suspension layout. Noteworthy features are the lifting handle and wide mudguard*

# ES2 Norton

## of Effortless High-speed Cruising

*The lusty long-stroke power unit is notable for its good low-speed pulling characteristics*

opening. Power reserve is exemplified by the fact that maximum speed figures achieved by runs in opposite directions differed only by little over one m.p.h. The exhaust note was pleasant at moderate engine speeds but was obtrusive at large throttle openings.

It was a simple matter to effect clean gear changes. When changing up at low r.p.m. it was sometimes necessary to feel in the gears by engaging the clutch before pressure was removed from the gear pedal. At higher engine speeds, however, silent changes could be made, upward or downward, as quickly as the controls could be operated. Indeed, the more quickly and lightly the controls were manipulated, the sweeter was the gear change. Third and top gear ratios are pleasantly close. Neutral could be located easily from either bottom or second gear. With the engine idling, engagement of bottom gear from neutral was noiseless. The gear box was quiet in the indirect ratios.

Steering and cornering were first class. At no time was the steering damper required. In fact, its use, even lightly, tended to spoil low-speed cornering. Straight-ahead steering was positive and unaffected by road bumps provided that the rider resisted a subconscious tendency to pull on the handlebar owing to the long reach from the seat. Rippled surfaces produced a slight tendency for the machine to wriggle. Negotiation of slippery city streets showed excellent stability. If either wheel was locked at low speed, it skidded in a straight line. On slow corners or fast bends, the Norton could be heeled well over with complete confidence. Any desired line could easily be held on a bend.

Both front and rear springing were hard and could not be made to bottom. Normal movement of the rear wheel with the machine ridden solo was approximately one and a half inches, though the potential maximum movement permitted by the layout is 3½in. Road holding at high speeds was good.

Both brakes were smooth and reasonably powerful. Considerable pressure was needed on the front-brake lever to obtain good results. The heavy Bowdenex control cable gave a very solid feel to this lever; there was an entire absence of sponginess. The movement of the rear brake pedal necessary

for full application of the brake was too long for comfort.

The main headlamp beam enabled the machine's maximum performance to be used at night; the pilot light was felt to be insufficiently conspicuous. Full lamp load was balanced by the dynamo at 30 m.p.h. in top gear. During the test, the dynamo ceased to charge; a replacement instrument, fitted by the dynamo makers' service department, proved satisfactory.

By means of the convenient side lifting handles, the machine could be easily placed on its excellent centre stand. The prop-stand fitted to the front of the engine cradle is efficient but proved inaccessible with the footrests set in the preferred position. The toolbox thumbscrew earned full marks for convenience.

Particularly effective was the 7½in-wide rear mudguard. A criticism can be levelled at the chromium plating of the exhaust pipe, which showed rust inside a week during which the machine was exposed to the elements; conversely, handlebar and tank were not similarly affected.

## Information Panel

*The 490 c.c. Norton ES2*

### SPECIFICATION

**ENGINE :** 490 c.c. (79 × 100 mm) single-cylinder o.h.v. Fully enclosed valve gear. Ball and roller bearings supporting mainshafts. Compression ratio 6.16 to 1. Dry sump lubrication ; oil-tank capacity, 4 pints.

**CARBURETTOR :** Amal, with lever-operated throttle-stop for easy starting. Twistgrip throttle control. Gauze air filter in intake.

**IGNITION AND LIGHTING :** Lucas Magdyno with manual ignition advance and retard control. 7in-diameter headlamp.

**TRANSMISSION :** Norton four-speed gear box with positive-stop foot control. Bottom, 14.2 to 1. Second, 8.4 to 1. Third, 5.75 to 1. Top, 4.75 to 1. Multi-plate clutch with Ferodo inserts. Primary chain, ⅜in × 0.305in in pressed-steel oil-bath case. Secondary chain, ⅝in × ¼in. R.p.m. at 30 m.p.h. in top gear, 1,900.

**FUEL CAPACITY :** 3½ gallons.

**TYRES :** 3.25 × 19in Avon studded front and rear.

**BRAKES :** Both 7in diameter 1⅛in wide ; hand adjusters.

**SUSPENSION :** Norton Roadholder telescopic front fork with hydraulic damping. Pivoted-fork rear springing employing coil springs and hydraulic damping.

**WHEELBASE :** 56½in unladen. Ground clearance, 5½in unladen.

**SEAT :** Norton dual-seat. Unladen height, 30½in.

**WEIGHT :** 405 lb fully equipped and with approximately one gallon of fuel.

**PRICE :** £164. With Purchase Tax (in Britain only), £209 11s 1d.

**ROAD TAX :** £3 15s a year ; £1 0s 8d a quarter.

**MAKERS :** Norton Motors, Ltd., Bracebridge Street, Birmingham, 6.

**DESCRIPTION :** *The Motor Cycle*, 2 October 1952.

### PERFORMANCE DATA

**MEAN MAXIMUM SPEED :** Bottom :* 28 m.p.h.
Second :* 48 m.p.h.
Third :* 70 m.p.h.
Top : 79 m.p.h.
*Valve float occurring.

**MEAN ACCELERATION :**

|        | 10-30 m.p.h. | 20-40 m.p.h. | 30-50 m.p.h. |
|--------|--------------|--------------|--------------|
| Bottom | —            | —            | —            |
| Second | 4.2 secs     | 4 secs       | —            |
| Third  | —            | 6.4 secs     | 6 secs       |
| Top    | —            | 8 secs       | 8 secs       |

Speed at end of quarter-mile from rest : 68 m.p.h.
Time to cover standing quarter-mile : 18.8 secs.

**PETROL CONSUMPTION :** At 30 m.p.h. 96 m.p.g. At 40 m.p.h., 77 m.p.g. At 50 m.p.h., 65 m.p.g. At 60 m.p.h., 50 m.p.g.

**BRAKING :** From 30 m.p.h. to rest, 33ft (surface, damp tar macadam).

**TURNING CIRCLE :** 16ft 6in.

**MINIMUM NON-SNATCH SPEED :** 20 m.p.h. in top gear, with ignition fully retarded.

**WEIGHT PER C.C. :** 0.81 lb.

## ROAD TESTS OF CURRENT MODELS

### The 497 c.c. o.h.v. Model 7 "DOMINATOR"

# NORTON

## A High Performance Twin with an Economical Appetite

*The new rear suspension gives a comfortable ride. (Right) Contact-breaker accessibility is a feature. (Below) A close-up view of the "Dominator's" twin cylinder, o.h.v. engine.*

### TESTER'S ROAD REPORT

**Maximum Speeds in :—**

| | | | | | Time from Standing Start |
|---|---|---|---|---|---|
| Top Gear (Ratio 5·00 to 1) | 88 | m.p.h. | 5700 | r.p.m. | 36 secs. |
| Third Gear (Ratio 6·05 to 1) | 80 | m.p.h. | 6150 | r.p.m. | 20⅕ secs. |
| Second Gear (Ratio 8·85 to 1) | 55 | m.p.h. | 6250 | r.p.m. | 8⅗ secs. |

**Speeds over measured Quarter Mile :—**

Flying Start ...87·36... m.p.h. Standing Start ...53·56... m.p.h.

**Braking Figures On** TARRED GRAVEL **Surface, from 30 m.p.h. :—**

Both Brakes ..32.. ft. Front Brake ..44.. ft. Rear Brake ..56.. ft.

**Fuel Consumption :—**

30 m.p.h. 86·4 m.p.g. 40 m.p.h. — m.p.g. 50 m.p.h. 72 m.p.g.

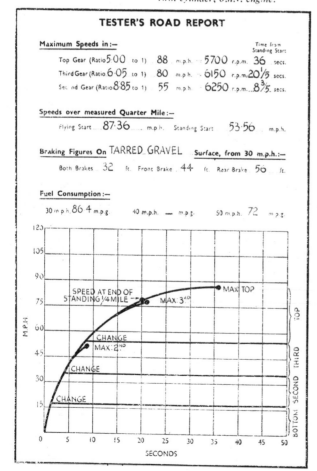

THIS road-test report of the 497 c.c. Norton Model 7 "Dominator" makes history in that, for the first time since the war, premium grade fuel was available to obtain the performance figures. Many miles were also covered with "Pool" in the tank and, before assessing the machine's capabilities, it may be stated that surprisingly little difference was observed in the general behaviour on the two different grades of spirit. With the better-quality fuel, the most obvious improvement was in consumption, and the test figures indicate that with the "Dominator," an inherently economical machine, the price increase per gallon may well be offset by the greater resulting mileage.

To the reputation for high performance established during the years that followed the introduction of the machine, in 1949, can

*In its latest form, the " Dominator"
Norton is a handsome model capable
of a speed approaching 90 m.p.h.*

now be added the further claim of remarkable comfort, for the incorporation of swinging-arm-type, hydraulically damped, rear-suspension and a well-made dual seat has resulted in a motorcycle on which excellent averages can be maintained without personal stress or strain.

A single-tube cradle forms the front half of the frame and, onto this, a pair of triangulated tubes, attached to the top and bottom of the seat down-tube, carry the rear fork pivot and the attachment points for the tops of the hydraulically damped spring units. "Roadholder" front forks are, of course, fitted and the petrol tank, of 3¾ gallons capacity, is of distinctive shape. Silencers of unusual section are part of the new specification.

When considering the riding position, the factory chose to provide a layout that is admirably suited to " leaning on the wind " and is ideal for fast mainroad stretches. Without some support from a self-made breeze, the wrists and arms tend to react to the fact that the handlebars are low and well forward, a position not entirely suited to those with short arms and, in fact, noticeable also to those with arms that are not so short. All controls and the footrests are adjustable and the riding position can be altered to permit the knees of even the tallest rider to fit to the inset knee-grips on a tank in which the width is nicely proportioned. At maximum depression, the footbrake tends to foul the exhaust pipe, but this occurs only when the brake pedal is set low in the first case.

Almost uncannily, the engine would fire at the second prod, even after standing in the open at night, when temperatures were well below zero.

Controls worked smoothly and the clutch withdrew easily, but required firm pressure. From neutral, first gear engagement was noiseless and the movement of the pedal sufficient without being excessive. Clean gearchanges could be made and the definite manner in which the gears " went in " indicated the racing experience which lay behind the Norton nameplate. At whatever speed the gearchange was made, fast or slow, ratios could be swapped positively and noiselessly. In the earlier stages, the first-to-second movement tended to " hang on " very occasionally; with increased mileage this eased off and would occur only when clutch and gearchange movements were poorly co-ordinated. The ratios are well selected and, in particular, third gear is nicely related to the top ratio. On those occasions when a burst of acceleration was necessary, a snap change into " third " would start the speedometer needle on its way round the dial.

Good acceleration is an outstanding feature of the machine and this has not been obtained at the expense of tractability. The engine did not appear unduly sensitive and, even with " Pool " in the tank, could not, when driven more harshly than warranted, be made to " pink." Quite happy when pulling at 25 m.p.h., the unit would accelerate from this speed even if the throttle was used without particular care. At the other end of the range, 65 m.p.h. could be maintained smoothly; 70 m.p.h. followed without fuss and bursts of 85 m.p.h. were well within the machine's scope when conditions permitted. Following one high-speed trip, " running-on " occurred; subsequent experience showed that, with a change to Lodge FE100 plugs, this disappeared entirely. The standard F70 plug will, however, be entirely suitable for all but most exceptional conditions.

Mention has already been made of the comfortable manner in which the machine performs and to this must be added the satisfactory way in which it sits on the road. The change to a swinging-arm system at the rear has produced an almost indefinable weight characteristic which, after a brief mileage, can be ignored. In cold weather the front fork movement was noticeably stiffer than the rear, but when the oil warmed both units worked well together.

The noise level of engine, transmission and exhaust was commendably low. Neither pistons nor rocker gear could be heard and at high engine revs. only was a slight high-pitched whine apparent. At normal throttle openings no offence could be given by the exhaust through the twin silencers. Higher in the range, the note had a not unpleasant " tang," never, however, reaching an objectionable stage.

No engine vibration could be discerned until the unit was working hard. Some very slight period was noticed via the petrol tank and knees as the road speed reached 65 m.p.h. in third gear or 75 m.p.h. in top gear.

Widely different characteristics were apparent in the movement of the brake controls. At the front, firm pressure, short travel and positive feel were the points noted; with the footbrake, the reverse was the case and, in application, a long, soft movement was needed. Both units worked well but a more powerful front brake would be in keeping with the spirited performance of the machine.

Well disposed, the head lamp provided a beam for night driving that could hardly be bettered. In the dipped position—effected by a conveniently placed thumbswitch on the nearside bar—the beam gave no offence.

The crankcase remained clean throughout the test, but small traces of oil smear appeared on the rocker-box covers. Tappet adjustment would be best carried out with the tank removed, but routine adjustments are easily made. Some difficulty was experienced with the oil filler cap which, when opened, fouls the dual seat and restricts the size of the orifice. Although no necessity arose to make use of the facility, it was noted that the rear wheel may be detached without removing either chain or brake unit.

---

### BRIEF SPECIFICATION

**Engine:** Vertical twin, o.h.v.: bore, 66 mm., stroke, 72.6 mm., capacity, 497 c.c.; C.R. 6.7 to 1; single chain-driven camshaft; dry sump lubrication by gear-pump; totally enclosed and positively lubricated valves and rockers; forged high-tensile steel cranks with cast-iron central flywheel; rocker box integral with cylinder head: ball bearings on timing side, roller on drive side; H-section R.R. 56 Hiduminium light-alloy connecting rods; phosphor-bronze small-end bushes; three-piece built-up crankshaft and plain steel-backed shell big-end bearings; flat top light-alloy pistons, each with one scraper and two compression rings; fully floating gudgeon pins; iron monobloc cylinder and iron head; Lucas magneto driven by separate chain; automatic advance and retard; Amal carburetter, type 76/AK.

**Transmission:** Separate Norton four-speed gearbox with built-in, positive stop, foot-operated gearchange; ratios, 5.0, 6.05, 8.85, 14.88 to 1; multi-plate clutch embodying a dual-action vane-type shock absorber; primary chain, ½ by .305 in.; rear, ⅝ in. by ¼ in.; oilbath primary chaincase.

**Frame:** Cradle-type; swinging arm, hydraulically damped rear wheel suspension; Norton "Roadholder" hydraulically controlled, telescopic front forks; steering damper; spring-up central stand and prop stand; bolt-up front stand; dual seat; fully adjustable handlebars; side-lifting handles.

**Lighting:** Separate Lucas 6-volt, 48-watt dynamo; battery mounted under saddle; 7-in. Lucas head light.

**Wheels:** WM2/21 front rim, WM2/19 rear; Avon tyres, 3.00-in. by 21-in. front; 3.50-in. by 19-in. rear.

**Brakes:** 7-in. by 1¼-in. front and rear; finger adjustment.

**Tanks:** Welded steel fuel tank, 3¾-gallons capacity; oil tank, 4 pints; both with quick-opening, hinged filler caps; reserve fuel tap.

**Finish:** Black enamel, with matt silver petrol tank and Norton motif; bright parts chromium plated.

**Equipment:** 120-m.p.h. Smith's speedometer, internally illuminated; electric horn; tool kit.

**Dimensions:** Wheelbase, 54½ ins.; overall length, 84 ins.; overall width, 28 ins.; ground clearance, 5½ ins.; saddle height, 31 ins.; weight, 413 lb.

**Price:** £187, plus £51 18s. 11d. P.T.= £238 18s. 11d.

**Makers:** Norton Motors, Ltd., Bracebridge Street, Birmingham, 6.

*May 6, 1954*

## ROAD TESTS OF CURRENT MODELS

# The 490 c.c. o.h.v. Model ES2
# NORTON

### New Rear Suspension and Improved Mechanical Silencing Characterize a Popular Machine

*(Left) The Norton proved to be possessed of remarkable stamina. (Below) The rear suspension; also shown is the enclosure of the C.V.C. unit in the capacious tool box.*

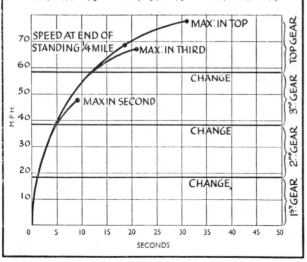

*The latest ES2 Norton engine and foot-operated gearbox present a commendably clean exterior.*

### TESTER'S ROAD REPORT

**Maximum Speeds in:—**

|  |  |  |  |  |  | Time from Standing Start |
|---|---|---|---|---|---|---|
| Top Gear (Ratio **4.75** to 1) | **77** m.p.h. | = | **4780** r.p.m. | **32 3/5** secs |
| Third Gear (Ratio **5.75** to 1) | **67** m.p.h. | = | **5030** r.p.m. | **23** secs |
| Second Gear (Ratio **14.4** to 1) | **48** m.p.h. | = | **5170** r.p.m. | **9** secs |

**Speeds over measured Quarter Mile:—**

Flying Start ... **75** m.p.h    Standing Start ... **48.39** m.p.h

**Braking Figures On DRY CONCRETE Surface, from 30 m.p.h.:—**

Both Brakes **31** ft.    Front Brake **40** ft.    Rear Brake **52** ft.

**Fuel Consumption:—**

30 m.p.h. **118** m.p.g.    40 m.p.h. **95** m.p.g.    50 m.p.h. **82** m.p.g.

SPEED AT END OF STANDING ¼ MILE

MAX. IN TOP

MAX. IN THIRD

CHANGE · TOP GEAR

CHANGE · 3ʳᵈ GEAR

MAX IN SECOND

CHANGE · 2ⁿᵈ GEAR

CHANGE · 1ˢᵀ GEAR

MPH — SECONDS

THOSE who, for the sake of pocket or preference, seek a machine in the single-cylinder range, find that the Norton 490 c.c. ES2 appeals strongly. For one thing, it is a long-established model, built to provide 100% reliable transport in solo or combination form. It is completely modern, but, in general design, it retains much of the inherent " one lunger " simplicity, and, equally important, accessibility, which is not always achieved in a " multi."

*Motor Cycling* last tested this model in 1950 and mention was then made of

*With swinging-fork rear springing the latest model ES2 scales 379 lb.*

the high standard of mechanical quietness. In the case of the 1954 test just completed, the yet further improvements made in this direction were a strong first impression which deserves initial emphasis in the report.

At normal ride-to-work-or-seaside speeds, no one engine component made its activities particularly audible. Gear and chain whine were absent; the tappets emitted a subdued ticking sound, but there was no undue noise from the rocker mechanism nor evidence of piston slap, even when the engine was first started from cold. Altogether, the power unit of the ES2 seems now to be among the quietest of its kind. Using the performance to the full, i.e., carrying out test runs against the clock in search of maximum-speed figures, and at the end of a spell of fast main-road work, a degree of loosening-up was noticeable, this resulting in slightly increased mechanical noise. Another likeable feature was the crisp but subdued exhaust note.

Overall gear ratios are slightly lower than they were four years ago, and that factor probably contributed to the rather steeper performance-curve, recording a maximum speed attained in slightly more than 32 sec. instead of 34, as previously. It must, of course, be recognized that premium-grade petrol, unobtainable in 1950, somewhat nullifies further comparison of old and new performance figures. Provided that such figures conform generally to an expected standard—and in this case the graph shows that they do—interest centres chiefly on attributes such as ease of starting, handling, reliability, comfort and ease of maintenance.

An affirmative answer to the easy-starting question is given without qualification. Almost infallible first-kick firing, followed by a slow, steady tick-over, was another early impression of the ES2 which earned good marks. Physical ease in getting this result depended somewhat upon the stature of the rider. The level of the dual seat is some two inches higher than that of the saddle previously fitted and that, coupled with the elevation of the sprung rear-end in an unloaded condition, tends to impede the full swinging kick which text books advise. This, however, is a characteristic of nearly all modern swinging-fork, dual-seat-equipped motorcycles and one to which the rider, accustomed to the conventional saddle, readily adapts himself.

For believers in a comparatively high riding position the ES2 provides full justification. From town speeds up to maximum m.p.h. the steering of the model tested was first class, for the geometry of the new rear suspension appears to be harmonic with that of the sturdy "Roadholder" forks. The positions of the seat, handlebars and rests were just right and the longest non-stop run—in the region of 130 miles—was carried out with complete satisfaction from the comfort point of view. Rests and handlebars are fully adjustable.

On main-road journeys of that kind, using 70 m.p.h. bursts when conditions permitted, but also dawdling behind "heavies" and through 30 m.p.h. areas, an average m.p.g. figure of approximately 78 was recorded. On a premium-grade diet the engine "plonked" like a side valve in top gear and would pull away in that ratio (4.75:1), silkily and swiftly. The only criticism of the handling of the model is that a rider unused to the ES2 finds it difficult at first to accept the somewhat limited steering lock, necessarily restricted by stops in order to avoid the fork shrouds impinging on the tank panels.

The four-speed Norton gearbox was smooth in operation: gear selection was foolproof and positive, and the clutch, though light to handle, stood up to every aspect of the test and needed no adjustment or attention of any kind.

Since the previous test an 8-in. diameter brake has been fitted at the front, and the benefit of this useful "stopper" was most marked. Using this brake alone it was possible to pull the machine up in 40 ft. from 30 m.p.h. The 7-in. diameter rear brake was efficient, bringing the model to a standstill in 52 ft. Applied together the brakes served to record a stopping distance of 31 ft., which is good. Throughout prolonged tests of this type there was no sign of brake fade.

Although the new swinging-fork rear suspension components add slightly to the weight at the rear end, the model can be lifted on to the substantial centre stand without difficulty. For general parking purposes, however, the side-stand, spring controlled and located beneath the primary chaincase, gives excellent service. It is held extended or folded back by spring tension and the foot is sufficiently well-dimensioned to give support on soft ground without sinking in and allowing the machine to topple over.

Full marks also go to the electrical equipment. The headlamp beam provided satisfactory illumination throughout the period that the machine was in our possession, the only maintenance carried out being a routine topping-up of the battery. A point worthy of mention is the complete protection given to the Lucas C.V.C. unit, which is housed in a special toolbox compartment.

The machine came to us during a period of drought; therefore, throughout the test, there was scant opportunity for assessing handling characteristics on really wet roads. It was felt, however, that road-holding qualities would remain unimpaired in damp conditions and that weather protection would be good.

We took delivery of the ES2 in practically brand-new condition and normal running-in maintenance, including tappet adjustment and the tightening of the head race, was carried out. The tools supplied were adequate for these and all other items of owner-maintenance, but the kit could, with advantage, be supplemented by a special spanner for the Q.D. wheel nuts. None of the standard tools seemed sufficiently long to give good leverage, while the holes provided originally in the spoke flange for a box spanner, are now screened by the speedometer drive box.

These constructive criticisms do not detract from the impression that the ES2, now completely modern in every respect, is as fine a value-for-money proposition as ever it was.

## BRIEF SPECIFICATION

**Engine:** Single cylinder, single-port o.h.v. with push-rod operated valves; 79 mm. bore by 100 mm. stroke = 490 cc. Compression ratio 6.16 : 1; cast-iron cylinder head; valve gear positively lubricated; high-tensile steel H-section connecting rod with double-row roller-bearing big-end; coil valve springs; dry sump lubrication; Amal carburetter with twist-grip operation; rear-mounted chain-driven Lucas Magdyno.

**Transmission:** ½-in. pitch by .305-in. primary chain; totally enclosed in oil bath; ⅝ in. by ½ in. final drive, protected on upper and lower runs. Four-speed gearbox; ratios 4.75, 5.75, 8.4 and 14.4 : 1; multi-plate clutch, incorporating dual-action, vane-type shock absorber, operated by positive stop foot-change gear mechanism.

**Frame:** Solid drawn steel tube cradle type, incorporating swinging-fork rear suspension assembly pivoting on "Silentbloc" rubber bushes; hydraulically damped spring units.

**Front Forks:** Norton patented "Roadholder" telescopic front forks with hydraulic damping.

**Lighting:** Lucas 6-v. Magdyno lighting; compensated voltage control; Lucas 7-in. headlamp.

**Wheels and Tyres:** Chromium-plate rims taking 3.25-in. by 19-in. front and rear tyres; wheels carried on non-adjustable ball journals, a double row type on brake side.

**Brakes:** 8-in. by 1¼-in. front brake; 7-in. by 1¼-in. rear brake.

**Equipment:** Smiths 120 m.p.h. speedometer, centre and prop stands.

**Finish:** Black enamel; bright parts chromium-plated with Norton motif on silver fuel tank.

**Tanks:** 3½-gal. petrol tank, rubber mounted; separate oil tank under saddle, capacity 4 pints; built-in rubber knee grips.

**Dimensions:** Saddle height 31 in.; wheelbase 54½ in.; overall length 84½ in.; overall width 28 in.; ground clearance 6½ in.; weight 379 lb.

**Price:** £170 10s. plus £34 2s. P.T. = total £204 12s.

**Annual Tax:** £3 15s. Quarterly £1 0s. 8d.

**Makers:** Norton Motors Ltd., Bracebridge St., Aston Cross, Birmingham, 6.

## The 490 c.c. 16H and 596 c.c. Big Four model

# NORTONS

## Part 2.—Work on Transmission and Cycle Components

THE removal of the engine from the frame for work discussed in the previous article in this series, has probably involved dismantling the primary drive, the back of the chaincase and the clutch assembly, and, therefore, it is most likely that this week's activities can be continued simply by lifting out the gearbox and carrying on the dismantling work on the bench. It is usual to have some sort of jig, preferably mounted in the vice—a short length of rod suffices—to act as a holder upon which the box can be retained by one of its two fixing lugs.

### Dismantling Procedure

For those tackling the transmission side of the work first, or as a separate operation, however, and leaving the engine intact, a word on the subject of clutch construction is timely.    There is a steel band pressed around the clutch sprocket member to prevent excess oil entering the clutch-plate area.    While the plates can be slipped out with the band in position, it must be taken off before the owner can examine the driving slots in the sprocket member.    A circlip retains the clutch plates; there are six plain steel plates and five Ferodo-insert plates.

The driving clutch plates transmit power through the medium of a rubber cush-centre component, this being the only shock absorber between the engine and the rear wheel.    It is usually necessary to employ a " C " spanner, or similar tool, to rotate the serrated clutch centre and compress the large rubber segments, while the smaller ones are extracted. Nortons supply a special threaded clutch body extractor which, screwing into the centre of the body, carries a central bolt. This bolt, slowly tightened, impinges upon the end of the gearbox mainshaft and breaks the joint between the shaft and the clutch body.

Make certain that the surface of each of the clutch inserts is standing proud of the surrounding metal of the carrier plate. It is desirable, if the insert plates are worn, to renew all the Ferodo parts and not just one or two.    Make sure that, when the new inserts are fitted, there is flat and even contact with the steel plate surface on both sides of the insert members.

Inspect the splines on the body and the slots in which the clutch plates drive or are driven.    Worn, or pocketed, contact points should be filed or ground smooth in order that free movement of the plates is not interrupted during the declutching operation. Pay particular attention to the back plate which, in an old or misused machine, occasionally takes on a slight warp; in this condition it can never contribute to 100 per cent. efficient clutch operation.

The gearbox is almost identical with that introduced in 1948 for the high-duty require-

ments of the " Dominator " twin.    In most respects it is the 1955 gearbox and, to a great extent, the owner of a 1948-53 " 16H " or " Big Four " model can use the current instruction book for guidance in his overhauling jobs and, of course, in like manner the current spares list is largely applicable.

The design retains the features of the old pattern thought to be good, in particular the slotted cam plate for control of the gear selection and the positive-stop members, which, for simplicity, continue as a spring-loaded selector-plate-cum-ratchet assembly linked with the cam wheel.    New, is the location of the positive-stop mechanism within a cavity formed by the outer and inner gearbox covers on the kickstarter side.

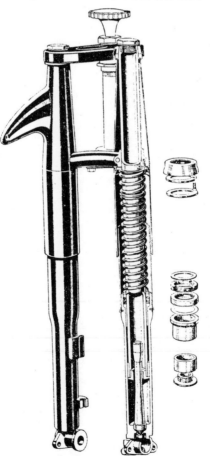

*An impression of the components in the famous " Roadholder " telescopic front forks which are fitted to the s.v. Nortons in both models.*

## USEFUL DATA

### Gearbox :

**Bearings :**

Mainshaft sleeve-gear bearing, ball type, bore 1¼ in. by O/D 2½ in. by ⁹⁄₁₆ in. Mainshaft (cover end), bore ⅝ in. by O/D 1⅜ in. by ⁷⁄₁₆ in. Layshaft (drive side) bore 17 mm. by O/D 40 mm. by 12 mm.

**Bushes :**

In hollow K.S. spindle : .6865/.6872 in.   In sleeve pinion : .8140/.8145 in.
Cam plate and quadrant spindle bushes : .4995/.5005 in.

**Gear Ratios :**

Solo : 5, 6.05, 8.85 and 14.82 : 1
Sidecar : Big Four 5.6, 6.76, 9.9 and 16.6 : 1
16H : 5.93, 7.17, 10.5 and 17.6. : 1.

### Transmission :

**Chains :**

Primary : ½ in. pitch x .305 in.   74 pitches.
Secondary : ⅝ in. pitch x .25 in. 91 pitches.

Also retained is the long-established Norton Acme-threaded worm-type thrust spindle and the attendant actuating lever.    These parts however, are now housed within the outer cover and there is an inspection plate provided for adjustment purposes.

With the clutch out of the way, the owner may now continue work on the kickstarter side of the box by removing the kickstarter crank, the gear indicator and gear-change lever.    Screw down the clutch cable adjuster as far as possible and, by using a large screwdriver and adjustable spanner, rotate the clutch worm lever in a clockwise direction until the cable nipple can be cleared.

Take out the seven cheese-headed screws which hold the outer cover in position; a certain amount of oil will escape as the parts are separated and note should be made at this early stage to replenish this cavity when putting the gearbox together again.    The previously-mentioned inspection aperture can be used for this purpose.

Remove the eight nuts which secure the inner cover and withdraw this part, being careful not to tear the paper washer which, if the assembly has been properly carried out by the previous owner, should be between it and the face of the gearbox shell.

The footchange mechanism is dismantled by removing the two nuts which secure the U-section outer plate and withdrawing this plate, followed by the lever return spring, core carrier and ratchet plate. There is a spacing shim fitted behind the ratchet plate. The clutch worm is simple to remove by completely unscrewing it from the nut.    By taking out the nut one has access to the mainshaft bearing which, if it is in need of renewal, can be driven out or, alternatively, heated and knocked out.    This bearing in standard form is of the ball type and the dimensions are provided in the Useful Data panel.

The inner gearbox cover also carries the kickstarter spindle which is counter bored and bushed internally to support the layshaft on this side.    The bush dimension, too, is provided in the Useful Data panel.    The manufacturers state that the kickstarter cam and stop pieces, which are riveted into the cover, should never need renewing; on the other hand, continued usage may result in their working loose and in this case they can be re-riveted in position without difficulty.

When taking out the gears note the position of each, check the condition of the mainshaft second gear which is carried on a fully-floating bush. Unscrew the striker fork shaft by means of the two flats which are machined on its outer end and remove it, together with the layshaft second gear and striker fork. Withdraw the mainshaft or, as the manufacturers' instruction book has it, the main axle, together with the third gear and striker fork.

You will find that the main gear wheel, or sleeve gear, remains in position. Within the bore of the sleeve gear is a 13-roller bearing and if the sleeve is to be left undisturbed, these rollers may be safeguarded by inserting a roll of stiff paper shaped to simulate the diameter of the mainshaft. In the majority of cases, however, the overhaul at this stage is designed to be comprehensive and the rollers forming this bearing will, therefore, be extracted and laid on one side pending reassembly.

Located on the mainshaft next to the sleeve pinion is a thrust washer of bronze material; this little part should be most carefully checked for wear, indicated by grooving across the face. The washer carries most of the end thrust each time the clutch is withdrawn and it is, therefore, subjected to considerable pressure stress. For this reason you should have no hesitation about fitting a new part, particularly if there has been previous indication of excessive clutch end-float.

The main gearbox bearing supporting the sleeve pinion is of a special Norton type; it is a double-row ball journal component

which can, if necessary, be driven out under heat. Below this bearing in the gearbox shell is the drive side layshaft bearing which is of the roller type and a number of proprietary bearings of suitable dimensions are available. Nortons, of course, can also supply spares.

To dismantle the cam-plate take off the domed hexagon nut located at the bottom of the forward side of the gearbox; this nut anchors the cam-plate indexing plunger, which will drop out, so releasing pressure. Take off the two bolts securing the cam-plate and quadrant—both these parts, once released, may be pushed through into the hollow shell. It is stated that it is unlikely for the cam-plate spindle bushes to need renewing.

### Re-assembly

There is a pen-steel washer fitted either side of the sleeve gear bearing, and the smaller of the two should be dropped into the bottom of the bearing housing before a new component is driven in. Now fit the 13 rollers, retaining them within the bore of the sleeve gear by a roll of paper or thin tube; fit the large pen-steel washer over the shank of the sleeve gear and press the part through the bearing, fit the final-drive sprocket, tighten the nut and lock it up by means of the locking washer and pin.

Slide the bronze clutch thrust washer on to the mainshaft in such a position that the face with the three oil grooves will be against the main sleeve gear when fitted. Carefully insert the shaft, simultaneously removing the protective roll of paper. During the remainder of the assembly it is of assistance to fit a short length of tube in place of the clutch and to add the clutch nut.

Now fit on to the layshaft the third gear wheel (20T) and top gear wheel (18T)

and fit the inner race with rollers and cage to the end of the shaft. Grease the rollers and put the assembly into the gearbox.

The cam-plate should be set in the second gear position, viz., with the indexing plunger in the groove next to the shallow neutral groove. Assemble the striking fork with the mainshaft third gear (22T) and fit to the mainshaft, meshing this pinion with the layshaft gear already in position. The second striking fork should be assembled with the layshaft second gear (24T) and the pegs on the striking forks should now fit conveniently into the cam-plate slots.

The remainder of the gearbox assembly is largely a reversal of the dismantling procedure; make sure of the good condition of the paper washers between the gearbox shell and the inner plate and also that between the faces of the inner plate and outer cover. Top up with the manufacturers' recommended oil.

### Hub Details

Both these side-valves were equipped with wheels conforming with current specifications. Double-row ball-bearing journal assemblies support the brake side of the wheels front and rear: the dimension of this type of bearing is bore 17 mm. by O/D 40 mm. by 16 mm. On the opposite side on each case, the wheel carries a single row ball journal bearing, the dimension of which is, bore 17 mm. by O/D 40 mm. by 12 mm.

Grease nipples are provided in the hub for routine lubrication but it is advisable periodically to pack out the hubs in order to avoid over-zealous work with the grease gun and possible percolation into the brake drums.

### Suspension

From 1949 until their demise the Norton s.v. machines were equipped with "Roadholder" telescopic front forks, the sum total of maintenance for which comprises replenishment of damper fluid at approximately 5,000-mile intervals. This task involves removal of the hexagon-headed filler plug from the top of each fork leg and the unscrewing also of the drain plug at the lower end of each fork. Oil should drain out and then the forks should be moved up and down several times in order to eject the last drops of lubricant.

Now replace the drain plugs and refill each leg with a measured quarter pint of S.A.E. 20 oil. Finally, work the forks up and down a few times to dispose of air locks and replace the filler plugs. The general design of the Norton forks, the helical impact sprint, taper damper mechanism and main bushes is seen from the accompanying sketch.

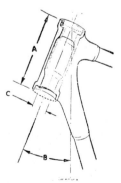

*Norton head lug data: (A) overall depth 6$\frac{15}{16}$ in.; (B) 27 degrees; (C) head races, thrust type 2$\frac{3}{16}$ in. by 1.173 in., each carrying 17$\frac{5}{16}$-in. dia. balls.*

*The parts in the Norton four-speed gearbox and positive stop footchange mechanism.*

# 497 c.c. Norton Model 88 Twin

**Stylish High-performance Roadster With First-class Steering, Roadholding and Brakes**

SO successful was the Norton duplex-loop frame on the factory racing machines in 1950 and subsequently, that a roadster combining a similar frame with the 497 c.c. Dominator parallel-twin engine was an obvious development. The superb handling qualities inherent in the "featherbed" frame (as it was nicknamed from the start) were unmistakably demonstrated in classic and minor road races; what more natural than that fast tourists should covet such high-class steering and road-holding? Known as Model 88, the new roadster was restricted to oversea markets for the first two years of its production and was made available in Britain in 1954.

Because of its indirect racing associations, the Model 88 has always been surrounded by an aura of speed, and there was for some time a widespread misconception that the model was of the super-sports type. In point of fact it was, until late 1955, essentially a touring mount with an unpretentious camshaft and a modest compression ratio (6.8 to 1). From that time onward, however, pistons giving a compression ratio of 7.8 to 1 have been standardized, as has the Daytona camshaft evolved in connection with the famous American races. As a result of those modifications the Model 88 now has a speed and acceleration potential which place it in the super-sports bracket, while the use of a light-alloy cylinder head (introduced for 1955) makes it possible for the engine to sustain its high power output without tiring.

As would be expected, the outstanding impressions remaining after an extended road test are of surging acceleration and of the stylish way in which the model could be heeled through bends and corners, especially at high speeds. No steering damper is fitted; nor was one felt to be remotely desirable, for steering was extremely positive under all conditions. Neither pitching nor snaking was ever experienced. All that was necessary in order to execute a graceful curve, almost regardless of road-surface irregularities, was to heel the Norton over to the required degree. On ultra low-speed corners slightly lighter steering would have been appreciated and a more generous steering lock would be an advantage when manœuvring the model in confined spaces.

*Left: Brake-pedal return spring and stop, and the stop-light switch spring are concealed on the 1957 model*

*Below, left: Combining smooth appearance with great power, the front brake has an iron liner cast in the new light-alloy hub*

*Below: The battery is concealed within a box which fits neatly in one corner of the left-hand frame loop*

*Sleek lines characterize the 497 c.c. Model 88 Norton*

Contributing partially towards the absence of pitching was the relatively short and firm action of the front and rear springing. Roadholding at high speeds is unimpeachable although at slight expense in comfort—insulation of the rider from road shocks could be better, especially when the model is ridden without a pillion passenger. The softer of the two settings for the rear shock absorbers was used when carrying passengers of light or medium weight and they expressed appreciation of the comfort.

Minimum width of the seat at the front (12in) is dictated by the spacing of the frame loops and is rather too great for maximum comfort for short-legged riders. The footrests are adjustable for height and the most satisfactory setting for riders of various statures was with the hangers lowered one serration from the horizontal position in which they leave the factory. In relation to the seat, siting of the footrests is a shade too far forward for a high-performance machine; in consequence, several consecutive hours of high-speed riding produced a mild ache in the rider's thighs and forearms. This effect could be minimized by improvizing a backrest on the dual-seat of, say, spare riding gear, assuming no pillion passenger was carried. All controls, whether hand or foot operated, could be readily adjusted for convenient reach and were smooth in use.

The engine revelled in high r.p.m. rates. Indeed the effect of the Daytona camshaft is such that the best results, both from the viewpoint of power and comparative fuel consumption, are obtained in the upper engine-speed ranges. On long main-road journeys a throttle opening of two-thirds was most frequently used and, in average circumstances, that gave an indicated cruising speed of 75 to 80 m.p.h. This, and higher speeds if required, could be maintained indefinitely under suitable road conditions; with a slightly favourable side wind, a speedometer 90 m.p.h. was achieved while the rider was normally seated. During sustained fast riding some oil found its way from the crankcase breather on to the rear of the machine while seepage from the oil-tank cap soiled the right leg of the rider's trousers.

When the Norton was ridden at a steady 30 m.p.h. (such as in built-up areas) the engine pulled top gear quite happily, but acceleration from that speed revealed a trace of hardness in the transmission and, as would be expected, sweeter, as well as brisker, results were obtained by using one of the lower gears for acceleration. A minor vibration period was perceptible over a small speed range in the region of 50 m.p.h. in top gear and at corresponding speeds in the lower gears. Between 75 and 80 m.p.h. in top gear a rhythmic vibration could be felt though

## INFORMATION PANEL

### SPECIFICATION

**ENGINE:** Norton 497 c.c. (66 x 72.6mm) overhead-valve vertical twin. Valve gear operated from a single camshaft. Light-alloy connecting rods; plain big-end bearings. Crankshaft supported in roller bearing on drive side and ball bearing on timing side. Compression ratio, 7.8 to 1. Dry-sump lubrication; oil-tank capacity, 4½ pints.

**CARBURETTOR:** Amal Monobloc; air slide operated by handlebar lever.

**IGNITION and LIGHTING:** Lucas magneto with auto-advance. Separate Lucas 60-watt dynamo. Lucas 6-volt, 12-ampere-hour battery. Lucas 7in-diameter headlamp with pre-focus light unit.

**TRANSMISSION:** A.M.C. four-speed gear box with positive-stop foot control. Gear ratios: bottom, 12.7 to 1; second, 8.41 to 1; third, 6.31 to 1; top, 4.75 to 1. Multi-plate clutch with moulded inserts running in oil. Primary chain, ½ x 0.305in in oil-bath case. Rear chain, ⅝ x ¼in with guard over top run. Engine r.p.m. at 30 m.p.h. in top gear, 1,830.

**FUEL CAPACITY:** 3½ gallons.

**TYRES:** Avon; front, 3.00 x 19in. Speedmaster; rear, 3.50 x 19in Safety Mileage.

**BRAKES:** Front, 8in diameter x 1¼in wide; rear, 7in diameter x 1¼in wide; finger adjusters.

**SUSPENSION:** Norton telescopic front fork with hydraulic damping. Pivoted-fork rear springing employing coil springs and hydraulic damping; two-position manual adjustment for load.

**WHEELBASE:** 56in unladen. Ground clearance, 5¼in unladen.

**SEAT:** Norton dual-seat; unladen height, 31in.

**WEIGHT:** 406 lb fully equipped, with full oil tank and approximately half a gallon of petrol.

**PRICE:** £210. With purchase tax (in Great Britain only), £260 8s.

**ROAD TAX:** £3 15s a year; £1 0s 8d a quarter.

**MAKERS:** Norton Motors, Ltd., Bracebridge Street, Birmingham, 6.

**DESCRIPTION:** *The Motor Cycle, 20 September 1956.*

### PERFORMANCE DATA

**MEAN MAXIMUM SPEED:** Bottom: *43 m.p.h.
Second: *65 m.p.h.
Third: *85 m.p.h.
Top: 90 m.p.h.
*Valve float occurring.

**HIGHEST ONE-WAY SPEED:** 92 m.p.h. (conditions: moderate three-quarter wind; rider wearing bulky two-piece suit and overboots).

**MEAN ACCELERATION:**

|  | 10-30 m.p.h. | 20-40 m.p.h. | 30-50 m.p.h. |
|---|---|---|---|
| Bottom | 2.8 sec | 2.6 sec | — |
| Second | 3.8 sec | 3.6 sec | 3.7 sec |
| Third | — | 5.5 sec | 5.3 sec |
| Top | — | 8.5 sec | 8.8 sec |

Mean speed at end of quarter-mile from rest: 79 m.p.h.
Mean time to cover standing quarter-mile: 16.7 sec.

**PETROL CONSUMPTION:** At 30 m.p.h., 80 m.p.g.; at 40 m.p.h., 75 m.p.g.; at 50 m.p.h., 68 m.p.g.; at 60 m.p.h., 60 m.p.g.

**BRAKING:** From 30 m.p.h. to rest, 29ft 6in (surface, dry tarmac)

**TURNING CIRCLE:** 18ft.

**MINIMUM NON-SNATCH SPEED:** 20 m.p.h. in top gear.

**WEIGHT PER C.C.:** 0.82 lb.

*Neatly mounted in the headlamp shell, the speedometer is easily read from the saddle. Layout of the handlebar controls is clean and convenient*

this period, like the minor one, was more noticeable in the indirect gears. Speedometer flattery was approximately 2 m.p.h. at 30 m.p.h., 4 m.p.h. at 60 and 6 m.p.h. at maximum speed.

Probably the most endearing characteristic of the Dominator power unit was its rapid acceleration. Provided the engine was turning over moderately fast, its response to throttle opening was extremely brisk and the revs would continue to build up unhesitatingly to valve-float point or the maximum possible in the circumstances, according to which gear was engaged. Nor was it necessary for the rider to curb his use of the available engine performance unduly to avoid embarrassment; for while the exhaust note is deep and healthy it is not unpleasant or offensive.

Ease of starting deserves full marks. The test was carried out during very harsh weather with the air temperature sometimes below freezing point. Yet provided the carburettor was liberally flooded (but not excessively so) and the air lever closed, one hearty swing on the kick-starter would always bring the engine to life from cold. Partial opening of the air lever was then necessary to ensure even firing and the lever could be opened fully after about a mile had been covered. When the engine was warm a first-kick start required only a smart thrust on the pedal. Just as soon as the unit was moderately warm it would idle slowly and reliably when the twistgrip was rolled back fully.

The moulded clutch inserts are claimed to be unaffected by the presence of oil and no precautions are taken to keep the oil

in the primary chaincase away from the friction surfaces. At all times the clutch was most firm in taking up the drive yet it freed completely when withdrawn. As a result engagement of bottom gear with the model stationary and the engine idling was accompanied by only a mild click and neutral was easy to find from bottom or second gear whether the machine was moving or at rest. The gear change was a trifle stiff but the stiffness could be largely mitigated by precise movements of the controls. Upward changes required least pressure on the pedal if all three controls (throttle, clutch and gear pedal) were operated simultaneously. For the lightest possible downward changes it was necessary to blip the throttle quickly as the pedal was moved. So long as these methods were used, clean and speedy gear changes in both directions were achieved.

No matter at what speed they were applied, the brakes were always smooth, controllable and very powerful, and, as the performance data show, the stopping distance is well in keeping with the machine's speed capabilities. Though the shoe mechanism of the front brake is unchanged since drum diameter was increased from 7 to 8in three years ago, a sleek new shoe plate was introduced for the current year, as was a slim aluminium hub with cast-in liner. Another modification for 1957 was the tidying-up of the operating mechanism and the stop-light switch for the 7in-diameter rear brake. Both the pedal stop (in the form of a tab washer) and the return spring are concealed from view by a shroud incorporated in the pivot boss. Transfer of the return spring from the cam lever to the pedal considerably lessens the effort required to operate the finger adjuster. The stop-light switch is actuated by a spring concealed within the body of the switch.

Further changes in the interest of neatness are the restyled end cover for the dynamo, the discarding of a remote ignition button in favour of one in the contact-breaker cover and the fitting of the speedometer directly in the headlamp shell rather than in a separate panel screwed to the shell. The new speedometer mounting overcomes the former difficulty of operating the trip return. A sleek line is given to the petrol tank by the use of separate chromium-plated side panels, framed in plastic beading, while the near-cylindrical shape of the new silencers and the absence of tail pipes contributes much to the improved appearance of the current model.

The headlamp furnished an intense and concentrated beam which made night riding a pleasure, while the offset of the dipped beam to the left was appreciated alike by the rider and other road users. Stowed beneath the dual-seat and reached after removal of two wing-nuts, the tool kit was of average quality but contained no spanner to turn the steering column locknut when adjustment was required.

To sum up, the latest Model 88 is a good-looking five-hundred twin with a zestful and tireless engine, remarkably powerful brakes and a well-subdued exhaust. Steering is in the best Norton tradition and will please the many enthusiasts who rightly insist on first-class high-speed handling.

*Separate, chromium-plated fuel-tank panels and stylish silencers help to give the Model 88 a distinctive appearance*

# Inside Information

*Norton brains trust. Above is a study of managing director Herbert Hopwood, M.I.Mech.E., and on the right, chief engineer Douglas Hele, A.M.I.Mech.E.*

## By BOB CURRIE

## THE FULL STORY BEHIND THE 1958 NORTON
## EXPERIMENTAL RACING ENGINES

WHATEVER else 1958 may have brought, it certainly produced as fine a crop of rumours in the racing field as the most rabid fan would wish to hear. "Did you know?" one knowledgeable type would exclaim to another (in print, too, on occasion), "Nortons are lending so-and-so a 90-bore engine for the Senior T.T.!" Or maybe it was to be a 93-bore, or something with a very hush-hush crankshaft assembly.

Yes, we knew. And we, too, had heard the rumour that there was even a desmodromic-valve Norton engine in existence. But to a direct query as to the significance of any particular move the Norton technicians would smile gently, would admit that perhaps a certain engine was partly experimental—but would say little more than that. However, it was clear that something was in the wind; that the Bracebridge Street folk were under way with a development programme more intensive than for many seasons past—even without the help of an official racing team.

Promised managing director Herbert Hopwood, "We'll tell you all about it later,

when the season is over and we have had time to assess the results of our various experiments." And, as always, he kept his word. By now, the 1958 races have passed into history; and in his office in the Norton factory Mr. Hopwood, assisted by Douglas Hele (chief engineer and the man chiefly responsible for racing-engine development) felt free at last to tell the full story of those intriguing non-standard Nortons, and of the lessons which have been learned from them.

But first it is necessary to paint in a little of the background to the recent experimental programme. Apart from minor changes here and there basic design of the Manx engines had remained static for a number of years; and yet for each new season the wizards of the racing shop had managed to produce just a few more rabbits from the hat, just that little extra in power output.

However, the annual uplift in urge was beginning to throw an ever-increasing strain on engine components that had previously proved completely reliable, and big-end bearings, connecting rods and camshaft-drive bevels were showing signs

of protest. A respite from camshaft-drive troubles was obtained by introducing, for 1957, a redesigned drive with coarser-pitch bevel pinions which incorporated a hunting tooth—in other words, driving and driven bevels had an unequal number of teeth, so that wear could be spread more evenly.

Next on the list came overheating and inlet-valve distortion. A quick (though somewhat expensive) way out of trouble was found by introducing a sodium-filled inlet valve, generally similar to the exhaust valve used with success for a number of years. Of this step, Bert Hopwood says: "Could we have foreseen the future we might have sought some other solution." Admittedly the new valve was lighter than a comparable solid component, and it cured the distortion trouble; furthermore, it had an under-head profile which improved the gas flow and thus the cylinder filling. But it was a mixed blessing. Further research last year led to the nimonic steel valve standardized for the 1959 Manx models, in which the efficient under-head shape of the sodium-filled valve has been incorporated.

But the new inlet valve and camshaft drive were only palliatives. Nortons envisage the extraction of still more power from the Manx engine in the future, and it was evident that more extensive research would be necessary if the machine was to retain its long-standing reputation for reliability. At the same time, the development work about to be undertaken would provide an opportunity to probe whatever restrictions may lie ahead in the ultimate development of the single-cylinder engine. It is, remarks Bert Hopwood, a relatively simpler task to obtain sheer racing power—maximum b.h.p.—from a twin or four than from a single. Then will Nortons eventually switch to a racing multi? Possibly, but for the moment they feel that the single has certainly not reached its limit of development. And both Bert Hopwood and Doug Hele regard the extraction of those remaining horses as a personal challenge.

There would be time enough to seek higher r.p.m. once they had satisfied themselves that the crankshaft components would stand up to the extra loads that would be imposed. And so it was towards the strengthening of the lower part of the engine assembly that the emphasis of the programme was directed. Many years of racing experience had taught that it was desirable to retain the roller big-end bearing. Nevertheless, it would be an advantage to have a replaceable bearing instead of running the rollers direct in the hardened connecting-rod eye—and that, in turn, would mean more metal round the eye and

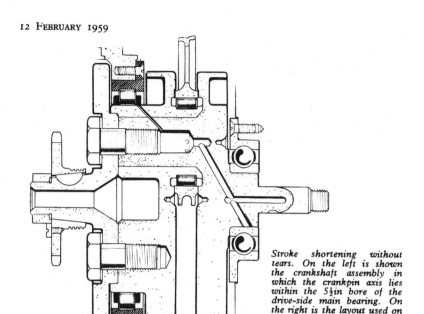

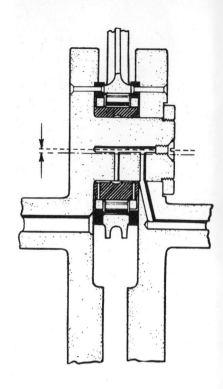

*Stroke shortening without tears. On the left is shown the crankshaft assembly in which the crankpin axis lies within the 5½in bore of the drive-side main bearing. On the right is the layout used on the 93mm-bore engine which has an eccentric crankpin bush*

*The picture below shows a 1959 five-hundred Manx engine ready for bench test. Behind the rig are Doug Hele and test-house chief Ivor Smith*

consequently a heavier rod. All the more reason for pressing on with the programme.

To minimize inertia loads the thoughts of Doug Hele turned to the short-stroke engine. The usual rule in engine design is that the length of the connecting rod should be approximately four times the crank throw; hence a shorter stroke would result in a shorter (and, of course, lighter) connecting rod. Also, a shortened crank throw reduces the centrifugal loading on the big end. The truth of the theory was demonstrated when the familiar wear on the underside of the crankpin (due to inertia loading) gave place to wear on the top side—due to punch.

Already in existence, a veteran of earlier days, was a five-hundred with bore and stroke dimensions of 90×78mm; this was the legendary "90-bore," an engine with inside flywheels and with the cylinder off-set $\frac{1}{16}$in rearward—the opposite way to the ordinary désaxé. The theory behind this unusual layout was that connecting-rod angularity on the firing stroke would thereby be increased; with the piston at top dead centre the thrust from the connecting rod would be slightly ahead of the crank pin centre-line, and hence at the moment of full power there would be less of a direct bump on the big-end. An incidental advantage of the cylinder offset was that the tappets were more centrally placed above the valve stem ends since the cambox position is fixed in relation to the crankshaft.

There might have been something in the theory, though Mr. Hele was not really convinced. However, four more 90mm-bore engines were constructed, two of them with the offset cylinder; they were troublesome to build, and bench tests showed that while the supposed advantages were all very well in theory, in practice there was little to be gained. An offset of perhaps as much as 1in would have been needed before any marked result would be apparent. For all that, preliminary tests indicated that a short-stroke engine was certainly not inferior in overall performance to the standard "square" engine. And the attractions of a reduction in weight of the reciprocating parts were real enough. It might even be worth while trying out a still shorter stroke.

Meanwhile, back to the big-end bearing. Over the years the Norton big end had been little altered apart from an increase in size. The rollers were located between flanges on the crankpin, and the roller retaining cage had of necessity to have a large outside diameter. With increasing crankshaft speeds, there had been a growing tendency for the cage to fling radially outward. In extreme cases it could pick up

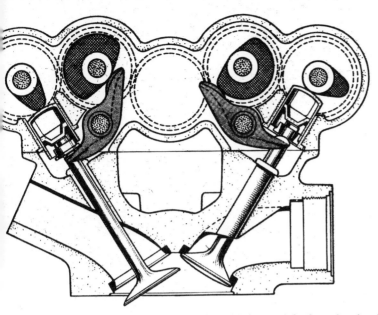

*Above is a sketch showing the comparatively simple layout of the desmodromic valve gear. The opening cams operate through hollow tappets and the closing cams through forked rockers actuating collars retained by split collets. Alongside is a photograph of the desmodromic cam box on a cylinder head. Below are details of the splined camshaft drive standardized on 1959 Manx models*

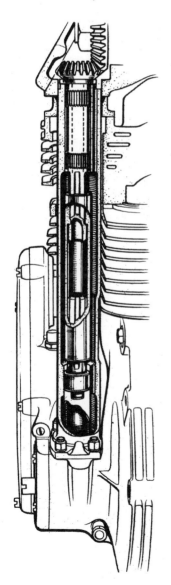

on the bore of the big-end eye and drag the rollers round the crankpin, thus causing serious scuffing.

The answer was to locate the rollers laterally by two hardened steel rings riveted to the inner cheeks of the flywheels, dispense with the crankpin shoulders and locate the cage on the pin. The connecting-rod eye could then be narrower (a further saving in weight) and the cage would be lighter and have a smaller outside diameter. Should there still be a tendency for the cage to fling outward it could only contact the bores of the hardened rings and little harm would result. Experiments with the new-style bearing were distinctly encouraging, although it has not yet been found practicable to adapt it for production Manx models.

Short of using a split roller bearing—a rare and tricky expedient found on the early post-war Moto-Guzzi Gambalunga five-hundred—incorporating a roller big-end bearing makes it necessary to employ a built-up crankshaft assembly. Obviously, with this type of construction there is a limit to the shortness of stroke of the engine, for a point is ultimately reached where a crankpin nut fouls a main bearing or its housing.

The plan was to go beyond the apparent limit, to investigate an ultra-short-stroke engine while retaining built-up crankshaft construction. Hence the engine which, maybe, promoted more T.T.-time rumours than any other. In the Norton factory it was referred to affectionately as the B.B.C. —the "big-bearing crankcase" engine.

Big bearing? The drive-side roller bearing was immense, with an internal diameter of no less than 5½in, located on a wide spigot on the outside of the drive-side flywheel. In the early hours of one practice morning the hush-hush job was fitted into the frame of the Pip Harris sidecar outfit —principally because the frame of that machine could be modified to accept it more readily than anyone else's.

No, the engine was not a short-stroker; bore and stroke dimensions were strictly standard. But what was unique was the crankshaft construction. Formed integrally with the drive-side flywheel, the hollow crankpin boss was located on an inwardly projecting shaft (hollow and internally threaded) on the timing-side wheel, the two parts being clamped together by a bolt screwed into the end of the shaft and located within the bore of the main bearing. An outer disc incorporating the drive-side mainshaft was bolted to the flywheel and thus held the bearing inner race in position.

Had the experiment proved successful with an engine of normal stroke, then there would have been no difficulty in devising a much shorter-stroke unit. And the experiment was indeed a success; true, Harris did not finish the race, but his trouble was in no way associated with the unorthodox lower half of the engine, and examination afterwards confirmed the designer's hopes.

Well, that was one way of doing the job; but Doug Hele had another ace up his sleeve. His alternative plan was so simple as to make any engineer cry "Why didn't I think of that?" The 90-bore engine had proved its reliability—and so he took one of them and clamped an eccentric bush around its crankpin. Immediately, he had a means of varying the stroke at will within the limits of bush eccentricity. With the bush set to provide the minimum stroke the bore worked out at 93mm—which diameter may raise a chord of memory.

The 93-bore was thoroughly tested, with such encouraging results that a duplicate engine was made, and the two units were lent to Alan Holmes and Keith Campbell for the Senior T.T. Holmes in particular put up an excellent showing, and he was a good fourth in the race until a broken carburettor needle clip—of all things— dropped him from the leader board to finish somewhere among the silver-replica winners. Fate can be harsh at times.

Development of the bottom end of the engine was beginning to pay dividends. Experiments with the short-stroke unit, with its lighter piston and connecting rod (incidentally, it is an easier matter to carve away metal from the inside of the 93mm-bore piston—there is more room to work) not only produced a substantial reduction in big-end bearing wear, but also the power flow was smoother and acceleration had improved.

Research then switched to something completely different, a type of engine rumoured to be in existence years ago but never seen in public. Yes, there *is* a Norton with desmodromic valve gear, but its running has been strictly confined to the test bench. To outward appearance the cambox assembly is little different from that of the standard Manx engine, although internally there is, of course, a considerable change. Additional cams are incorporated with what are normally the intermediate pinions of the gear train, operating rockers which act on the underside of valve stem collars to give positive valve closure.

Bert Hopwood explains: "Our desmodromic-valve engine was designed with the same valve-lift curve as for a standard Manx engine; the intention was not, at first, to seek a higher power output, but rather to compare friction losses in the two types of valve gear. After a little development we achieved about the same power output as with a standard Manx; we were learning."

They were indeed, and at that stage development headed in yet another direction. The unusual engine was provided with "square cams"—cams with an unusually fierce profile to give very quick opening and closing of the valves. The result of that experiment was that the vertical drive shaft gave in its notice! Doubtless the existing drive could have been strengthened, but Doug Hele decided to scrap the Oldham couplings which had been for so long a feature of the drive and start afresh.

The redesigned drive was extremely robust, yet simpler than before, and its ability to withstand punishment on the desmodromic unit prompted its adoption for 1959 on the over-the-counter Manx models. Basically it comprises a single-tube light-alloy casting which carries pairs

*Ace driver Pip Harris (right) installs the big-bearing - crankcase engine in his Norton outfit a few days before last year's Sidecar T.T.*

of needle-roller bearings at top and bottom; within the casting is an internally splined coupling tube, into which the short shafts which carry the upper and lower bevels are a tap-in fit. Secured to the crankcase bevel housing, and spigoted into place there and through the cylinder-head casting, the drive forms a complete unit. Not much chance of error, therefore, when an engine has to be stripped and rebuilt in a hurry!

Will the desmodromic system be subjected to further development? Perhaps, say the technical team, but until it begins to show clear-cut advantages the positive-closure mechanism will not be adopted on the standard engines. Before then there are other fields to be explored.

Doug Hele thinks that experiments can now go ahead with the combustion chamber, for example. At present it is necessary to use 38 degrees of ignition advance to ensure complete burning of the mixture, and one result is that very high stresses are imposed on the big-end bearing while it is still climbing towards top dead centre. It may be that a twin-plug system, with both plugs firing simultaneously, would

promote more rapid combustion; the degree of advance could then be lessened and hence crankpin load lightened. We shall see.

Meanwhile the valve-gear experiments did bring one minor but important improvement, now adopted for 1959. Previously, a hardened-steel bearing housing, pressed into the cam-box cover, had a flange which also served to locate the valve tappet; however, should the housing move inward then the tappet could become trapped. In the complete redesign the housing is of larger diameter (to accommodate a standard journal roller bearing instead of itself serving as the bearing outer race), while the screwed plug on the outside of the cover now engages with a thread at the rear of the bearing housing thus preventing inward movement.

So much, then, for 1958. Soon, racing will be getting under way once more; and, inevitably, the rumour-mongers will again be with us. "Have you heard?" they will say; and the Norton chief will smile gently, will admit, perhaps, that the machine used by a particular rider embodies certain experimental features. . . .

*Alan Holmes heels the 90mm-bore Norton into Parliament Square during the 1958 Senior T.T. He lay fourth when slowed by carburettor trouble*

# ROAD TESTS OF CURRENT MODELS

### The 249 c.c. o.h.v.
### High-camshaft

# NORTON
# "Jubilee 250"

*"Motor Cycling" Presents First On-the-Road Impressions of a Lightweight Twin that Sets New Standards of Design and Performance in the 250 c.c. Class*

WITH the commencement, last month, of 100% flow production of " Jubilee 250 " models, Nortons were as good as their Showtime word by entrusting to *Motor Cycling* an off-the-line twin for a first full Press road test. Carrying out this task has entailed assessing the brain-child largely of one man—the managing director, Mr. Herbert Hopwood, M.I.Mech.E.—whose ideas and drive now extend Norton interests from the 650, 500 and 350 c.c. fields to that

of 250 c.c. Here the " Jubilee 250 " occupies a rather special place in that it has no peer in the form of any other production lightweight of similar technical character.

The " Jubilee 250 " is, first and foremost, a lightweight from which a comfortable, safe maximum speed in the region of 70-75 m.p.h. is anticipated by the makers, though

the massive crankshaft and main-bearing components—similar to those of bigger twins in the range—would obviously stand up to the effect of any further top-end development with increased performance in view. Considerably over-square engine dimensions subscribe to high-revving characteristics with relatively low piston speeds. But there is a useful supply of pulling power freely available; for this reason, and because the over-all gearing is somewhat on the low

## TESTER'S ROAD REPORT

**Maximum Speeds in:—**

Time from Standing Start

Top Gear (Ratio 6·8 to 1) __73__ m.p.h. == 5300 r.p.m. __33__ secs.

Third Gear (Ratio 8·8 to 1) __65__ m.p.h. == 7900 r.p.m. __22__ secs.

Second Gear (Ratio 12·5 to 1) __52__ m.p.h. == 8600 r.p.m. __11__ secs.

**Speeds over measured Quarter Mile :—**

Flying Start __71·5__ m.p.h.    Standing Start __45__ m.p.h.

**Braking Figures On WET TARMACADAM Surface, from 30 m.p.h.:—**

Both Brakes __30__ ft.    Front Brake __46__ ft.    Rear Brake __54__ ft.

**Fuel Consumption :—**

30 m.p.h. __100__ m.p.g.    40 m.p.h. __91__ m.p.g.    50 m.p.h. __82__ m.p.g.

*Each sparking plug is connected to a separate contact-breaker forming part of the Wico-Pacy electrical system in which D.C. feeds the ignition, the lights being supplied by the A.C. generator charging the battery via a rectifier. Attention to the contact-breakers is easy, as shown.*

*An important chore, that of valve tappet adjustment, is readily carried out by means of these accessible eccentric rocker-mountings, turned by a screwdriver to give the correct clearance between valve-heel and rocker-arm.*

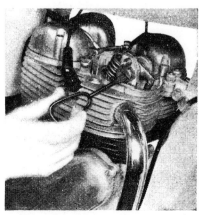

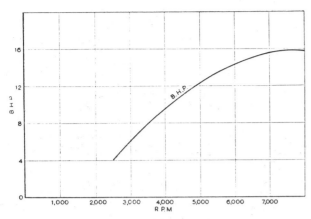

side—a good fault—the model is extremely flexible with a minimum top-gear dawdle as low as 15 m.p.h. · The built-in vane-type shock absorber imparts smoothness to the transmission from the 15-20 m.p.h. speed bracket up to the 70-75 m.p.h. level, and it is feasible to use this top-gear performance, accelerating gently but progressively without sign of distress either in the form of pinking or chain snatch.

## Clutch and Gears

Following a small mileage the clutch started dragging. Immediately adjustment was carried out a return was made to the excellent gear changes which had been gratefully noted right from the moment the machine was taken over at the factory. Feather-light pressure at the clutch lever and gear pedal normally resulted in a satisfyingly slick and silent gear-change. This and other nominal maintenance jobs provided reason to look at the toolkit, which appeared to be adequate for the general run of work carried out by the average owner. One notable omission was an Allen key, an item which, so it is understood, is to be included from now on.

The tool-roll nestles in a tray immediately beneath the dual seat and the latter is quickly and completely detachable, being located by double pegs at the nose and two open-ended spring clips that pass through apertures in the mudguard pressing to snap home over a transverse bar at the rear. Housed within the centre frame structure is the oil tank: the top of the filler orifice, complete with cap and integral dip-stick, is level with the tool tray and, therefore, accessible

*How the power builds up. A typical b.h.p. reading using the following carburetter settings : choke .781 in.; main jet, 120. Ignition, 32 deg. b.t.d.c. Barometer, 29.6; temp. 71 deg. F. Fuel 90 octane*

*"Motor Cycling's" man demonstrates the ease of centre stand operation.*

Timely maintenance of the 6v. 12 a.h. battery is encouraged by the positioning of the battery on a platform where it is secured by a cross-strap and two Allen screws. It is necessary first to take away the off-side centre panel which is Dzus-fastened at three points, but the coin-in-screw-slot method of turning the fasteners calls for a very strong wrist indeed! The battery-strap fixing nuts are trapped and, therefore, do not fall away when the two Allen screws are extracted.

Taking off the near-side panel, also Dzus-fastened, exposes the carburetter and, if it is necessary to remove the petrol tank, only a single bolt located beneath the saddle nose need be slackened and withdrawn,

leaving the tank, which has a spigot-type forward locating point, to be lifted away.

Inspection of the tappets revealed the ease with which the four light-alloy rocker covers —each secured by two Allen screws—can be taken off. Tappet adjustment is by means of eccentric mountings: the arrangement is one which makes tappet-setting a quick, easy job and is conducive to long spells of running without need for further attention. A trial showed that all these items— oil, battery and tappets, plus inspection of the double contact-breaker assembly and gearbox and chaincase oil levels—could be carried out in less than 15 minutes.

For maintenance work, or simply for

*(Right) Generous rear enclosure, ultra-modern styling but unimpaired accessibility are features of the "Jubilee 250."*

*The above last-mentioned fact is illustrated by the ready manner in which the fairings may be lifted away (left) to disclose components which may require maintenance.*

# R O A D   T E S T   O F   " J U B I L E E   2 5 0 "   N O R T O N

*Continued from previous page*

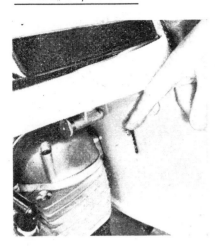

*Protruding through a slot in the enclosure is a lever actuating the carburetter tickler button—an example of detail work on the Norton.*

parking purposes, the model is lifted onto a sturdy centre stand: Nortons line up with those manufacturers who have designed easy-to-operate centre stands and add a lifting handle to make the job yet simpler. Completely enclosed by the centre panels, the float-chamber tickler is actuated by a hinged, long-travel lever extending through a panel slot on the near side. Gentle depression of the lever, the switching on of the ignition and a single prod on the pedal starter sufficed on all occasions to get the engine ticking over happily. The ignition control, one of two Wico-Pacy switches in the headlamp shell, also provides for emergency starting and repeated tests showed that the same first-kick results are forthcoming with the " E " circuit in use.

## Rapid Getaway

Normally the 19.7 : 1 bottom-gear ratio was employed only for getting under way: it was the means of accelerating off the mark very rapidly and, as a general rule, the 12.5 : 1 second ratio was selected at 20-22 m.p.h. By accident the model was put into second gear for starting and this occasion revealed, inadvertently but satisfyingly, the first-rate pulling qualities of the " Jubilee 250 " unit.

Third and top gears have been excellently

chosen and, to notch maximum speeds, it was necessary to hang on to the third 8.8 : 1 ratio right up to the mid-sixties. The standing-start quarter-mile speed test gave best results by staying in " third " to the end of the measured distance. Similarly, against a wind or to retain speeds of " sixty-plus " on long gradients, third gear proved to be a blessing and even at near-ceiling r.p.m. the performance forthcoming was vibrationless and a pleasure to use. At the maximum in each gear a high-frequency buzz came from the region of the headlamp shell or rim. It was instantly deadened by touching the rim.

## Tested at M.I.R.A.

The steering, though light at low speeds, had a rock-steady quality higher up the scale. In conformity with the character of the machine, the frame and forks are to a generally light specification, but the suspension is good and cross-bracing, plus the benefit derived from the use of an oval, fabricated front down tube, contributes to rigidity and good navigation when gathering speed, turning corners or stopping.       Separately and together the brakes matched the needs of the 55-60-m.p.h. day-long cruising rate of which the " Jubilee 250 " is well capable.

March winds await no tester's convenience and most of the speed and fuel measuring carried out on the wind-swept levels of the Motor Industry Research Association's Lindley terrain, was necessarily done in what are known domestically as good drying-day conditions. The fixed-speed m.p.g. figures, therefore, are quoted with some reserve, the head-on buffeting into fresh breezes on about one-third of the circuit possibly outweighing advantages gained on the remaining two-thirds. But they are conditions encountered daily by road users and, consequently, lend validity to a road-test report.

At over 60 m.p.h. the speedometer was fast and best runs were made with the needle creeping towards 80 m.p.h. In fact, the true speed was in the region of 76 m.p.h. and the maxima shown on the test report panel are the mean of many runs in varying conditions. And supplementing the fuel-consumption information are two other interesting readings. One was taken when the machine enjoyed a flat-out canter around the M.I.R.A. circuit, the speedometer ambitiously clawing at its optimistic 80 m.p.h. The result was 64 m.p.g. More realistic to the average user is the 85-m.p.g. return from tests under everyday riding conditions—to and from work, in speed-limit areas, in traffic and

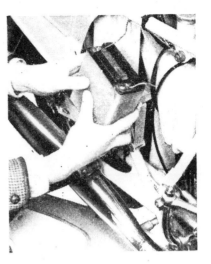

*The battery is mounted so that, although removal for attention offers little difficulty, it is in a well-protected location.*

with the throttle well open on the open road.

A feature of the " Jubilee 250 " is extensive fairing and extremely practical mudguarding so that inclement weather served to emphasize the value of these design features: especially satisfactory was the snub-nosed front mudguard. Surface water, carried up on the tyre tread, was flung into the closed mudguard end from which it tended to disperse instead of being blown back in quantity over the rider's knees. Deep valancing kept one's feet as dry as possible and the styled skirting of the side panels, extending in front and below the level of the passenger's shoes, was another thoughtful design point that was appreciated.

### Shush !

Mechanically very quiet, the test model was also endowed with a well-subdued exhaust note which, for all its fluffy diminuendo air, had been given respectability without detriment to performance. Electrical equipment was up to standard, with lighting adequate for normal cruising at night. Certainly the rider of a " Jubilee 250 " can see, but it is doubtful whether he is always heard: the warning note from the horn is by no means stentorian.

That and other minor items apart, the newcomer to the Bracebridge Street range adds to the stature of the Norton concern and strength to a class of British motorcycle fast returning to popularity.

--------**B R I E F   S P E C I F I C A T I O N**--------

**Engine:** 249 c.c. inclined parallel twin-cylinder four-stroke; bore 60 mm. by stroke 44 mm.; separate iron cylinders; light-alloy heads; o.h. valves; push-rod operated; c.r. 8.75 : 1; claimed b.h.p., 16 7,750 r.p.m.; Amal " Monobloc " carburetter, type 375, .781 choke; 120 main jet.
**Transmission:** Four-speed gearbox in unit with engine; positive-stop footchange; ratios, 6.8, 8.8, 12.5 and 19.7 : 1; primary drive by ⅜-in. duplex chain with tensioners; final drive by ½-in. by .305-in. chain.
**Frame:** Tubular pressed steel cradle; fabricated forward down member with bolt-up connections at the head; cross-bracing and built-up pressing provides centre support.
**Wheels:** WM2-18 rims, carrying 3.25 in. by 18 in. tyres; ribbed front; studded rear;

hubs incorporate 6-in. brakes.
**Lubrication:** Dry-sump lubrication; gear-type oil pump with high-pressure delivery through timing cover channels to the hollow mainshaft and big-ends; oil tank of 3½-pint capacity built into the frame structure.
**Electrical Equipment:** Positive-earth A.C. output Wico-Pacy generator; rectifier for battery charging; D.C. ignition with separate contact breakers and H.T. coils; 6-in. headlamp shell carries ammeter warning light and separate ignition and lighting switches with emergency-start control; bulb ratings: headlamp, pre-focus 6v., 30 24W. unit; pilot, M.E.S. cap 6v. 3W.; tail stop 6v. 3/18W.
**Suspension:** Telescopic front forks controlled by hydraulic damping; rear springing by swinging fork; movement controlled by

Girling units with hydraulic damping; spindle adjustment by means of abutment bolts.
**Tank:** Welded steel flat-base quickly detachable fuel tank, of 3-gal. capacity.
**Dimensions:** Wheelbase 53½ in.; ground clearance, 5½ in.; unladen seat height, 29 in.; dry weight, 330 lb.
**Finish:** Two-tone red dove grey with polished engine and timing covers; chromium-plated wheel rims and tank strip.
**General Equipment:** Full kit of tools; tyre pump; 80-m.p.h. speedometer; pillion footrests.
**Price:** £173, plus £42 16s. 4d. P.T. = £215 16s. 4d.
**Annual Tax:** £1 17s. 6d.
**Makers:** Norton Motors, Ltd., Bracebridge Street, Birmingham, 6.

# ROAD TESTS OF CURRENT MODELS

IN the Model 50 Norton, the race-bred frame and suspension developed for a pair of famous " road-burners " become the setting for a 350 c.c. single-cylinder engine of conventional design and moderate output. The result is a gentlemanly mount which combines the docility, reliability and economy of a " ride-to-work machine " with a standard of handling seldom found in this category.

For the man who *has* to get to work on time, perhaps very early on a frosty morning, the Model 50 would be ideal. The test example always started without any display of temperament. Lucas coil ignition, giving a " hot " spark at low cranking speeds, no doubt played its part.

The behaviour of the emergency system was completely reassuring; an emergency start was, in fact, indistinguishable from a normal one. YOK 686 was off-loaded from the delivery lorry with a completely discharged battery. Despite the fact that the tester was unfamiliar with the machine and did not know how much choke or flooding would be needed, he was able to effect an immediate start on " EMG."

Practice showed that little in the way of mixture enrichment was needed for a cold start and none when the engine was warm. Idling was reasonably reliable, although there was a tendency to " fluff " in pro-

### The 348 c.c. Single-cylinder o.h.v.
# MODEL 50 NORTON

*Race-bred Steering Combines with Easily Managed o.h.v. Engine to Produce a Gentlemanly General-purpose Machine*

## TESTER'S ROAD REPORT
### (NORTON MODEL 50)

**Maximum Speeds in :—**

|  |  |  | Time from Standing Start |
|---|---|---|---|
| Top Gear (Ratio 5·3 to 1) | 74½ m.p.h. = 4950 r.p.m. | 47 secs. |
| Third Gear (Ratio 7 to 1) | 66 m.p.h. = 5850 r.p.m. | 27 secs. |
| Second Gear (Ratio 9·3 to 1) | 52 m.p.h. = 6100 r.p.m. | 15 secs. |

**Speeds over measured Quarter Mile :—**

Flying Start 73½ m.p.h.    Standing Start 46 m.p.h.

**Braking Figures On Dry Tarmacadam Surface, from 30 m.p.h. :—**

Both Brakes 26½ ft.    Front Brake 40 ft.    Rear Brake 72 ft.

**Fuel Consumption :—**

30 m.p.h. 117 m.p.g.    40 m.p.h. 101 m.p.g.    50 m.p.h. 88 m.p.g.

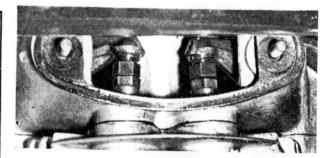

*(Above) Valve-clearance adjustment is hardly a chore when accessibility is so good. There is no need to remove the tank. (Right) A clean exterior! Enclosure of the final-drive chain prolongs its life; this design leaves the brake and chain-tension adjusters fully exposed for easy manipulation.*

longed traffic stops; otherwise, carburation was perfectly in order.

Bottom gear went home without " scrunch " and the clutch took up the drive sweetly once one had become accustomed to the fact that the operative part of the lever's travel was fairly small.

Acceleration was brisk enough. The heavy flywheels of the long-stroke motor demanded time to build up momentum in each ratio, but this characteristic was largely offset by the ease and speed of changes possible with the A.M.C. gearbox. No aptitude at all was required to bring about a quiet change, but it was advisable to pause before releasing the clutch on an upward change so that the motor could run down some of the flywheel energy on a closed throttle, otherwise the machine would surge forward.

As the clutch freed absolutely, this was no hardship. Indeed, when in a hurry it was possible to modify the gearchanging drill to take advantage of this storehouse of energy; the clutch did not appear to resent such abuse, for it required no adjustment. (The acceleration curve in the data panel was obtained with orthodox changing.)

Downward gearchanging was equally satisfactory except for the odd occasion, when coasting to a standstill at lights, on which the pedal seemed to " bring the dogs end-on " so that pressure had to be maintained until they moved into mesh.

Also noted was a reluctance to disengage from bottom gear at abnormally high engine speeds. Only a heavy foot enabled second to be selected on the upward changes when obtaining the data panel figures. Despite this, it was still possible to better 20 seconds for the standing-quarter-mile time.

Having selected top gear anywhere between 30 and 60 m.p.h., the rider could remain in that ratio for a commendably long time. Whilst the docile engine did not produce power beyond its capacity class, its heavy flywheels permitted speed to be maintained on hills longer than would otherwise have been the case. At lower speeds, when cantering round country lanes, the rubber shock-absorber built into the clutch enabled top to be held down to 25 m.p.h., with effective acceleration when wanted.

That top was useful below 30 m.p.h. is commendable, for the Model 50 pulls the high gear of 5.3 : 1—in effect, almost an overdrive. It is also praiseworthy that the maximum speed, without quibbling about the odd ½ m.p.h., was as high as 75.

Top gear, although too high for rapid acceleration, was delightful for giving that feeling of a slow-working engine which is so conducive to freedom from fatigue on a long journey (at 60 m.p.h. corrected speed, the r.p.m. are a modest 4,000). The exhaust was quiet and vibration was not pronounced except when peaking in the gears.

The overdrive effect undoubtedly played a large part in the establishment of excellent fuel consumption figures. The set-speed values shown in the data panel are very good, but even more impressive was the average of 83 m.p.g. for 10 gallons towards the end of the running-in period, when increasingly high speeds were being recorded. A normal owner on a reasonably traffic-free daily journey might well better this by 10 or 15 m.p.g.

The consumption figures quoted are corrected to allow for a mileage recorder error

*The Model 50 was whisked through swervery in traditional Norton " Unapproachable " manner, the road-holding being exemplary.*

of plus 4%. The speedometer was correct at 30 m.p.h. and some 6% fast at maximum.

Good though the fuel economy factor of the Model 50 is, it is overshadowed by the machine's two really oustanding attributes —braking and handling.

Near-record braking figures were recorded. To get below 30 ft. from 30 m.p.h. in a both-brakes stop is quite an achievement. The Model 50 recorded 26½ ft., a figure that had not been approached by a test machine for several years. It cannot be said that the brakes were specially fettled, for when the machine received its 1,500-mile check the tester asked for a tendency to " grab " at 60 m.p.h. to be investigated. The cause was found to be insufficient lining chamfer.

By itself, the full-width 8-in.-diameter front brake stopped the motorcycle in 40 ft., also a near-record. The back unit was sweet and controllable, though lazy in its pedal return action. Emergency stopping from speed, two-up, was of the kind that could cause embarrassment to following traffic.

However, if one had been working the Model 50 through some swervery it was hardly likely that anything would be on its tail. The steering was of that calibre. Using Norton's Featherbed frame and Roadholder forks, the machine is endowed with handling that cannot be faulted in any

way, either solo or with pillion passenger.

Admittedly the ride was firm; passengers even averred that their half of the seat was decidedly hard—a valid criticism. But the heavily damped, pitch-free action of the suspension was a small price to pay for steering of such a high order.

It proved impossible to " touch down " any part of the machine, even on an adverse-cambered slow corner. The grounding angle, on either side, was apparently in excess of that at which tyre adhesion was felt to be critical.

The pilot's half of the seat was resilient without being jelly-like and gave firm but chafeless support to the thighs. In fact, the riding position would have been ideal but for a handlebar bend of curiously inadaptable design.

Another source of annoyance was the use of a fuel tap with too small a knob, placed so high as to be shrouded by the projecting lower lip of the tank.

These detail points were the only debit items logged during 2,200 test miles on the Model 50. Against them stood the general picture of an excellent general-purpose machine, with race-bred roadholding and braking to lend colour to the more mundane qualities of economical running and unfailing reliability.

---

### BRIEF SPECIFICATION

**Engine:** 348 c.c. single-cylinder four-stroke; 71 mm. bore by 88 mm. stroke; overhead valves, push-rod operated; cast-iron cylinder; light-alloy head with detachable light-alloy rocker box; c.r., 7.3 : 1; built-up crankshaft assembly with roller-bearing big-end; Amal Monobloc carburetter of 1-in. bore with 230 main jet.

**Transmission:** Four-speed gearbox manufactured by Associated Motor Cycles. Ltd.; positive-stop footchange; ratios, 5.3, 7, 9·3 and 14.1 : 1; oil-bath single-row primary chain to Norton multi-plate clutch incorporating plates with bonded Ferodo friction material and rubber buffer vane-type shock absorber; final drive by enclosed rear chain.

**Frame:** Tubular all-welded structure of patented design with full loop duplex support for engine and gearbox; steering head cum engine steady brace.

**Wheels:** WM-2 x 19 rims carrying Avon tyres; 3.00 in. by 19 in. ribbed front; 3.50 in. by 19 in. studded rear; full-width light-

alloy hubs with q.d. rear wheel; 8-in. dia. front brake within hub and 7-in. dia. outboard rear brake.

**Lubrication:** Dry sump type with spur gear pumps; oil tank of 3½ pints working capacity; positive feed to o.h. rockers; oil bath for primary chain.

**Electrical equipment:** Lucas A.C./D.C. RM15 alternator with 6-v. full-wave rectifier; Lucas coil ignition firing K.L.G. FE80 three-point plug; Lucas PUZ7E 11 battery enclosed within pressed-steel compartment; Lucas 7-in. dia. block-lens light unit with No. 373 30 24-w. pre-focus bulb; 3-w. m.b.c. pilot bulb within reflector body; Lucas tail/stoplamp with No. 384 6 18-w. bulb; speedometer lamp; rear-brake stoplamp switch; Lucas horn.

**Suspension:** Roadholder telescopic front forks of Norton design, with two-way hydraulic damping; rear springing by swinging fork, movement controlled by Girling units with hydraulic damping and three-position setting; spindle adjustment by push-bolts.

**Tank:** Welded steel of 3½-gal. capacity; plunger-type tap with reserve.

**Dimensions:** Wheelbase, 55½ in.; ground clearance, 6 in.; unladen seat height, 30½ in.; certified kerbside weight, 399 lb.

**Finish:** Dark green stove enamel; wheel rims, exhaust system, handlebars and controls, detachable tank panels and sundry items chromium plated; many light-alloy parts buffed and polished; black dualseat.

**General equipment:** Kit of tools; tyre pump; 125 m.p.h. Smiths speedometer; pillion footrests; dualseat; prop and centre stands.

**Price:** £189 10s. plus £39 1s. 8d. P.T.= £228 11s. 8d.

**Extras:** Rear chaincase, £2 17s. 4d. including P.T.; non-standard colour scheme of black with silver tank, £2 14s. 4d. including P.T.

**Annual tax:** £3 15s.; quarterly, £1 0s. 8d.

**Makers:** Norton Motors, Ltd., Bracebridge Street, Birmingham, 6.

в 1

# The 349 c.c. NORTON

# 'NAVIGATOR'

### Fastest '350' twin

### roadster has superb

### handling and braking

## Specification

### ENGINE

| | |
|---|---|
| Type .. .. | Parallel-twin four-stroke |
| Bore .. .. .. .. | 63 mm. |
| Stroke .. .. .. | 56 mm. |
| Cubic capacity .. .. | 349 c.c. |
| Valves .. .. | Overhead (push-rod) |
| Compression ratio .. .. | 8.8 : 1 |
| Carburetter .. | Amal type 375, $\frac{7}{8}$-in. bore |
| Ignition .. .. | A.C.-output generator, battery and twin h.t. coils |
| Generator | Wipac 6v. crankshaft alternator |
| Makers' claimed output | 22 b.h.p./7,000 r.p.m. |
| Lubrication .. | Dry sump and double-gear pump |
| Starting .. .. .. | Kickstarter |

### TRANSMISSION

Unit construction gearbox with footchange.
Ratios .. .. 5.7, 7.4, 10.6, 16.7 : 1
Speed at 1,000 r.p.m. in top gear .. 13 m.p.h.
Speed equivalent to revs. at maximum power rating:

| | | |
|---|---|---|
| Second gear | .. .. | 49 m.p.h. |
| Third gear | .. .. | 71 m.p.h. |
| Top gear .. | .. .. | 91 m.p.h. |
| Primary drive | Duplex chain with tensioner | |
| Final drive .. | .. .. .. | Chain |
| Clutch .. | Multi-plate in oilbath | |
| Shock-absorber | Synthetic rubber in clutch | |

### CYCLE PARTS

| | |
|---|---|
| Frame .. | Pressed steel fabricated and tubular cradle type |
| Front suspension .. | Telescopic forks with two-way hydraulic damping |
| Rear suspension | Swinging fork with hydraulically-damped spring units |
| Tyres .. | Dunlop 3.00 x 19 in. ribbed front, 3.25 x 18 in. studded rear |
| Brakes .. | Front, 8-in. dia.; rear, 6-in. dia. Total lining area, 28½ sq in. |
| Fuel tank .. | Welded steel; single-bolt fixing; single tap |
| Oil tank | .. .. .. 3½ pints |
| Lamps .. | 30/24-w. head; 3-w. pilot; 18/6-w. tailstop |

| | |
|---|---|
| Battery .. .. | 12 a.h. Lucas |
| Speedometer .. | Smiths 100 m.p.h. non-trip |
| Seating .. .. | Single-level dual seat |
| Stand .. .. | Centre |
| Tool kit | ..3 open-ended spanners; 2 tyre levers; combined plug/wheel-nut spanner; box spanner; shock-absorber adj. spanner; pliers; Allen keys; feeler-gauge set; 2 tommy bars; screwdriver |
| Toolbox .. .. | Tray beneath seat |
| Standard finish .. | Black and dove-grey |

### OTHER EQUIPMENT

Tyre pump; pillion rests.

### PRICES

| | |
|---|---|
| Machine | £237 12s. 7d. (inc. £40 12s. 7d. P.T.) |
| Extras .. .. .. .. .. | none |
| Total as tested .. .. | £237 12s. 7d. |
| Tax .. .. .. .. | £3 15s. 0d. p.a. |
| Makers | Norton Motors, Ltd., Bracebridge Street, Birmingham 6. |

## 'Motor Cycling' Test Data

**Conditions.** *Weather: Cool with heavy showers.* (*Barometer 29.20 Hg. Thermometer 53°F.*) *Wind: S.W., 12 m.p.h., gusting to 18 m.p.h. Surface (braking and acceleration): Damp asphalt. Rider: 11½ stone, 5 ft. 8½ in., wearing one-piece suit, riding boots and safety helmet. Fuel: Super grade (100 research method octane rating).*

**Venue:** *Motor Industry Research Assoc. Station, Lindley.*

Speed at end of standing 1,000 yd.:
| | | |
|---|---|---|
| East | .. .. .. | 80.6 m.p.h. |
| West | .. .. .. | 72.8 m.p.h. |
| Best certified M.I.R.A. maximum (rider prone) | | 89.2 m.p.h. |

Braking from 30 m.p.h. (all brakes):
9½ yd.

Fuel consumption:
| | |
|---|---|
| At constant 30 m.p.h. .. | 96 m.p.g. |
| 50 m.p.h. .. | 78 m.p.g. |
| 500-mile Overall figure .. | 76 m.p.g. |

**Speedometer**
| | |
|---|---|
| 30 m.p.h. indicated = | 26.8 m.p.h. true |
| 40 m.p.h. indicated = | 37.6 m.p.h. true |
| 50 m.p.h. indicated = | 45.2 m.p.h. true |
| 60 m.p.h. indicated = | 54.0 m.p.h. true |
| 70 m.p.h. indicated = | 63.4 m.p.h. true |
| 80 m.p.h. indicated = | 72.2 m.p.h. true |
| 90 m.p.h. indicated = | 80.55 m.p.h. true |

**Mileage Recorder.** Over-reading 2%

**Electrical Equipment**
Top gear speed at which generator output balances:
Ignition only. Below minimum non-snatch speed.
Minimum obligatory lights 17 m.p.h.
Full lights .. .. .. 21 m.p.h.

**Weights and Capacities**
Certified kerbside weight (with oil and 1 gal. fuel) .. 351 lb.

Weight distribution, rider normally seated:
| | | |
|---|---|---|
| Front wheel | .. .. | 38% |
| Rear wheel | .. .. | 62% |

Tank capacity (metered):
| | | |
|---|---|---|
| Total | .. .. | 3 gal. |
| Reserve | .. .. | 1 pint |

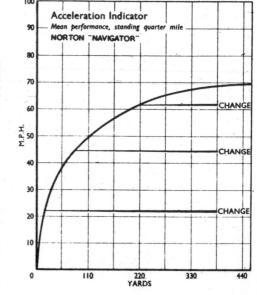

Acceleration Indicator
*Mean performance, standing quarter mile*
**NORTON "NAVIGATOR"**

CHANGE
CHANGE
CHANGE

M.P.H.

YARDS

# NORTON 'NAVIGATOR' ROAD TEST

A MAXIMUM speed, electronically timed, of over 89 m.p.h.; truly magnificent roadholding and steering; and powerful brakes which can be used to the full in complete safety.

Those are the chief findings, after a full road test under exacting conditions, on Norton's new 349 c.c. twin, the "Navigator"—second Earls Court attraction in the middleweight class to be tested by "Motor Cycling."

The tester's task was difficult, firstly, due to weather conditions that made headline news at the time and, secondly, because of the temptation to write in superlatives. It was at once apparent that in the "Navigator"—which is far from being simply a "grown-up" version of the 250 c.c. "Jubilee" — Norton's have a definite winner.

It is the fastest British standard roadster of its kind and also one of the safest, for the design team at Bracebridge Street have put into the "Navigator" all the experience of braking and steering that they have won on the Grand Prix circuits of Europe.

"Over-square" in bore and stroke, the engine is high-revving, with a usable ceiling around 7,000 r.p.m., at which rate the output is in the region of 22 b.h.p. A higher output than this has been obtained during the development phase, with correspondingly greater road speeds, but none will cavil at the near-90 m.p.h. maximum of the production version, with an acceleration curve which would have done credit to a sports "500" a few years ago.

To make the best use of the available power at all speeds, 100 octane fuel was recommended by the makers. It certainly suited the 8.8:1 compression ratio very well, though the utterly pink-free behaviour of the unit encouraged screwing open the twist-grip to steam up a gradient—the engine gulping in quantities of expensive petrol—when a change-down might have achieved the same result more economically This combination of a high-revving peak output with slogging side-valve characteristics at the other end of the scale gave the "Navigator" a most flexible top-gear range.

The gear ratios, based on the internal reductions of the "Jubilee" with 19t. gearbox and 52t. rear wheel sprockets, seemed to be ideal. The particularly useful 10.6:1 second could be used from walking pace to close on 55 m.p.h., though normally third gear would be brought in at a little over 40 m.p.h.

To extract the best possible standing quarter-mile acceleration, the "Navigator" was left in third, though ordinarily this 7.4:1 ratio was relinquished at about 60-62 m.p.h. Third gear could be used as a "low top" for short-term cruising or accelerating in the 60-70 m.p.h. bracket. At high speeds, incidentally, the Smiths speedometer was decidedly optimistic.

It was hardly surprising to find that such vigorous driving in the intermediate gears resulted in a higher-than-average fuel consumption. A check over 112 miles, which included all the high-speed testing—equal to a dash down M1—showed that at the end exactly 2 gallons had been used. More judicious riding gave an average m.p.g. figure nearer to 76.

Assuming a discreet reduction of speed to 30 m.p.h. or less after switching to the reserve supply, the reserve pint then available would last about 10 miles—not a great distance for the man in fuel trouble on, say, A41 at night, let alone abroad. A faint swish, audible from the opposite tank-well, suggested that a tiny supplementary reserve would be obtainable by tilting the machine.

Gear engagement was quiet. The four-plate clutch (three double and two single-side bonded-insert elements are used) freed to give a slick first-gear engagement and there was no difficulty in selecting neutral.

To the rocket-like performance of this twin are matched handling and steering of such an order as to put the new-comer almost into the racing category. A modified steering-head angle, together with the famous Norton "Roadholder" forks ("resprung" to suit the "Navigator's"

Removal of a cover plate reveals the twin contact-breakers. The "short" engine leaves ample overhead clearance for access to plugs and rocker-gear.

weight distribution) and a wheelbase an inch shorter than that of the "Jubilee" have produced navigation of such quality as to inspire the model's name.

One exhilarating experience was to swing around the M.I.R.A. circuit at full bore. Another was to fling back mile after mile of main road at a 55-60 m.p.h. cruising speed —a favourite "Navigator" pace—and feel the machine with you at the slightest change of course, the whole rock-steady as if part of the rider, and almost thinking with him. Adverse cambers, wet leaves . . . the conditions seemed never to matter.

The brakes were a revelation of how safe a fast middleweight could be. Norton's have not been content with minimum lining areas that will just do the job; instead, they have given the "Navigator" the best they make. The lightest touch would bring the powerful front "stopper" into action, slowing the machine without the slightest hint of grab or fade—this after the test model had been out for a day on flooded roads. Equally sensitive was the smaller

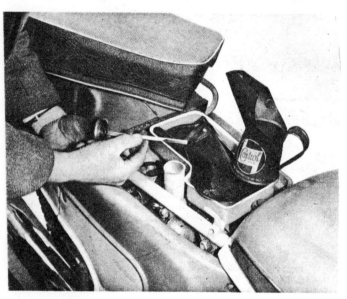

(Above) The cylinder-head steady lug is welded to the front down-tube. The remote carburetter tickler protrudes through a slot in the fairing, close to the petrol tap.

(Right) The front wheel has an 8-in.-diameter brake identical with that of the bigger Norton twins.

(Left) Oil filler cap, with integral dipstick, and tool tray are beneath the quickly detachable dual seat

but efficient rear brake. The two, applied with determination, gave a safe, reliable pull-up in less than the classical datum distance of 30 ft. from 30 m.p.h.—without streaks of rubber left on the road, or the alarm that accompanies a sudden wheel lock.

There was good protection from the wet weather prevailing two weeks ago. A deep front guard checked throw-back and the rear enclosure of the de-luxe test machine was very effective protection against water flung from the tyre. Chain condition indicated the results of a wet life—the chaincase available as an extra at £3 15s. 0d. would obviously be a good investment.

Seat and handlebars were well positioned for a rider of average stature and there was provision for handlebar adjustment by rotating the bars. Movement, however, was limited by the resultant angle of the clutch and front brake levers, which pivot in clevis lugs integral with the bars.

Separate switches control the lighting

and ignition circuits; they are mounted accessibly, and visibly, with the ammeter and speedometer in the top of the headlamp-shell. An emergency-start circuit caters for flat-battery conditions. There is no "ignition-on" warning device, except for the discharge shown by the ammeter needle. The horn, which has a piercing note, is mounted on the front down-tube.

Weighing less than 360 lb. with two gallons of petrol aboard, the de-luxe version was no burden to manhandle. The centre stand went into action easily and supported the machine with the rear wheel clear of the ground. A toolkit similar to that of the "Jubilee" is carried in a tray beneath the seat. Adjacent is the filler cap of the built-in 3½-pint oil tank, with a dipstick attached.

Each of the four rocker covers is accessible, and the tappets are adjusted by rotating the eccentric rocker spindle so that the rocker arm moves towards, or away

from, the tip of the valve stem. Three coin-slotted Dzus screws secure each side panel; removal lays bare the Amal "Monobloc" carburetter, and battery. The contact-breaker and ignition timing can be adjusted after taking off the circular inspection plate on the offside engine-cover (two screws).

To get at the twin h.t. coils, the fuel tank is rapidly removed by taking out the single retaining bolt at the rear and disconnecting the fuel line. The tank keys into position at the front and rests on rubber buffers.

The 19-in. front wheel, with a 3-in. ribbed tyre and 8-in. diameter brake— identical with that of the bigger twins— has a knock-out spindle, the rear 3.25 by 18-in. wheel with 6-in. brake being on a fixed spindle.

Maintenance generally, in fact, promised to be commendably easy—a bread-and-butter virtue admittedly, in comparison to the main characteristics of this outstanding machine. As to them, perhaps the chief impression remaining is one of eminently *usable* performance. If a motorcycle will sell on safety as well as speed, there is no doubt about the future of the Norton "Navigator."

# The 497 c.c. NORTON 'DOMINATOR 88 S/S'

**BIG SPORTSTER TESTS**

### 100-plus sports version of

### a race-bred roadster

### with faultless handling

## Specification

### ENGINE

| | |
|---|---|
| Type .. .. .. | Parallel-twin four-stroke |
| Bore .. .. .. .. | 66 mm. |
| Stroke .. .. .. .. | 73 mm. |
| Cubic capacity .. .. | 497 c.c. |
| Valves .. .. | Overhead (push-rod) |
| Compression ratio .. .. | 8.5 : 1 |
| Carburetters .. Twin Amal "Monobloc," | |
| | 1-1/16 in. bore |
| Ignition .. .. .. Lucas battery and coil | |
| Generator .. Lucas 6-v RM15 alternator | |
| | with full-wave rectification |
| Maker's claimed output 36 b.h.p. at 7,000 r.p.m. | |
| Lubrication .. Dry sump with gear pump | |
| Starting .. .. .. Kickstarter | |

### TRANSMISSION

| | |
|---|---|
| Ratios .. .. .. | 5.0, 6.1, 8.5, 12.8 : 1 |
| Speed at 1,000 r.p.m. in top gear .. | 15½ m.p.h. |

Speed equivalent to revs. at maximum power rating:

| | | |
|---|---|---|
| Second gear | .. .. .. | 65 m.p.h. |
| Third gear .. | .. .. | 90 m.p.h. |
| Top gear .. | .. .. | 109 m.p.h. |
| Primary drive.. | Single-row chain in oilbath | |
| Final drive .. | .. | Single-row chain |
| Clutch .. | Bonded multi-plate in oilbath | |
| Shock-absorber | Vane-type in clutch centre | |

### CYCLE PARTS

| | |
|---|---|
| Frame .. | Full duplex cradle, brazed and welded |
| Front suspension | Telescopic forks with coil springs in compression and two-way hydraulic damping |
| Rear suspension | Swinging fork with adjustable, three-position hydraulically damped Girling spring units |
| Tyres .. | Avon 3.00 × 19-in. ribbed front and 3.50 × 19-in. studded rear |
| Brakes .. | 8-in. dia. front, 7-in. dia. rear. Total lining area, 30 sq. in. |
| Fuel tank .. | Welded steel; two-position tap |

| | |
|---|---|
| Oil tank .. .. .. | 4½ pint |
| Lamps .. 30/24-w. head, 3-w. pilot, 6/18-w. | |
| | tail/stop; 1.8-w. speedometer |
| Battery .. .. .. | Lucas 6-v., 12 a.h. |
| Speedometer .. | Smiths 120 m.p.h. trip type |
| Seating.. .. .. .. | Dual seat |
| Stands .. .. | Centre and prop |
| Tool kit Spanners: 3 open-ended, 3 box, | |
| | Girling. 2 tommy bars; Allen key; |
| | 2 screwdrivers; pliers; 2 tyre levers; |
| | tool roll |
| Toolbox .. | Open tray beneath seat |
| Standard finish .. | Green and dove-grey |

### OTHER EQUIPMENT

Tyre pump.

### PRICES

| | |
|---|---|
| Machine .. | £291 5s. (inc. £50 16s. P.T.) |
| Extras .. .. | None |
| Total as tested | £291 5s. (inc. £50 16s. P.T.) |
| Tax .. | £4 10s. p.a.; £1 13s. for four months |
| Makers .. Norton Motors, Ltd., Bracebridge | |
| | Street, Birmingham 6 |

## 'Motor Cycling' Test Data

**Conditions.** *Weather: Mild, dry (Barometer 29.35 in. Hg. Thermometer 54°F.). Wind: South-west, 10 m.p.h. Surface (braking and acceleration): Dry asphalt. Rider: 11½ stone, wearing one-piece racing leathers, boots and safety helmet, normally seated (except for "Best certified M.I.R.A. maximum" and "Flying lap speed"). Fuel: "Super" grade (101½ research method octane rating).*

**Venue:** *Motor Industry Research Association Station, Lindley.*

Speed at end of standing 1,000 yd.:

| | |
|---|---|
| East .. .. .. | 92½ m.p.h. |
| West .. .. .. | 77½ m.p.h. |
| Best certified M.I.R.A. maximum (rider prone) | 111.0 m.p.h. |
| Flying lap speed (rider prone) | 97.6 m.p.h. |
| Braking from 30 m.p.h. (all brakes) .. .. .. | 9 yd. |

### Fuel consumption

| At constant 30 m.p.h. | Not recorded |
|---|---|
| 50 m.p.h. .. | 79 m.p.g. |
| 70 m.p.h. .. | 62 m.p.g. |
| 500-mile overall figure .. | 62 m.p.g. |

### Speedometer

| | |
|---|---|
| 30 m.p.h. indicated = | 27.4 m.p.h. true |
| 40 m.p.h. indicated = | 37.2 m.p.h. true |
| 50 m.p.h. indicated = | 46.9 m.p.h. true |
| 60 m.p.h. indicated = | 56.5 m.p.h. true |
| 70 m.p.h. indicated = | 65.1 m.p.h. true |
| 80 m.p.h. indicated = | 76.1 m.p.h. true |
| 90 m.p.h. indicated = | 86.0 m.p.h. true |
| 100 m.p.h. indicated = | 95.4 m.p.h. true |
| 110 m.p.h. indicated = | 103.2 m.p.h. true |

**Mileage Recorder** .. Over-reading 1%

### Electrical Equipment

Top gear speed at which generator output balances:

| | |
|---|---|
| Ignition only .. .. | 18 m.p.h. |
| Minimum obligatory lights | 23 m.p.h. |
| Headlamp main beam .. | 27 m.p.h. |

### Weights and Capacities

| | |
|---|---|
| Certified kerbside weight (with oil and 1 gal. fuel) .. .. | 408 lb. |
| Weight distribution (rider normally seated): | |
| Front wheel.. .. .. | 42% |
| Rear wheel .. .. .. | 58% |
| Tank capacity (metered): | |
| Total .. .. .. | 3.49 gal. |
| Reserve .. .. .. | 1¼ pints. |

**Acceleration Indicator**
*Mean performance, standing quarter mile*
**NORTON "DOMINATOR 88 S/S"**

CHANGE

CHANGE

M.P.H. / YARDS

FROM a "Sports Special" version of a fast roadster which is already a by-word for its race-bred handling, one obviously expects a great deal. The highest possible praise for Norton's new "Dominator 88 S/S" is to say simply that it is no disappointment.

At the M.I.R.A. track, its best one-way speed of the day was 111 m.p.h. Making allowance for a gentle tail wind, this indicates a still-air maximum of 103-104 m.p.h.—about 7 m.p.h. higher than that of the standard model.

Wind and the configuration of the track, incidentally, had the opposite effect upon the recorded flying lap speed of nearly 98 m.p.h., which would have been higher in still air.

An extra 6 b.h.p. has been extracted from the twin by fitting two carburetters with the bore increased to 1⅛ in. and larger inlet valves and ports to suit, and by using the 650 c.c. "Manxman" camshaft and light push-rods, as well as special valve springs—with a stiffer crankshaft to handle the output. The split-skirt pistons give a modest 8.5 : 1 c.r. For those who want even more top-end performance there are 9+ : 1 pistons for the asking. . . .

The price of a 36 b.h.p./7,000 r.p.m. motor has not been paid in bad manners or difficult starting. This is almost certainly due, amongst other things, to the fitting of a special silencer and small-bore pipes (of the siamesed pattern) which increase the exhaust-gas velocity at low engine speeds, when this is an advantage.

The only drawback we found was a tendency to foul K.L.G. FE100 plugs with pure "lampblack" in prolonged city usage. The reasons seemed to be a plug grading which was "over-hard" for general use, aggravated by mixture richness at the bottom end. For everyday riding, FE75 plugs were more practical wear.

On the road, the tester was greatly impressed by the way in which power would surge in at about 45 to 50 m.p.h. in top. Below this speed, top-gear acceleration was decidedly useful—even brisk—yet when everything "got into step" the motor really pulled at the leash.

This buoyancy persisted even at 85 in top. A twitch of the grip at this speed (when "500s" are usually tailing off markedly) and yet more power came in. There was no need to look at the speedometer—one could feel the handlebars straining forward and the shiny seat of one's Barbour suit slipping inexorably to the rear. If the "88 S/S" acceleration graph is plotted on top of those of many other "500s," then the point is forcibly borne home.

It was usual to extract high revs for maximum pick-up; 7,000 is not abusing this motor, and indeed Nortons quote this as the peak-power rate. We habitually ran the test machine up to 65 m.p.h. indicated in second and the top side of 90 in third. No distress at this continued treatment appeared and there was no more vibration than could be comfortably tolerated.

The exhaust was quiet enough by sports standards. The new silencer gave it a throaty, chuckling quality, as though the sound were being generated at the bottom of a deep well; obviously the pitch has been modified more drastically than the volume. We thought this silencer was definitely a step in the right direction—towards less noisy motorcycles.

Roadholding was—Norton. Handling was truly superlative on bends or straights, bumpy or smooth, fast or slow.

## TWO-PAGE DRAWING OVERLEAF

"Siamesed" pipes leave the nearside of the engine clear. The caps which give access to the valve-clearance adjusters can be removed without disturbing the tank. The primary chaincase is retained by a single nut on the footrest hanger.

# NORTON 'DOMINATOR 88 S/S' Road Test (continued)

(Left) Checking the camshaft chain after resetting the slipper-type adjuster. (Below left) Adjusting the clutch. (Below right) A plastic mesh filter is fitted in the banjo connection above each float chamber.

amount of oil was ejected—enough to coat the left wall of the rear tyre. Oil also got past the tank filler cap.

Otherwise, the unit was free from oil stains and when stationary left no more than a few spots under the crankcase from the engine breather.

The lights generally rated "adequate" on the tester's check card. But the owner of a 100 m.p.h. roadster might well want more watts. In daytime the "88 S/S" will cruise apparently for ever at 80 to 85 m.p.h. indicated on a motorway (still more if wind pressure is tolerated), and it is frustrating to be limited to 70-ish just because the sun has set.

The Lucas equipment not only kept the battery charged, but continued charging at a rate of 4 to 6 amp. when the battery was right "up"; the deduction is that the A.C. generator system was insufficiently sensitive to battery state.

The horn note was comfortingly loud to the rider's ears and, normally, had a reasonable effect on vehicles in front. But again, for a motorway cruiser, rather more sheer "blasting" power is needed, and would be welcomed as an optional extra.

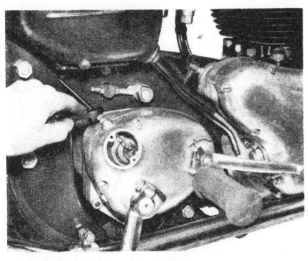

There was ample ground clearance; it would be more than a good man who could "graunch" the head of the silencer pinch-bolt—it would be a foolhardy one! This exhaust system has been tailored with the Thruxton production-machine race in mind and there's no restriction, on either side, to the laying-down process—other than tyre adhesion.

The "Roadholder" front forks and Girling-controlled rear end gave a reasonable degree of comfort. The ride was firm, but not unbearably so. The dual seat had just the right qualities—resilience without sogginess—and the controls, rests and bars were well placed.

The riding position was highish and of the leaning-on-the-wind variety. The near-straight bars could have a more natural set to the ends, and might well be narrower on a mount which never needs physical force to dominate the steering. The horn button would benefit if it were not sited by a screwed-on attachment.

The brake and gear pedals could be adjusted exactly to suit the height selected for the footrests. The twin carburetters did not make the twistgrip heavy to operate; the plastic grip, however, was a sliding fit.

Braking was faultless. In power the stoppers were fully equal to the requirements of a sports mount driven to the limit. Both units were waterproof, neither needed adjustment during 1,700 test miles (the machine was supplied run-in), and the operating pressure of each was just right.

It was observed that the rear anchor could be locked slightly more readily than those of other Nortons we have tested. This may have resulted from the forward riding position, with its attendant greater weight (2%) on the front wheel. Despite the greater load on the front unit, no fade was encountered.

Gearbox and clutch were above criticism.

The secondary transmission required only negligible adjustment; this may have been due to somewhat copious lubrication from the oil-tank vent pipe. The tester was careful never to exceed the ordained level (indicated by a mark), yet at very high speeds a certain

Details on the "full marks" side included the prop and centre stands, both of which were serviceable, and the q.d.-est dual seat imaginable. One coin-slotted Dzus fastener held the seat; its removal exposed the tool compartment. We also liked the easy access to the valve-clearance adjusters, primary chaincase contents and clutch adjuster.

The rear wheel came out readily and the push-bolts to the spindle were accessible; these required only a half-turn during the whole test. The wheel was genuinely q.d. and came out without disturbing the brake or chain. Front wheel removal was foolproof. It was easy to get at the camshaft chain.

In detail, as in general character, the "88 S/S" shows what can be done by the development of a basically excellent and (as the aircraft people say) "stretchable" design. This is a mount that is going to make a name for itself on the highways of Britain, and will almost certainly make its mark wherever production-machine races are held.

# The 497 c.c. NORTON 'DOMINATOR

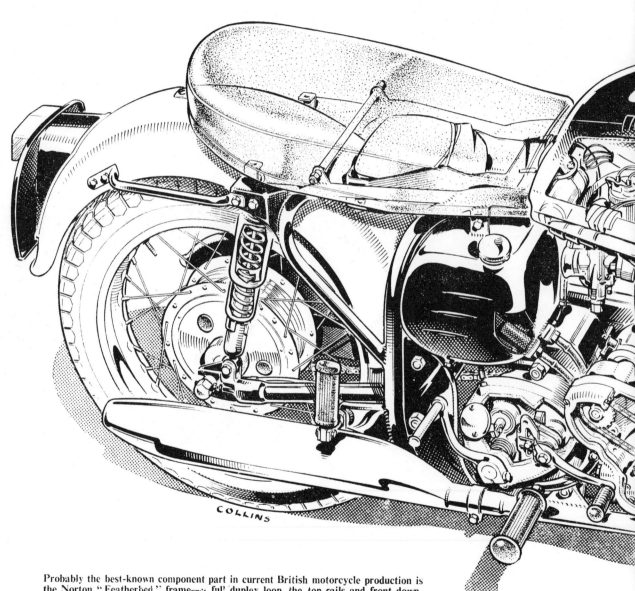

COLLINS

Probably the best-known component part in current British motorcycle production is the Norton "Featherbed" frame—a full duplex loop, the top rails and front down-tubes of which cross at the steering-head. The roadster version is "waisted" to reduce the width between the rider's knees. The alloy-head engine has a chain-driven camshaft with inclined pushrods and tappets in the front of the cylinder block. "Siamesed" pipes are the most conspicuous difference between the "Sports Special" and the standard "Dominator 88."

# S/S'

**FULL ROAD TEST REPORT ON**

**PAGES 52, 53 and 56**

# NORTON DOMINATOR TWINS

## SERVICE SHOP LORE No. 8

**THE DOMINATOR** family is larger than you think. It sprung, back in 1949, from the 497 c.c. No. 7 which had a brazed-lug, plunger-sprung frame and the lightly damped version of the Roadholder front fork.

Only one other Dominator had that sort of frame and front fork (though its rear fork was pivoted). That was the No. 77, a 597 c.c. twin marketed for a short while for sidecar duty.

**By far the best known of the Dominators, of course, are those with the so-called featherbed frame—that is, the welded duplex-loop type famed first on the factory racers in Geoff Duke's day—and the race-bred variant of the front fork.**

**I**N this group are the five-hundred 88, six-hundred 99 and the 650, all of which at some time or other have appeared in standard, de luxe and super-sports guise.

But all Dominators have so much in common that, for servicing, they can be lumped together.

A year ago the instruction book was completely revised and it is now quite exceptionally informative and helpful. In most respects it applies equally to the earlier models. But the bulk of Dominator owners won't have seen it. Here, then, is a selection of tips based on service-shop experience.

## TRANSMISSION

**FIRST, CHAINS.** On pivoted fork models a common mistake is to overtighten the rear chain by setting the up-and-down play to the recommended ⅜in with the machine on its wheels but unladen. Then, when the suspension settles under the rider's weight the chain becomes board hard.

The setting varies from slackest at the extremes of suspension travel to tightest midway between them (when the rear-wheel axis is dead in line with those of the gear-box sprocket and fork pivot).

It is with the suspension at mid-travel that the chain should have ⅜in up-and-down play half way along the run. The simplest way to make this check is to straddle the rear number plate with your chest on the dual-seat; then pull upward on the fork with the right hand while feeling chain tension with the left.

Only rarely should the primary chain call for adjustment. The drill is first to overtighten the chain slightly by pulling the gear box back with the rear nut on the drawbolt; then back off that nut and ease the box forward with the front nut until there is ½in up-and-down play in the middle of the run.

The idea is to take up the backlash in the drawbolt eye as a safeguard against the box being jerked backward under the greater pull of the rear chain.

## NEVER TIGHT

AS WITH the transmission chains, the two timing chains should never be run tight. Since they tend to tighten with the warming (and consequent expansion) of the crankcase, there should be ⅜in free

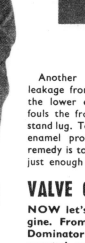

*Rear suspension must be compressed halfway when checking chain tension. This is a simple way to do it*

movement when cold.

Removal of the timing cover for checking, though, takes the outer support from the intermediate-gear spindle and that may be disturbed if too much force is used on the chains.

The service-shop dodge is to fit a scrap timing cover with windows cut for access to the chains.

When checking the camshaft chain you should ensure that its lower run is hard against the slipper; this may necessitate turning the camshaft anti-clockwise a shade with a spanner on the sprocket-retaining nut.

Before you finally replace the original timing cover, do see that the synthetic rubber seal is still on the oil-pump nozzle. The penalty for neglecting that could well be a wrecked engine.

## OIL-TIGHT CASE

GOT the outer half of the primary chaincase off? If you want the case to be oil-tight on reassembly it is most important not to overtighten the large chrome-plated retaining nut.

This should be done up until only one or, at the most, two threads protrude from the outside.

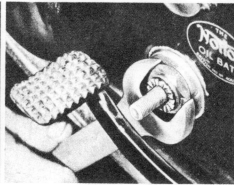

*Overtightening the primary chain slightly then moving the gearbox forward to the correct setting helps prevent the adjustment from shifting*

*This cutaway timing cover supports the intermediate gear spindle while chain tension is checked. It may be necessary to turn the camshaft a shade to get the slack in the top run*

*The primary chaincase will leak if you overtighten the retaining nut. Only one or two threads should protrude beyond the nut face*

Another possible cause of leakage from the case is that the lower edge of the cover fouls the frame tube or prop-stand lug. Telltale marks on the enamel provide a clue. The remedy is to file back the edge just enough to give clearance.

## VALVE CLEARANCES

NOW let's look at the engine. From 1959 onward all Dominator cams have incorporated quietening ramps. These blend the flanks very gradually into the base circle and so take up the running clearance more quietly.

But they make it risky to set the valve clearances the old-fashioned way, at top dead centre, since the cam follower could be somewhere on the ramp and not on the base circle unless your positioning of the piston is very precise.

The way to make sure the follower is plumb in the middle of the base circle is to set the corresponding valve in the other cylinder at full lift. And even with the earlier camshafts there is nothing at all against this method—it is foolproof.

## HEAD OFF

YOU want to lift the cylinder head? Then make a point of slackening the exhaust-port ring nuts while the engine is still hot at the end of a run. Once it has cooled right off you might find them too obstinate for the standard C-spanner.

Actually it is possible to lift the cylinder head and block as one unit (yes, including the carbs) and separate the parts on the bench. (Of course, the pistons should be at bottom dead centre.) But this is not advisable.

Often the head sticks rather obstinately to the block and it is easier to break the joint before the block is slackened. Levering between the fins is not the way to do this, it merely breaks the fins.

The safest drill is to hold a stout piece of wood (preferably hard) against the roof or the underside of an exhaust port and jar the wood with a mallet.

Lowering the block over the piston rings without breaking any is easily done if the piston skirts are first brought down gently on to two long bolts or tommy-bars placed transversely across the crankcase mouth.

How to engage the pushrods with the valve rockers when refitting the head? Take the two 5/16in × 26 t.p.i. cylinder-head nuts that came off the studs between the exhaust ports and place them on the top fin of the block, one at each side, before lowering the head.

They will keep the joint far enough apart for you to mate the rods and rockers by using a wire hook through the exhaust-valve inspection holes.

## TWIN CARBS

IF YOUR engine has two carbs, the mixing chambers are probably joined by a short, straight plastic tube. It is worth while scrapping this, turning the banjos to face the rear and joining them with a U-shape loop.

Why? Because the left-hand pilot screw is then easier to reach when you are synchronizing the idling settings.

While we're on carbs, the front and rear joint faces of the inlet manifold on the 650 Standard and de luxe are not parallel. Should the manifold be fitted upside down, the carburettor will be tilted upward excessively.

It is easy to see which position gives the less downdraught—in any case the embossed part number should be at the bottom.

## GAP IMPORTANT

NOW FOR a few random hints. If you puncture you may want the quickly detachable rear wheel out—quickly! Too bad to find it won't come away from the brake drum. So, when you've time to spare, it's a good idea to separate the parts, clean any rust or paint off the central boss of the hub and grease if before re-entering it in the drum.

Should your SS model have a plastic pipe on the contact-breaker breather—pull it off and point the banjo downward. Also keep an eye on the contact points gap (0.012 to 0.015in).

The pipe can lead to condensation and consequent erosion of the points. This widens the gap, which overadvances the ignition timing. In the end burning of the pistons can result.

If the foot-change return spring breaks, make sure you replace it with the latest pattern which has the legs crossed when installed. The action of this spring tightens the spring coils instead of opening them and so stresses the wire much less.

Replenishing the front fork with oil (featherbed frame models)? The correct quantity is 5 fluid ounces per leg, not 7 which is right only for the Manx fork with external springs and hence greater internal capacity.

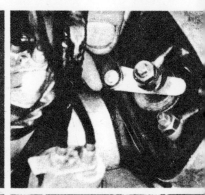

*Valve-clearance check. The right-hand inlet valve is at peak lift while the clearance of the left-hand valve is checked*

*Cylinder-head joints are apt to stick. Jarring the head with mallet and hardwood breaks the joint without damage*

*Supporting the pistons on rods across the crankcase mouth makes it easier to lower the cylinder block safely over the rings*

*Twin carburettors should be joined by a U-shape pipe rather than a short straight pipe to provide access to the left-hand pilot air screw*

# ROAD TESTS OF NEW MODELS

*Mudguards are chrome plated. The starter motor nestles behind the cylinder block*

# 384cc NORTON ES 400

APART from its extra 35 cc, three up-to-the-minute features distinguish the 384 cc Norton ES 400 twin from its famous sister, the Navigator. They are 12-volt electrics, push-button starting and grip-tip winkers. Other, less obvious, differences are that the steering head on the ES 400 is gusseted while the rear brake is of 7in diameter compared with the Navigator's 6in.

*With the engine not too cold, the electric starter worked a treat. But it was hard put to spin the crankshaft fast enough for reliable starting when the ES 400 had just spent a frosty night in the open. The best drill then was to use the kick-starter initially—a couple of prods sufficed—and press the button for subsequent starts.*

Incidentally, it is not necessary for the gears to be in neutral when using the electric starter. If a gear is engaged you merely declutch.

Along with the headlamp dip switch and horn button, the starter button is incorporated in a Wipac Tricon ring switch just inboard of the left hand-grip. On the other side of the bar, the winker switch could not be operated without releasing the twistgrip; an improvement would be to change this switch to the left.

Grip angle proved comfortable though reach to the clutch and front-brake levers was a shade on the long side. The footrests were low enough to give a wide knee angle but the starter-drive case fouled the rider's left leg.

**Burbling unobtrusively through dense traffic or swinging along the open road at 70 mph came alike to the ES 400. Though healthy, the exhaust note was not objectionable; the twistgrip could be tweaked hard without giving offence.**

Bottom-end punch was good without being startling—the engine gave its best results in the middle and upper rpm range. On the open road it was usual to let speed build up to an indicated 45 mph (true 42) in second and 60 mph (true 56) in third before changing up.

The needle would climb steadily to the 70 mark and anchor itself there on half throttle. Full throttle brought a further 5 mph and under favourable conditions, with the bulkily clad rider normally seated, the needle would hover on 80 indefinitely.

Provided the engine was allowed to spin freely, hill climbing was first class; only the steepest main-road gradients pulled the speed down appreciably.

Few vertical twins are vibrationless but the ES 400 is no great sinner. A tremor was felt through the handlebar when the engine was spinning fast but was never at any time uncomfortable.

**Light and smooth in operation, the clutch showed no objection to a succession of six full-throttle standing starts when the performance figures were obtained. But, before the first start of the day it was advisable to free the plates by pumping the kick-starter with the lever pulled up to the handlebar.**

Well chosen, the lower three gear ratios are slightly higher than on the Navigator, though top is the same.

Movement of the gear pedal was light and short. Noiseless upward changes were easily made but downward changes required precise blipping of the throttle if slight clashing of the dogs was to be avoided.

There was not the slightest difficulty in identifying the characteristically precise Norton steering. Absence of top hamper contributes to effortless handling and the ES 400 could be placed almost to a hair and cornered with utter confidence.

With the footrest rubbers well chamfered in the 2,000 miles already logged by the ES 400, the only limits to cornering angle were the centre-stand extension on the left and footrest hanger bolt on the right. Stability on slippery surfaces was remarkable.

Firm at low speeds, the front fork cushioned road shocks well at higher speeds. In contrast the rear-suspension units were soft in action and this gave rise to slight pitching and occasional weaving on fast bumpy bends.

# SPECIFICATION

*ENGINE:* Norton 384 cc (66x56 mm) overhead-valve parallel twin. One-piece forged-steel crankshaft supported in ball bearing on timing side and roller bearing on drive side; shell-type plain big-end bearings. Separate light-alloy cylinder heads; compression ratio 7.9 to 1. Dry-sump lubrication; oil-tank capacity 5 pints.

*CARBURETTOR:* Amal Monobloc; air slide operated by handlebar lever.

*ELECTRICAL EQUIPMENT:* Coil ignition with twin contact breakers. Wipac 85-watt alternator, with rotor mounted on left-hand end of crankshaft, charging two Exide 6-volt 12-amp-hour batteries (in series) through rectifier. Separate Lucas electric starter driving crankshaft by chain. Wipac 7in-diameter headlamp with 50/40-watt pre-focus light unit.

*TRANSMISSION:* Norton four-speed foot-change gearbox in unit with crankcase. Gear ratios: Bottom, 15.4 to 1; second, 9.62 to 1; third, 6.98 to 1; top, 5.72 to 1. Multi-plate clutch with bonded friction facings running in oil. Primary chain, ⅜in duplex in cast-aluminium oil-bath case. Rear chain ½ x 0.305in with guard over top run. Engine rpm at 30 mph in top gear, 2,400.

*FUEL CAPACITY:* 3 gallons.

*TYRES:* Avon: front 3.00 x 19in Speedmaster Mk II; rear 3.25 x 18in Safety Mileage Mk II.

*BRAKES:* 8in diameter front, 7in diameter rear, both with finger adjusters.

*SUSPENSION:* Norton telescopic front fork with hydraulic damping. Pivoted rear fork controlled by Girling spring-and-hydraulic units with three-position adjustment for load.

*WHEELBASE:* 50½in. Ground clearance, 6in. Seat height, 30in. (All unladen.)

*WEIGHT:* 354 lb. fully equipped, with full oil tank and approximately one gallon of petrol.

*PRICE:* £259 10s including British purchase tax.

*ROAD TAX:* £4 10s. a year; £1 13s. for four months.

*MAKERS:* Norton Motors, Ltd, Plumstead Road, Woolwich, London, SE18.

*DESCRIPTION:* Motor Cycle, 31 January 1963.

# PERFORMANCE DATA

*MEAN MAXIMUM SPEED:* Bottom, 36 mph.*; second, 58 mph*; third, 75 mph; top, 78 mph. *Valve float occuring.

*HIGHEST ONE-WAY SPEED:* 83 mph (conditions: light tail wind; 13-stone rider wearing two-piece waxed-cotton suit and overboots).

*MEAN ACCELERATION:*

|  | 10-30 mph | 20-40 mph | 30-50 mph |
|---|---|---|---|
| Bottom | 3.4 sec | — | — |
| Second | 5 sec | 5.4 sec | 5 sec |
| Third | — | 7 sec | 7.2 sec |
| Top | — | 9 sec | 9 sec |

Mean speed at end of quarter-mile from rest: 73 mph.

Mean time to cover standing quarter-mile: 17.8 sec.

*PETROL CONSUMPTION:* At 30 mph, 81 mpg; at 40 mph, 79 mpg; at 50 mph, 64 mpg; at 60 mph, 51 mpg.

*BRAKING:* From 30 mph to rest, 38ft (surface, dry tarmac).

*TURNING CIRCLE:* 15ft.

*MINIMUM NON-SNATCH SPEED:* 16 mph in top gear.

*WEIGHT PER CC:* 0.92 lb.

The head-on view on the left emphasizes the slimness of the ES 400 and the excellent positioning of the flashing turn indicators on the ends of the handlebar

*Below:* The ES 400 shares with the three-fifty Navigator its enviable reputation for unsurpassed roadholding. Stability on wet roads was outstanding

Brakes on the model tested were below Norton standard—both lacked bite and the rear was particularly spongy. However, stopping power from high speed was considerably better than is suggested by the figure in the performance panel.

**Headlight intensity was markedly good, the wide beam spread allowing daytime cruising speeds to be used in absolute safety after dark, but a sharper cut-off to the dipped beam would have been appreciated by oncoming drivers.**

It was a change to ride a machine with a strident horn note; that of the Norton was loud enough even for high-speed motorway riding.

Most routine maintenance tasks were easily carried out—but not so valve adjustment. This entailed removing the petrol tank; and detaching the exhaust rocker covers was a bit of a fiddle because of the proximity of the steering-head gusset plates. The adjustment itself, by means of eccentric spindles, is straightforward.

Some difficulty was experienced in replacing the tool box lid because of its distortion; it is secured by a single slotted screw.

Throughout the 700 miles of the test the power unit remained completely oiltight and oil consumption was negligible. Since the petrol tap has no reserve position a careful check had to be kept on mileage.

With hard riding, the refuelling range was about 150 miles—on the short side for a machine of this type.

**Smartly finished in black and matt silver, with chromium-plated mudguards, the ES 400, provides a lot of fun and is certain of an enthusiastic following among those who want a "three-fifty" with the plus of more power and luxury.**

*Above can be seen the cast aluminium case enclosing the chain drive from the Lucas electric starter to the left-hand end of the crankshaft*

*Right: A separate set of contact points serves each cylinder. Access for adjustment merely involves removal of a cover held by two screws*

*Below: Matching the oil tank on the other side, the left-hand pannier compartment houses the tool roll and quickly detachable batteries*

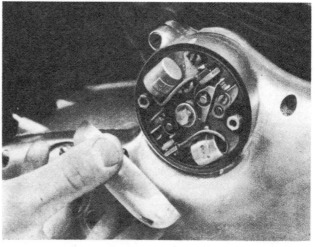

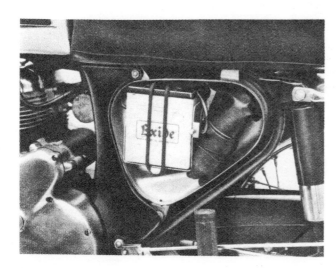

# 647 cc by DAVID DIXON
# DUNSTALL DOMINATOR

## Road tests of new models

HOW about this for a dream? Two-miles-a-minute top whack; out-accelerate a Manx Norton; cover a standing-start quarter-mile in sprint time yet easily restart on a 1 in 4 gradient; tick-tock idling at 500 rpm. This dream travels under the name, Dunstall Dominator. On road and track it provided me with some of the most scintillating miles I've ever covered on a production bike.

Draped with Dunstall goodies, it attracted almost embarrassing attention, not only from youngsters but mums and dads. It even lit up many an old grandfather's eyes. This lavishly bedecked Norton is one of the most arresting creations ever to grace a road. Dunstall does for the 650SS what Francis Beart achieves with his Nortons—creates a work of art. Dunstall, though, sells the goodies over the counter. The customer gets to work and can thus trim the bike as he pleases.

*Left: The 650 SS engine. Raised compression ratio and improved breathing give added zip. Exhaust pipes and rear-set footrests are Dunstall extras. Above: Bend-swinging is a joy at all times*

Most economical way is to order a new 650SS with the full Dunstall treatment. Then it costs only £35 above list price. If you want even more urge, invest another £30 on internal mods.

The model I used had been given the full treatment, inside and out. A glance at the specification panel will give you the full picture.

Believing that dropped bars and rearward rests are best for the track, I took the beauty to Brands Hatch for a few laps, where Dave Degens had already tried to wear it out. With KLG FE220 plugs in, the bike was ready for racing. And a shattering performance it gave. Taking the revs to the recommended limit of 6,800 in the gears, I soon found that I easily had the legs of five-hundred Manx Nortons.

# *Specification and Performance*

**ENGINE:** Norton 647 cc (68 × 89mm) overhead-valve parallel twin. Crankshaft supported in ball and roller bearings; plain big-end bearings. Light-alloy cylinder head; compression ratio, 10.5 to 1. Dry-sump lubrication; oil-tank capacity, 4½ pints.

**CARBURETTORS:** Two Amal Monoblocs; air slides operated by handlebar lever.

**ELECTRICAL EQUIPMENT:** Lucas magneto with auto-advance. Lucas 12-volt lighting system with RM/19 alternator charging twin Lucas six-volt, 13-amp-hour batteries. Lucas 7in-diameter headlamp with pre-focus light unit.

**TRANSMISSION:** AMC four-speed foot-change gear box. Gear ratios: bottom, 11.6; second, 7.57; third, 5.52; top, 4.53 to 1. Multi-plate clutch with bonded friction facings. Primary chain, ⅜ 0.305in in pressed-steel oil-bath case. Rear chain, ⅝ ¼in with guard over top run. Engine rpm at 30 mph in top gear, 1,750.

**FUEL CAPACITY:** 5 gallons.

**TYRES:** Avon; 3.00 19in Speedmaster Mk II front; 3.50 19in Grand Prix rear.

**BRAKES:** 8in-diameter front; 7in diameter rear; both 1⅛in wide; finger adjusters.

**SUSPENSION:** Norton Roadholder telescopic front fork with hydraulic damping. Pivoted rear fork controlled by Girling spring-and-hydraulic units with three-position adjustment for load.

**DIMENSIONS:** Wheelbase, 55½in. Ground clearance, 5½in. Both unladen.

**WEIGHT** 364 lb with full oil tank and one gallon of petrol.

**SPECIAL EQUIPMENT:** Dunstall exhaust pipes and silencers; glass-fibre seat and five-gallon fuel tank; racing brake linings; rear-set footrests, gear change pedal and brake pedal; clip-on handlebars; light-alloy mudguards, wheel rims and front-fork ring nuts; chromium plated primary chain-case, oil tank, rear chainguard, instrument mounting bracket, suspension springs (not on test machine), headlamp shell and brackets, and battery-box lid.

**SPECIAL ENGINE MODIFICATIONS:** High-compression pistons (10.5 to 1); 1⅜in-bore Monobloc carburettors; 1⅜in-bore inlet tracts and enlarged inlet- and exhaust-valve throats; finned, light-alloy induction spacers; lightened and polished rockers and cam followers; increased-feed oil pump.

**PRICE:** Complete, £416 0s 10d, including British purchase tax.

**ROAD TAX:** £8 a year, £2 19s for four months.

**SUPPLIER:** Paul Dunstall, Ltd., 156 Well Hall Road, Eltham, London, SE9.

## PERFORMANCE

**MEAN MAXIMUM SPEEDS:** Bottom, °46mph; second, °71 mph; third, °98 mph; top 120 mph. °Taken at peak power, 6,800 rpm.

**HIGHEST ONE-WAY SPEED:** 121 mph (conditions; still air top gear, 4.32 to 1 : 12½-stone rider wearing racing leathers).

**MEAN ACCELERATION:**

|  | 10-30 mph | 20-40 mph | 30-50 mph |
|---|---|---|---|
| Bottom | 2.2 sec | 2.6 sec | |
| Second | 3 sec | 3.2 sec | 3 sec |
| Third | — | 4.8 sec | 4.6 sec |
| Top | — | 5.8 sec | 5.4 sec |

Mean speed at end of standing quarter-mile: 96 mph. Mean time to cover standing quarter-mile: 13.8 sec.

**WEIGHT PER CC:** 0.56 lb.

*Left: This jewel is chromium plated. Dunstall extras include the glass-fibre petrol tank, racing seat and clip-on handlebars. Below: The Dominator being whanged around Brands Hatch*

Power was right there from the moment the twistgrip was tweaked—brutal, searing urge right up to maximum. And that sort of performance is just what pays off on the short straights of Brands. Before shutting off for Paddock Bend, I had a glimpse of 110 mph on the speedometer, with plenty more to come.

To the notorious Paddock Bend itself, the Dommy clung as only a Norton can, with just a suggestion of tail wag at the bottom of the drop—even the best bred tails wag here.

Then, when clamping the anchors hard on for Druids, I recognized what a wise investment racing linings are on a super-sporting lot such as this. Contemporary Norton brakes are among the best on the road; with the addition of racing linings they are easily the greatest.

Diving downhill out of Druids into Bottom Straight, and around the ripples of Kidney, the Dominator proved remarkably steady for a production machine—a tribute, I would think, to the matched Girling racing rear-suspension units.

A pity that many production racing enthusiasts don't realize that an unsteady front end can often be cured by fitting a decent pair of matched suspension units. . . .

Tyres are a very personal fad with racing men—some get on better with one make or type than with another, and the choice can make a world of difference to your reaction to a production racer.

I, for one, applaud Avons for continuing to market their GP rear covers with a high-hysteresis mix like that of the racing covers which went out

*Purposeful and fast. The crouch afforded by the dropped bars and rear-set footrests is comfortable for high-speed cruising*

*Spacers between the carburettors and head lengthen the induction tracts. They are intended to give more top-end power and keep the mixture cool*

of production about 18 months ago.

Identical in appearance with the old racing tyre, the GP fitted to the Dominator felt just as good as the pukka job. On the front was a standard ribbed Speedmaster Mark II.

The Dommy could be laid over until the right footrest and gear pedal caressed the road—and the rest is nearly 3in higher than standard!

(Before I rescued the bike from him, Degens had worn down to the side ribs of the front tyre and put flats on the bottom loops of the exhaust pipes. Later, Dunstall replaced these pipes with new ones guaranteed not to touch down until after the rider did!)

**How did lap times compare with those of a pukka racer?** Battler Degens, a **Brands scratcher in the best tradition, was wearing out the Dommy at the rate of about 61.6s a lap, compared with approximately 59.6s on the six-fifty Domiracer.**

No scratcher, Dixon was taking about 1.4s more than Degens on the Dominator.

Degens and Rex Butcher—another Brands ace—were both so tickled by the performance that Dunstall had to work hard to restrain them from entering his toy in the 1,000 cc races at Brands!

So much for track testing. Now for road work.

Perhaps I should put the record straight right now by repeating that I dislike dropped bars on the road because, apart from giving the impression that one is aping

the racers, the low riding position transfers too much weight to the wrists during traffic riding and may give one a crick in the neck.

Moreover, as I found on the Dominator, steering lock is restricted enough to make manoeuvring in confined spaces a headache. (This is shortly to be rectified by more cutaway on Dunstall's petrol tanks, so that the hands are not trapped on full lock.)

Let's be fair, though. The Dunstall riding position is tops when you are nipping along on a wide throttle opening—at over 90 mph.

**As I imply, speeds nudging the three-figure mark are small beer—105 mph is a touring gait. Tweak the grip and 110 comes up on the speedometer which, incidentally, proved no more than 2 mph fast up to 115 mph; then it was slow by 5 mph!**

What price do you pay in return for such spine-tingling performance? Certainly not hand-tingling vibration, for the Dominator engine had obviously been carefully built and was one of the smoothest Nortons I've ridden.

The megaphone-style silencers modelled on the old Gold Star BSA pattern—gave a sporty rasp when the engine was spinning smartly. No harm for motorway use but you required a disciplined right hand in built-up areas.

A handful of grip hard at low engine speeds—say below 4,000 rpm—provoked the tinkle of pinking, although 100-octane fuel was used. Obviously the 10.5-to-1 special pistons are right on the safe limit for road use.

Starting required a hefty swing on the crank and I found this easiest to do with the bike on the centre stud. Provided only that the air lever was closed, first-kick cold starts were usual.

Few engines of such performance will tick-over at 500 rpm or provide a woffling 2,000 rpm for traffic work, but the Dommy was docile enough for this.

And, with standard gearing, it would restart on the 1-in-4 test hill at the MIRA proving ground. Only moderate clutch coaxing was necessary for a protest-free pull-away. On the 1-in-3 gradient, only

slightly more clutch slipping was called for to avoid too much pinking.

How does the Dunstall Dominator compare with a standard 650SS? Back in February, 1962, colleague Vic Willoughby—who is two stones lighter than I am and considerably shorter—obtained a mean 111 mph, and a best of 118 mph with a strong three-quarter wind. He recorded a standing quarter-mile in 14 seconds and terminal speed of 95 mph.

My acceleration was hampered slightly by a damp track, provoking wheelspin.

Because the engine was over-buzzing, top gear was upped to 4.32 to 1 for mean maximum and fastest one-way speeds.

Two shortcomings common to Nortons applied to the Dunstall job. The test bike was fitted with the 1964 pattern $\frac{5}{8} \times \frac{1}{4}$in rear chain. It stretched with lightning rapidity during wet-weather riding. Latest models have the $\frac{5}{8} \times \frac{3}{8}$in chain.

In spite of being reinforced, the oil-tank top-mounting bracket fractured. And the right-hand exhaust pipe flange also fractured, allowing the pipe to come loose; these flanges have now been strengthened.

**These points apart, the Dunstall Dominator is one of the most scintillating mounts to have come my way. It looks just what it is—a thoroughbred sporting lot with a remarkable all-round performance.**

*That lean and hungry look—head on. The exhaust pipes are well tucked in to avoid grounding*

WITHOUT question, the Jubilee is a very pleasant little mount—lively, reasonably fast, comfortable, economical, and smart, and it handles well. But it is let down by poor factory spares service, indifferent electrics and, in some cases, by unreliability. That is the view of the majority; and to add force is the lowish overall mark they award the little Norton.

Of the 50 riders who returned our questionnaire forms, 31 said the Norton was a good buy. Thirty-two would buy another Norton. These figures, of course, represent percentages of 62 and 64.

As usual, there are extremes of opinion. Says Ronald Baker, 18, of Purley, Surrey: "Out of all the motor cycles my brother and I have owned or ridden, this fine little fellow deserves special mention."

On the other hand, 21-year-old telephone engineer Geoff Macintosh, of East Ham, London, is surprised that the "Jubbly" was considered a good enough bike for a riders' report!

With 520,000 Jubilee miles to their credit, the 56 contributors have an average age of 20 and they have been riding bikes for four years.

# 249 cc NORTON JUBILEE

gears are absolutely spot on.

"Forty-five in second comes up really quickly and the very good third will take me to 68 mph. A cruising speed of 50 to 55 mph can be held indefinitely."

Others place cruising speed rather higher—65 mph is average—and the Norton twin engine is generally acknowledged flexible.

One thing most are agreed on, though—the engine is noisy. Many complain of valve gear rattle, especially when a fairing is fitted.

Acceleration? Good, report our testers. The road test 19.4s for the standing quarter-mile is widely seconded.

## Starting

**EXCELLENT** is the first word—and the last, too. Everyone agrees that the Jubilee starts extraordinarily well.

It is usual to start without even flooding the carburettor. "The Jubilee takes first prize," opines one contributor.

## Fuel Consumption

**NO MOANS** here. Contributors' averages work out at 71 mpg overall; and everyone seems happy. This figure is well in line with that obtained in our road test.

## Performance

**TOP SPEED** of 75 mph, the average claimed by contributors, ties in very nicely with the figures obtained in our road test two years ago.

One or two, like Derek Cutcliffe of Barrow-in-Furness, find that they can never better 60-odd. But, on the other hand, claims of 80 or 85 mph are made by some.

"For an unsouped standard engine," reports 23-year-old Wilmot Sant of Winsford in Cheshire, "the performance is excellent. Second and third

*Above left: Timing-side view of the neat 249 cc power unit of the Jubilee. Above: Peter Fraser tests a 1963 model—handling is agreed as being one of the Norton's best features*

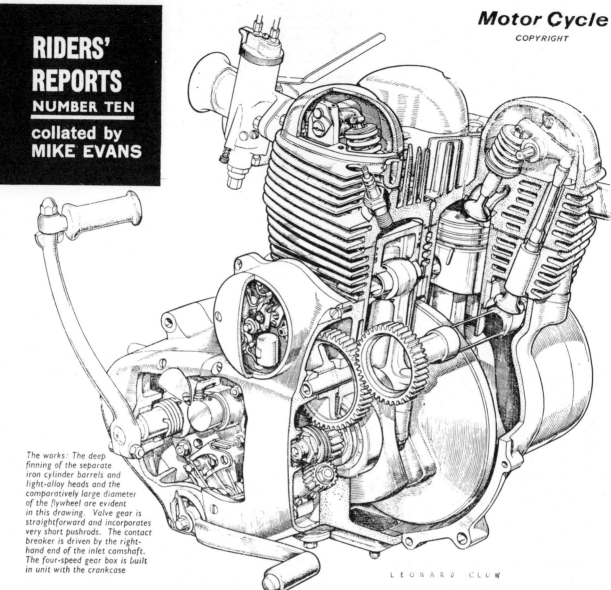

### RIDERS' REPORTS
#### NUMBER TEN
collated by
MIKE EVANS

*Motor Cycle*
COPYRIGHT

*The works: The deep finning of the separate iron cylinder barrels and light-alloy heads and the comparatively large diameter of the flywheel are evident in this drawing. Valve gear is straightforward and incorporates very short pushrods. The contact breaker is driven by the right-hand end of the inlet camshaft. The four-speed gear box is built in unit with the crankcase*

LEONARD CLOW

## Oil Tightness

THIS is a special category in this report since very few contributors fail to make comments on the oil-tightness. And only a few are complimentary.

Says Arthur Stephens of Wrexham, North Wales: "Oil leaks from the contact-breaker cover, from the top of the primary chaincase where the alternator leads emerge and from the base plate covering the return pump."

Many others particularly mention leaks from the rocker-box covers. Derek Cutcliffe says that his machine has never been free from leaks since he bought it.

Final word on this subject is a collective one from all contributors. They can award no more than 40 per cent for the Jubilee's oil-retaining capabilities.

## Handling

"GREAT! I can throw it around corners with great ease." And that's just one version of the general praise that comes the way of the little two-fifty.

"The safest of my eight machines," reports 58-year-old Fred Waller of Manchester. Confirms William Prosser, 20, of West Hartlepool, "Handling is excellent—on wet or dry roads, on smooth or rutted surfaces."

But there is a reservation from 18-year-old Graham Griffiths of Dewsbury: "Why must testers attempt to lead people to believe that the Jubilee handles like a featherbed?"

"Let's be fair, the Jubilee is average—but it can't possibly be compared with my latest bike, a Norton Atlas."

Some mention that front-fork damping could be better.

## Braking

PLENTY of power to stop you, avers one reader; best thing about the bike, reports another. They are in the minority.

"Considering the performance, I call the brakes only barely adequate and an 8in stopper similar to the Naviga-tor's would be much appreci-ated at the front end."

That's from my namesake, 21-year-old David Evans of Sutton-in-Ashfield, Notting-hamshire.

Agreeing, William Prosser says that the rear brake of his machine is reasonable—but only just; and the front is poor.

## Transmission

ONE of the best points of the machine, according to all accounts. "Beyond reproach," says one north-eastern reader. "The gear box gives no trouble whatsoever and always gives good service.

The clutch, like the rest of the transmission, is excellent, according to 18-year-old David

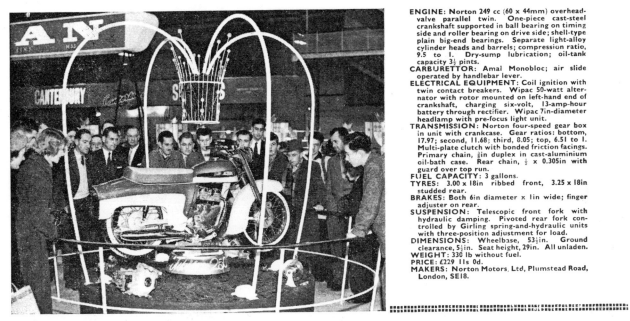

**ENGINE:** Norton 249 cc (60 x 44mm) overhead-valve parallel twin. One-piece cast-steel crankshaft supported in ball bearing on timing side and roller bearing on drive side; shell-type plain big-end bearings. Separate light-alloy cylinder heads and barrels; compression ratio, 9.5 to 1. Dry-sump lubrication; oil-tank capacity 3½ pints.
**CARBURETTOR:** Amal Monobloc; air slide operated by handlebar lever.
**ELECTRICAL EQUIPMENT:** Coil ignition with twin contact breakers. Wipac 50-watt alternator with rotor mounted on left-hand end of crankshaft, charging six-volt, 13-amp-hour battery through rectifier. Wipac 7in-diameter headlamp with pre-focus light unit.
**TRANSMISSION:** Norton four-speed gear box in unit with crankcase. Gear ratios: bottom, 17.97; second, 11.68; third, 8.05; top, 6.51 to 1. Multi-plate clutch with bonded friction facings. Primary chain, ⅜in duplex in cast-aluminium oil-bath case. Rear chain, ½ x 0.305in with guard over top run.
**FUEL CAPACITY:** 3 gallons.
**TYRES:** 3.00 x 18in ribbed front, 3.25 x 18in studded rear.
**BRAKES:** Both 6in diameter x 1in wide; finger adjuster on rear.
**SUSPENSION:** Telescopic front fork with hydraulic damping. Pivoted rear fork controlled by Girling spring-and-hydraulic units with three-position adjustment for load.
**DIMENSIONS:** Wheelbase, 53½in. Ground clearance, 5½in. Seat height, 29in. All unladen.
**WEIGHT:** 330 lb without fuel.
**PRICE:** £229 11s 0d.
**MAKERS:** Norton Motors, Ltd, Plumstead Road, London, SE18.

*Newcomer. The Jubilee was introduced in time for Earls Court in 1958—it was one of the highlights of the Show*

Grover, a mechanical engineering apprentice of Harrow.

He continues: "I have never experienced slip and the take-up is so smooth that sweet gear changes at any revs are the rule."

A few say that kick-starter springs and gear-change springs last no time at all. However, this is not the experience of the majority.

A tip comes from John Jordon, 34, of Glasgow: "Don't overdo filling of the primary chaincase."

## Electrics

**SOME** contributors like their electrical set up. But the majority are a bit scathing. Particular wrath is directed at flimsy switches and attachments.

Jokes Eddie Christian, 25, of Enfield, Middlesex: "I never had the chance to neglect my maintenance—the electrics saw to that. I was always working on the electrical system."

*Three-quarter overhead view—a point criticised by some reporters is the handlebar design. Universal patterns cannot be fitted*

"In 11,000 miles I went through £2 10s-worth of main bulbs," says David Beckerson of Chichester.

On the other hand, take the view of Colin Ibbertson, 18, of Rotherham: "Compared with electrics I have met on other bikes, I would say that the Wipac set-up on the Jubilee is reliable and well laid out."

"Very good," confirms Thomas Clark of Westminster, while Dennis Wakefield of Alcester leaves us gasping with his "perfection."

Bias is undoubtedly in favour of the "don't like" brigade—63 per cent is the score when disregarding the horn. If the horn is taken into account, the figure drops much lower!

Main grumbles are on the score of reliability, however. The lighting is acknowledged adequate.

Criticism of horns on the majority of English machines is usual in any riders' report. A charming piece of horn lore comes from Eddie Christian: "I finally got sick of the stupid thing and smashed it with my fist!"

## Detail Finish

"**BEAUTIFUL!**" exclaims Derek Cutcliffe. "In red and cream and sparkling chromium, it's a pleasure to see. I didn't buy this bike to learn on—I fell in love with it and just had to have it!

"The only thing is that I have a constant battle with the rust on the chromium of the front wheel. Weekly attention is needed to keep this rust-free."

For a contrary view, just read what another reader has to say: "Paintwork is pitifully inadequate and, at times, it is as if there is no undercoat, the way the paint dulls and flakes. The chromium work, with one or two exceptions, is also poor."

As usual, the true consensus of opinion lies midway between the two extreme views. Mediator is the 63-per-cent mark in the table of votes.

## Riding Comfort

**ONLY** one other category tops 90 per cent in the table and riding comfort is just a short way from being top of the poll.

Therefore, it is not surprising to find that few quibble over this aspect.

A couple of the sportier boys complain about the lack of racy equipment for the Jubilee. There isn't, they say, the proliferation of rear-sets or drop bars for this smallest Norton that is common for the bigger brothers.

But then, why should there be?

## Service

**COMBINE** factory and dealer service and you get a low result of 39 per cent. Take

*Below: Latest model, with its chromium-plated mudguards, is the smartest of Jubilees—full marks are given for appearance. Below left: This 6in front-brake unit receives little praise. Below right: Twin contact breaker is readily accessible*

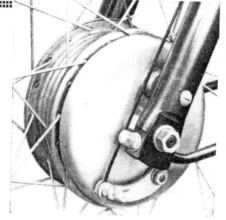

factory service alone and the 29 per cent is rather stunning.

To a large extent, factory service colours the service a rider receives from his dealer. If the dealer can't get spares from the factory he is going to be in the rider's bad books, whether or not it is his fault.

Typical comment comes from a London enthusiast: "I once waited eight weeks for a nut to secure the alternator rotor to the mainshaft.

"I eventually wrote a nasty letter to Nortons. Two days later I received a nut with the compliments of the service department, together with a catalogue of the latest Norton machines. The nut didn't fit!"

"Service? From Nortons, shocking; from Taylor Matterson, excellent." So says a 23-year-old Cheshire rider.

Gorbals, Glasgow, rider John Jordan always receives prompt information from the factory. But for spares he patronizes Harold Daniell: "Nothing's a bother to this chap—my wee bits were sent right to my cave."

Both Taylor Matterson and Harold Daniell are mentioned honourably in other letters.

An anonymous owner complains that he received his instruction book, containing the running-in tips, one week and 400 miles after the purchase.

However, this is not confined to Nortons—several manufacturers use this system of sending out the instruction book upon receipt of the guarantee card.

There is little doubt that this is a valid point. The instruction book should be with the bike when it is collected from the dealer.

Reports from readers who have had recent experience of factory-supplied spares strike a reassuring note.

"About a year ago Norton spares were a nightmare to obtain and often expensive, too. But the position seems to have improved."

That is the opinion of 20-year-old Ian Pointon of Burton-on-Trent.

Another reader, Colin Ibbertson, says that the longest he has had to wait is a couple of days.

## Reliability

VERY FEW contributors have kind words to say on this score. And several of them

## YOUR OPINION AT A GLANCE

After sending in their reports, readers were asked to complete a questionnaire in which they answered specific questions according to the formula good, middling or poor.

In calculating these figures we have allowed two points for good and one point for middling. Poor got nothing.

### THE MARKS ARE GIVEN AS PERCENTAGES

| | | | | | |
|---|---|---|---|---|---|
| Acceleration | 77 | Accessibility | 52 | Workmanship | 61 |
| Flexibility | 72 | Steering | 87 | Quality of finish | 63 |
| Smoothness | 65 | Suspension (front) | 68 | Lighting | 67 |
| Starting | 93 | (rear) | 86 | Horn | 12 |
| Oil Tightness | 40 | Smoothness of | | Other Electrics | 60 |
| Reliability | 59 | Controls | 77 | Tool Kit | 60 |
| Clutch | 70 | Riding Position | 92 | Spares from Factory | 29 |
| Gear Box | 71 | Brakes | 63 | Spares from Dealer | 49 |
| Delivery Tune* | 70 | Mudguarding | 77 | | |

*Secondhand machines not taken into account.

Is the machine a good buy? 62 per cent say yes.
Would you buy another Norton? 64 per cent say yes.
OVERALL MARK (averaging the above percentages): 65 per cent.

## OUR ROAD TEST VIEW

MEAN MAXIMUM SPEEDS: Bottom, 35 mph; second, 55 mph; third, 70 mph; top, 73 mph.
HIGHEST ONE-WAY SPEED: 75 mph.
STANDING QUARTER-MILE: 19.4s with terminal speed of 66 mph.
BRAKING: From 30 mph to rest, 30ft.
FUEL CONSUMPTION: At 30 mph, 104 mpg; at 40 mph, 88 mpg; at 50 mph, 76 mpg; at 60 mph, 64 mpg.

have only short experience with the Jubilee.

"Although I had the bike for 21 months," reports David Evans, "it was in running order for only about half that time—and when it was on the road there was often some minor defect apparent. I spent £80 on repairs—including fitting new pistons, main bearings, big ends and gear box."

Another reporter says that the machine is reliable in that there are no unexpected breakdowns, but general wear is above average. At 10,000 miles new big ends and main bearings were required on his Jubilee. At 18,000 miles new cam followers were fitted and the cams were either built up or replaced.

Yet with 10 years' motor cycling behind him, Fred Waller says that the Jubilee is the most reliable of his eight machines!

Wilmot Sant points out that it's a good job he can strip the engine himself or he would run up a fortune in bills. Three years' riding have seen main-bearing and big-end replacements at 12-monthly intervals. And one new crankshaft has been fitted.

Perhaps it is a coincidence that his summing-up paragraph is headed "Overhaul View?"

## Accessibility

THE 52-per-cent mark is rather low in view of the number of seemingly happily satisfied readers. "Everything dead easy to work on," reports Wilmot Sant.

Robert Dykes, 27, of Featherstone, Staffs, rates accessibility as good: "The tank is really qd—but oh! those rocker covers!"

Accessibility is not so good in the view of William Prosser: "For example, to replace the clutch cable it is necessary to remove the exhaust pipe and silencer, the footrest, the timing-side rear panel and the rocker covers!"

Many more mention this particular aspect—and it is probable that this is mainly responsible for the low mark. Nevertheless, the factory maintains that all this dismantling work is unnecessary if you go about the job the right way.

## Overall View

A NEAT summing up comes from David Evans: "The Jubilee fills a vacant spot in the current range of British bikes, that of a 250 cc four-stroke twin, for which there is an obvious demand. But unfortunately it doesn't fill it as well as it might."

David Grover points out that the Norton is a fine touring machine which will give good performance consistently if maintained regularly.

He thoroughly recommends it to anyone buying their first bike, for it is docile and easily controlled; yet it will satisfy the newcomer long after he has passed his test.

Even more enthusiastic is Wilmot Sant: "If you're mechanically minded it's a great British two-fifty. A really beautiful bike to look at and to listen to."

The Jubilee does have many endearing qualities—it handles well, it runs well, it is manoeuvrable and good to look at.

Yet out of some 50 reporters, about two-fifths of them wouldn't recommend it. Why?

Obviously some opinions have been influenced by the slow spares service that followed the factory move from Birmingham to Woolwich. This disruption was felt all along the line for far too long. Happily, there has been some improvement this year.

Then again, as David Grover says, the Jubilee is basically a straightforward roadster without claims to the super-sports class. Some readers seem to have expected too much and probably used every ounce of performance on tap.

Perhaps it should be borne in mind, too, that a high proportion of Jubilee owners are learners or are comparatively inexperienced and are, therefore, harder on their machines than experienced riders.

Above: Battery is handy on later models—although owners of enclosed Jubilees experience difficulties

This 1965 model was borrowed from Comerfords for a test ride. Here Mike Evans gets the feel of the little Norton

# 745cc NORTON COMMANDO

**No new model introduced in the past decade has made such a big impact as the Norton Commando. It was first seen at the London Show last September and greeted with enthusiasm, though in some cases the welcome was reserved until production machines were available.**

*Motor Cycle* road test

They were ready in May and experience on the road showed that the Norton marque had come back with a bang. The terrific power of the modified 745 cc Atlas twin was a new experience now it was rubber-mounted in an ingenious frame which did, in fact, virtually eliminate the effects of high-frequency vibration.

The sceptics retired to swallow their doubts. Overnight the Commando became the most-sought-after large-capacity roadster on the market.

Something more exhaustive than an orthodox road test was called for if the full potential of this bike was to be assessed. Thus TYT 63F was flown across the Channel in July after the routine performance figures had been obtained at the MIRA proving ground.

To say that the Commando showed up well would be grudging praise. In a 2,000-mile trip it proved a distance-devourer *par excellence*. Yet it was equally satisfying to ride in heavy traffic; on byroads in Italy and Switzerland, and high on alpine passes. It gave a new dimension to the sort of riding we have known on parallel twins in the past 20 years.

In short, the Commando provides an over-115 mph maximum speed, an acceleration graph like the side of a house, relatively light fuel consumption at high cruising speeds, woofling docility when required and a riding position that ensures complete comfort. All this, with a commendably low level of mechanical and exhaust noise.

## At home

The basic Atlas engine is no newcomer. Its Commando application involved far more than installing it with a forward inclination in rubber mountings. Much development work has been completed. While it retains its capacity for producing beefy torque at low revolutions it is equally at home revving freely at

6,800 rpm and pushing out nearly 60 bhp.

In fact, with the standard 19-tooth gear-box sprocket fitted, the maximum speed of 117 mph obtained equals 7,200 rpm. The engine has ample margins and revs of this order are completely safe, but a 21-tooth sprocket is available if preferred. For high-speed riding it is, in practice, rarely necessary to exceed 5,000 rpm in any gear. The spread of power is so wide that, for example, a whiff

**The comfortable riding position and taut feel of the Commando enable it to be ridden with satisfying verve on twisty roads**

of throttle in top gear moves the speedometer needle very smartly from, say, 75 to 100 mph—invaluable when mile-eating on the fast, though far-from-straight, major roads in eastern France.

With such an ample supply of power, pass storming in the Alps was a really enjoyable exercise. Gradient and traffic baulks could be dealt with by the zippy yet unobtrusive acceleration.

### Less orthodox

It was no hardship to use the indirect gears when necessary. The ratios are happily chosen and could be engaged rapidly and positively—from third to top as easily and quietly without clutch operation as with it.

The clutch is one of the Commando's less orthodox features. It has a diaphragm (with four friction plates) and is capable of dealing with more torque than the earlier, coil-spring clutch. It takes up the drive a shade more quickly but, apart from that, is better in every way. It proved light to operate, freed completely at all times and showed no signs of slipping or becoming overheated.

Handling is well up to the traditional Norton standards. The Commando has that taut, manageable feel at all speeds that encourages clean, stylish cornering. It keeps on line, can be flicked confidently through close-coupled S-bends and does not waver when banked over on bumpy surfaces.

The silencers limit banking angle but not to an unrealistic extent. Side and centre stands are well tucked away though they are slightly difficult to reach and push down with the foot.

### Slight flutter

Steering is rock steady at all speeds above about 40 mph. Below that, there is slight handlebar flutter if the hands are re-

moved from the grips. It is unnoticed in normal circumstances and might never be apparent unless the no-hands test is made.

The twin-leading-shoe front brake was, as expected, excellent, but the single-leading-shoe rear brake lacked power and occasionally failed to free properly. On the whole, braking was satisfactory (31 ft from 30 mph) but no more.

As mentioned earlier, the rider is well insulated from engine vibration. This factor alone is a comfort boost, especially on a 400-plus daily mileages such as undertaken during the text. But there is more to Commando comfort than this.

The riding position—the placing of the seat, handlebar grips, footrests and

**Inclined forward in the new frame, the 745 cc, twin-cylinder Atlas engine packs beefy power right through the range**

controls—is spot on and the only possible criticism might be that the well-padded dualseat, at 31 in from ground level, is a bit high for some riders.

Starting was invariably easy—usually one prod on the pedal was enough. With the engine cold the only difference was to close the air lever. With next-to-no warming up, the engine would idle re-

**The Commando has a completely new frame layout yet retains the powerful, thoroughbred lines long associated with high-performance Nortons**

liably at only a shade over 600 rpm. Despite much hard riding, the twin Amal Concentric carburettors retained their slow-running settings and balance.

The electrical side, too, was faultless. During the continental trip it proved to be properly weatherproofed. The bike was usually parked in the open and on one occasion it was ridden for 10 hours in continuous rain. The engine never missed a beat.

Lighting permitted 80-mph cruising in the dark. A much-appreciated practical feature is the easily-operated toggle switch in the headlamp shell. Very useful, too, is the headlamp-flasher button in the dipswitch/horn console on the left side of the handlebar.

Another practical feature is the rear-chain oiler. It kept the chain lightly lubricated without surplus oil reaching the wall of the tyre. The chain needed adjustment at approximately 800-mile intervals.

Over the long continental mileage, some of it at high cruising speeds, the fuel consumption worked out at a shade over 50 mpg—lighter than usual with some machines of smaller capacity. Premium-type fuel, 98 octane, was used. The engine could be made to pink on this fuel but not seriously enough to warrant a higher-octane diet.

Oil consumption was 300 miles to the pint. This is thought to be higher than average but there was no obvious explanation. The exhaust was not smoky and the engine remained free from serious leaks.

Accessibility for servicing is good. A quickly detachable panel on the left below the seat nose reveals the battery.

**Staffman Peter Fraser, who used the Commando for his visit to the ISDT venue at San Pellegrino in Italy, refuelling on his way back across France**

# 745 cc NORTON COMMANDO

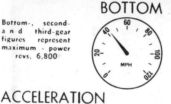   

Bottom-, second- and third-gear figures represent maximum - power revs, 6,800

## ACCELERATION

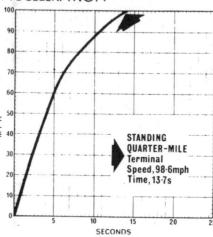

STANDING QUARTER-MILE Terminal Speed, 98·6mph Time, 13·7s

## FUEL CONSUMPTION

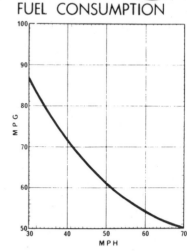

The seat itself can be removed in seconds without spanners. Tools are stored in a compartment in the glass-fibre tail fairing.

A single-bolt fixing for the cast-aluminium primary chain-case makes inspection and servicing unusually easy.

The Commando has set a new high in the field of big-capacity machines for which Britain has been famous for so long. It deserves the welcome it received when production started and the big reputation it is building now more and more machines are reaching world markets.

# specification

**ENGINE:** Capacity and type: 745 cc (73 x 89mm) overhead-valve, parallel twin. Bearings: crankshaft supported in a roller bearing on the drive side and a ball bearing on the timing side; plain big ends and small ends. Lubrication: dry sump; oil-tank capacity, 5 pints. Compression ratio: 8.9 to 1. Carburettors: twin Amal Concentric, 30mm-diameter choke; air slides operated by handlebar lever. Impregnated-paper air-filter element. Claimed power output: 58 bhp at 6,800 rpm.
**TRANSMISSION:** Primary by ⅜in. triplex chain with movable gear box for adjustment; secondary by ⅝ x ⅜in chain. Clutch; multi-plate, with diaphram-spring. Gear ratios: 12.4, 8.25, 5.9, 4.84 to 1. Engine rpm at 30 mph in top gear: 1,850.
**ELECTRICAL EQUIPMENT:** Ignition by capacitor and twin coils. Charging

by 110-watt alternator through rectifier and diode to 8-amp-hour battery. Headlamp: 7in-diameter, with 50/40-watt main bulb.
**FUEL CAPACITY:** 3¼ gallons.
**BRAKES:** 8in-diameter, twin-leading-shoe front; 7in-diameter rear.
**TYRES:** Avon ribbed front, 3.00 x 19in; Avon GP rear, 3.50 x 19in.
**SUSPENSION:** Norton Roadholder telescopic fork with two-way hydraulic damping; pivoted rear fork controlled by Girling spring-and-hydraulic units with three-position adjustment for load.
**DIMENSIONS:** Wheelbase, 56¾in; ground clearance, 6in; seat height, 31in; all unladen.
**WEIGHT:** 418 lb, including half a gallon of fuel and full oil tank.
**PRICE:** £456 19s 4d, including British purchase tax.
**ROAD TAX:** £10 a year; £3 13s for four months.
**MANUFACTURERS:** Norton Villiers Ltd, Norton Matchless Division, 44 Plumstead Road, London, SE18.

# performance

(Obtained by "Motor Cycle" staff at the Motor Industry Research Association's proving ground, Lindley, Leicestershire.)

**MEAN MAXIMUM SPEED:** 116 mph (14½-stone rider wearing two-piece trials suit).
**HIGHEST ONE-WAY SPEED:** 117 mph (still air).
**BRAKING:** From 30 mph to rest on dry tarmac, 32ft.
**TURNING CIRCLE:** 13ft 9in.
**MINIMUM NON-SNATCH SPEED:** 18 mph in top gear.
**WEIGHT PER CC:** 0.56 lb.